FORMAT

Use white, standard-size pap[...]
  from a spiral binder or ver[...]
For handwritten work, use v[...]
  lines) and black or dark blu[...]
For typewritten work, double[...] use a black ribbon.
Type or write on only **one** side of each page.

Give your name in the upper right corner of the first page and,
  below it, the name or number of the course, the name of your
  instructor, and the date on which you will submit the paper.

Center the title of your essay on the top line of a lined page or about
  2 inches from the top of an unlined page; do **not** set the title off in
  quotation marks unless it is entirely composed of a quotation of
  another person's words; if you include a quotation in your title, set
  off only the quoted words. For longer papers, your instructor may
  require a separate title page.

Leave blank at least one line, or the equivalent space, between the
  title and the first line of your essay.

Write or type the number of each page after the first in the upper
  right corner, using Arabic numerals. (If you have a title page, do not
  include it in the numbering.)

Leave margins about 1½ inches wide at the left side and at the top
  and bottom of each page; in a typewritten paper, leave a right-hand
  margin of about one inch.

Indent the beginning of each paragraph the equivalent of a five-letter
  word.

Spell out all numbers below ten unless you are using several close
  together (many authorities recommend spelling out all numbers
  below one hundred). Spell out any number, no matter how large,
  that begins a sentence.

Avoid splitting words at the ends of lines; split words are difficult to
  read. Instead, leave the space at the end blank. If splitting a word is
  necessary, check your dictionary for the correct syllable divisions,
  and use a hyphen to mark the split.

In a typewritten paper, skip two spaces after all terminal punctuation
  and one space after all internal punctuation except dashes. Indicate
  a dash by two hyphens with **no** space before, after, or in between.
  Add in ink any symbols that your typewriter does not have.

In a handwritten paper, make your writing as legible as you can.
  Make capital letters distinctly larger than lowercase letters.

Proofread your final copy with the greatest possible care. Read
  carefully for errors in spelling, punctuation, or grammar. Correct
  slips of your pen or typewriter by firmly crossing out the error and
  neatly writing the correction above it. Avoid erasures. If you find
  several errors on a page or if an error involves several words,
  recopy the page.

Fasten the pages of your paper together with a clip, staple, or binder.
  Ask your instructors which they prefer.

Dear Jeremy

May the true spirit of christmas bring you peace + happiness

love
Mom xx
1990

A HANDBOOK
for EXPOSITION

A HANDBOOK
for EXPOSITION

Georgia Dunbar

HOFSTRA UNIVERSITY

Clement Dunbar

LEHMAN COLLEGE,
THE CITY UNIVERSITY
OF NEW YORK

Harper & Row, Publishers, New York
Cambridge, Philadelphia, St. Louis, San Francisco,
London, Singapore, Sydney, Tokyo

Acknowledgments can be found on page 492, which constitutes a continuation of the copyright page.

Sponsoring Editor: Lucy Rosendahl
Project Editor: Carla Samodulski
Text Design: Delgado Design, Inc.
Cover Design: Delgado Design, Inc.
Text Art: Vantage Art, Inc.
Production Manager: Jeanie Berke
Production Assistant: Paula Roppolo
Compositor: ComCom Division of Haddon Craftsmen, Inc.
Printer and Binder: The Murray Printing Company
Cover Printer: Lehigh Press

A Handbook for Exposition

Library of Congress Cataloging-in-Publication Data

Dunbar, Georgia Dolfield Sherwood, Date
  A handbook for exposition.

Includes index.
  1. English language—Rhetoric. 2. Exposition (Rhetoric) I. Dunbar, Clement. II. Title.
PE1429.D76 1989   808'.042   88-32790
ISBN 0-06-041806-0

88 89 90 91 9 8 7 6 5 4 3 2 1

CONTENTS

Contents

Contents

Contents

Contents

Contents

PREFACE

Students need two kinds of help with writing assignments: with the **process of writing** an essay—gathering and interpreting material, and composing and revising the essay—and with **presenting the product**. At the heart of the composing process is a search for words and sentence structures that will make our meaning clear and forceful. Therefore, we begin this book with a discussion of English as a language, emphasizing the richness of its vocabulary and the flexibility of its syntax. Because composing involves continual **choosing**, we stress **actively and consciously making choices** while composing.

We explain conventions of English usage and demystify grammatical terms by giving **full definitions, including etymologies** to show the underlying logic of the terms. Succinct advice and dictionary-style definitions are often misunderstood even by students with a thorough traditional preparation; students without such preparation may find them incomprehensible.

Most examples draw on **familiar subject matter**, often repeating topics so that comparison is easy and differences are clear. This feature minimizes the need to decode each example, saving both time and study effort. Sample paragraphs by published writers draw on topics from the laboratory and social sciences as well as the humanities to reaffirm the need for good writing across the curriculum.

The **sequence of the book is flexible**. Which sections to assign and in what order will, of course, depend on the specific purpose of the course. **Frequent cross-referencing** makes the book easily adaptable to other sequences—for example, beginning with the whole essay and ending with the individual word, or beginning with the paragraph as a miniature essay and then as part of a larger unit before examining sentences and words, and so on. **We begin with words** and a brief history of the English language because a discussion of language begins most easily at the word level and, more important, because the immense vocabulary of English offers so great a range of choices in diction and syntactic structures. Although we place this section first, it can be a useful stimulant at any point in a composition course.

Section 2 includes methods for improving spelling that can help students develop greater confidence. Although discussion of spelling so early in the book is not the current fashion, spelling is often a major clue to word origins and meaning; more important, it need not be the bugbear that students often imagine it.

Sections 3 through 29 examine **the syntactic structures available in English sentences** and **the conventions of standard edited English**. For students with a thorough preparation in standard English, these sections offer help with specific problems of syntax and usage; for students with less preparation, they offer basic principles and detailed explanations.

Sections 30 through 35 explore **strategies for composing effective sentences and paragraphs**. They emphasize the many syntactic choices available and show how these choices not only help to make our meaning clear but also sometimes help to discover fresh aspects and interpretations of our material. Section 32 includes **two drafts of a short student essay** that show how the writer strengthened word choice and sentence structure by revising. The **student's notes on planning and writing the essay** explain the thinking behind the choices of detail and sentence structure and provide examples of the composing and revising process that are closer to the usual student experience than are the notes of professional writers.

Part Six discusses choices in the **composing process**, with detailed examples of the many patterns available for developing a thesis. We show how these patterns help in **discovering and exploring material** and **generating ideas** and how they are related to the writer's purpose, materials, and intended readers. We apply these patterns to a single topic so that students can easily analyze each pattern, compare the patterns, and see the relationship between the writer's purpose and choice of pattern. Part Six includes the **drafts of a 500-word student essay, showing all the stages of development**. It includes the student's log describing the multiple choices and decisions involved in composing and revising—again, a more persuasive parallel for student writers than the comments of professional writers. **Section 45** covers standard **outline forms** for the humanities and sciences.

Part Seven presents the research paper. **Sections 46 through 52** give detailed information on each stage of preparing a research paper, explaining both the **MLA and APA** styles for documentation and **presenting examples of fifty types of sources**. To encourage students to extend their research, Section 52 includes examples of references to **legal materials** and to such **non-print sources** as recordings, computer programs, and opinion surveys. **Section 53** includes **two very different sample research papers**: one, essentially a library report, examines several magazines and newspapers published on the same date, a topic especially accessible for class discussion; the other analyzes a short poem. The **student writer's log** accompanies each, detailing the process of gathering information, composing, and revising.

Part Eight covers standard formats for business letters and includes a sample job application letter and résumé. The book ends with a **Glossary of Usage**.

Acknowledgments

We thank the many people whose help has made this book possible—our editor at Harper & Row, Lucy Rosendahl; our former editor, Phillip Leininger; Lucy's assistant, Allison Philips; and our project editor, Carla Samodulski. We also wish to thank the readers whose suggestions and careful attention to the details of the manuscript have been creative and constructive: Ray Anschel, Normandale Community College; Evan Antone, University of Texas; Manuel B. Blanco, Laredo Junior College; Elizabeth Byers, Virginia Polytechnic Institute; Albert DeCiccio, Merrimack College; Robert Dees, Orange Coast College; Harriette Dodson, Florida Junior College; Susan Popper Edelman, Long Island University; Francis A. Hubbard, Marquette University; Joe Keller, Iowa Central Community College; Joyce Kinkead, Utah State University; Carol Niederlander, St. Louis Community College; Stephanie Russell, Collegiate School; R. Baird Shuman, University of Illinois-Urbana; Ronald A. Sudol, Oakland University; Ken M. Symes, Western Washington University; Arthur Wagner, Macomb College; Barbara Walvoord, Loyola College;

Mary Webb, University of Nevada-Reno; Stephen Wozniak, Palomar College; and Robert E. Yarber, San Diego Mesa College. Above all, we thank the many students whose difficulties and enthusiasms have made teaching English composition a challenging and rewarding experience for us.

Georgia Dunbar
Clement Dunbar

Part One
WORDS

1

1 ◆ ENGLISH AS A LANGUAGE

"Dr. Robinson, I am telephoning you to report an unusual occurrence that may interest you as director of our project and that I can personally verify because I was witness to the event."

"Lee, I want to tell you about something strange. I know it really happened because I was there. Since you work in the same field, I think you'll be very interested."

"Hey, Pat! Have I got something weird to tell you! And it's really true, so help me. I was there! Get a load of this, pal, 'cause it'll blow you away!"

"Hi, Chris. Do you want to hear something that's funny? It sounds kind of crazy, but it's true. I didn't make it up. I promise. It really happened. Every bit of it. I know it did. I was there. I bet you'll think it's funny too."

In writing and in speaking, we all adjust our style to fit the occasion. As the preceding examples show, in only a few minutes, one person may use four strikingly different styles of expression. In each, the speaker chooses words and sentence structures appropriate to the listener. The first two examples are standard English—entirely formal for a business associate, then simpler but moderately formal for a friend. The third, for a closer friend, uses colloquial English and slang, with short, informal sentence structures. In the fourth, for a young child, the speaker chooses a simple vocabulary, avoids slang that a child may not know, and breaks up the statement into many short, simply constructed sentences and fragments.

In brief, the characteristics that make the examples differ so much are these:

1. One sentence—33 words; no contractions; very formal word choice
2. Three sentences—32 words, including one contraction; moderately formal word choice
3. Five sentences—31 words, including 3 contractions; colloquial and slang word choice
4. Ten sentences—51 words, including 5 contractions; simple word choice

Our choice of words and sentence structures also determines the style and effectiveness of what we write. We shall focus on the kinds of word choice and sentence structure used in the first two examples because they are appropriate for formal occasions and for most kinds of writing.

To make sure that readers understand us, we need to know two things about the words we use. We must know the **precise meanings** of our words, and we must know the **roles** that they can play in sentences. For both, some **knowledge of the sources of English** and of how it developed as a language can help us to understand distinctions in meaning and ways to write effectively.

1a Principal sources of English

English draws on many sources and has many more words than any other modern language. The basic framework is Old English, also called Anglo-Saxon because it was the language spoken by the Angles and Saxons, Germanic tribes who invaded Britain in the fifth and sixth centuries A.D. and settled there, so that the country came to be called the land of the Angles, or England. Most of the words that hold our sentences together are from Old English: all our prepositions and conjunctions, such as *of, with, and, but,* and all our pronouns, such as *I, us, which, who.* Also from Old English come large numbers of our most common verbs, such as *be, have, go, love, eat;* nouns, such as *child, bed, house, food;* and adjectives and adverbs, such as *good, well, strong, early, true.* Even without having studied Anglo-Saxon, you may be able to understand some of this sentence, which was one of the laws of King Alfred:

> Gif mon sie dumb oððe deaf geboren þæt he ne mæge synna onsecggan ne geandettan, bete se fæder his misdæda.

> [If someone is born so dumb or deaf that he may not renounce or confess his sins, his father pays the fine for his misdeeds.]

French words, most of them of Latin origin, joined Old English after the Normans invaded England from France in 1066 and settled there. Because the Normans were the conquerors, their words were adopted for official matters and the leisure activities of the ruling class. Almost all our legal and military terms, including the words *legal* and *military,* come from French—for example, *court, judge, trial, captain, general, lieutenant,* and *battalion*—as do many of the words we associate with cultured and leisurely living, such as *dance, library, tennis, concert, theater, perfume,* and *tailor.* We call this transitional stage of

4

the language, when French words were being adopted in large numbers, Middle English. It is much closer to modern English, as you can see in this sentence written in 1391 by Geoffrey Chaucer, the greatest English writer of the Middle Ages, as part of the introduction to his treatise on the astrolabe, an instrument formerly used in astronomy:

> The first partie of this tretys shal reherse the figures and the membres of thyn Astrelabie by cause that thou shalt have the gretter knowing of thyn owne instrument.

By the sixteenth century the language had become fairly settled, thanks largely to the invention of the printing press, which made books available to more people. Spelling, however, remained very much an individual choice, as you can see in this sentence written by Sir Walter Raleigh in 1596, when he was exploring what is now Guyana in South America:

> I never saw a more beawtifull country, nor more lively prospectes, hils so raised heere and there over the vallies, the river winding into divers braunches, the plaines adjoyning without bush or stubble, all fair greene grasse, and the ayre fresh with a gentle easterlie wind.

A third invasion, this time by words and ideas, not military force, occurred in the sixteenth and early seventeenth centuries, when a revival of Greek and Latin learning, called the Renaissance, reached England from Western Europe. Through French, English had already acquired a large stock of words of Greek and Latin origin, but most of these had undergone changes in French before being absorbed by English and were then changed still more. The Greek and Latin words that entered the language in the Renaissance remain close to their original forms. Examples include *agriculture* (from Latin *ager* = field + *cultura* = cultivation), *sympathy* (from Greek *syn* = together + *pathos* = feeling), and *rhythm* (from Greek *rhythmos* = measured motion).

Because English draws on many sources, it has more words than does any other language, and therefore it gives us more ways to indicate precise shades of meaning and degrees of formality. For example, "report an unusual occurrence" and "tell you about something strange," quoted at the beginning of this chapter, have exactly the same meaning, but the first is very formal and the second is informal. Notice that the following words all have the same basic meaning, but each has a special effect, so they are rarely interchangeable: *happy, glad, gleeful, exultant, merry, joyous, joyful, ebullient, cheerful, pleased.*

To make sure that the words you have chosen express your meaning accurately, check them in a good dictionary before you make the final copy of each paper. Keep a desk-size dictionary beside you when you write, especially when you revise. A pocket-size edition can help with spellings and definitions when you write in class, and an unabridged dictionary will help with complicated problems. But the desk-size edition, often called a college edition, is what you should keep within easy reach. It is small enough to be picked up with one hand, but detailed enough to contain all the information you will ordinarily need.

Three widely respected American dictionaries have up-to-date desk-size editions:

The American Heritage Dictionary of the English Language, published by Houghton Mifflin

Webster's New World Dictionary of the American Language, published by Simon and Schuster and available in a softcover edition through college bookstores

Webster's Ninth New Collegiate Dictionary, published by Merriam-Webster

If your instructor does not require you to buy a particular dictionary, examine all three before you choose. Decide in which you find the type most readable, the abbreviations most understandable, and the diagrams and illustrations clearest. Comparing their entries for *infer* and *irregardless* will give you a good indication of how different their styles of presentation are and how conservative each one is.

Be sure to ask for them by the publisher's name as well as by the title, particularly the two called *"Webster's."* Any dictionary can use Noah Webster's name in the title, so his name is not a guarantee of quality. Look at the copyright date on the back of the title page to be sure that you are buying the edition with the latest information on new words and changes in definition and usage. Although their covers remain much the same from one edition to the next, these dictionaries are updated frequently.

1b Using the dictionary

Whichever dictionary you buy, study its opening pages carefully for directions on how to use it. Each has its own system for presenting information about the words and for abbreviating labels. Find out whether your dictionary lists definitions for a word in historical order, starting with the oldest, or by some other system. Find out where it lists names of places, foreign words and phrases, and biographical information on famous people—in separate sections or in the main body. Learn the pronunciation symbols and the abbreviations that appear frequently, such as the grammatical labels *v.* for "verb" and *n.* for "noun" and the historical labels giving the etymology such as *L.* for "Latin" and *OE.* for "Old English."

The following entry for *brave* comes from the second college edition of *Webster's New World Dictionary:*

EXERCISES

A.   How are the words *charms, spells, glamour,* and *enchantment* related to the words *grammar* and *spelling?* For each word, check your dictionary for all its meanings and its etymology—the other words from which it developed.

B.   The words in each of the following pairs are related but different and often cause confusion. Check your dictionary for their etymology, meanings, and uses.

infer *and* imply   incredulous *and* incredible
exalt *and* exult   enormity *and* enormousness
flaunt *and* flout   nauseous *and* nauseated
comprise *and* compose   punctilious *and* punctual
mitigate *and* militate   disinterested *and*
                                         uninterested

spelling

pronunciation

most common grammatical use (adjective)

etymology, in brackets, starting with
most recent source and going back
to earliest; including indication
that more information is available
under entry for *barbarous*

brave (brāv) *adj.* [Fr. < It. *bravo,* brave, bold, orig., wild, savage < L. *barbarus,* BARBAROUS] **1.** willing to face danger, pain, or trouble; not afraid; having courage **2.** showing to good effect; having a fine appearance **3.** fine, grand, or splendid [a *brave* new world]—*n.* **1.** any brave man ☆**2.** [< 17th-c. NAmFr.] a North American Indian warrior **3.** [Archaic] a bully—*vt.* **braved, brav′ing 1.** to face with courage **2.** to defy; dare **3.** [Obs.] to make splendid, as in dress —*vi.* [Obs.] to boast —**brave′ly** *adv.* —**brave′ness** *n.*

SYN.—**brave** implies fearlessness in meeting danger or difficulty and has the broadest application of the words considered here; **courageous** suggests constant readiness to deal with things fearlessly by reason of a stout-hearted temperament or a resolute spirit; **bold** stresses a daring temperament, whether displayed courageously, presumptuously, or defiantly; **audacious** suggests an imprudent or reckless boldness; **valiant** emphasizes a heroic quality in the courage or fortitude shown; **intrepid** implies absolute fearlessness and esp. suggests dauntlessness in facing the new or unknown; **plucky** emphasizes gameness in fighting against something when one is at a decided disadvantage —*ANT.* **craven, cowardly**

antonyms

synonyms with distinctions among them

one definition as intransitive verb

adverb based on word

noun based on word

numbered definitions as transitive verb

numbered definitions as noun, beginning
with most common—including American
use, marked with star—and ending
with definition of archaic use

numbered definitions as adjective,
beginning with most common and
giving example in phrase

9

C. Using a desk dictionary or, if you have the time, an unabridged dictionary, study the etymology and meanings of all the following words; then choose *five* that differ in the way they developed as words and in the way their meanings have changed and write a short paper giving the results of your study.

gas, gamut, lunacy, bedlam, juggle, jug, jeep, jeans, denim, anecdote, sarcasm, lady, umpire, furlong, caterpillar, sabotage, salary, tawdry, sacrilege, budget, sinister, gauche, boycott, lynch, supercilious, ampersand, junket, sandwich

1c Denotation, connotation, and levels of writing

English provides a larger number of synonyms and near-synonyms than does any other widely used language. Take advantage of this variety, but choose your words carefully. The **denotations** of two words—their literal dictionary definitions—may be the same, but their **connotations** are almost always different. Connotations are the associated meanings that a word acquires through use. For example, dictionaries commonly give *vehicle* as a synonym for *car,* but if you tell your friends that you drive a vehicle, they will probably think that you are being humorous or that you drive something other than a car.

To find additional synonyms for a word beyond those that your dictionary gives, consult a thesaurus (from Greek *thesauros* = treasure), or "treasury" of synonyms. The best known is *Roget's Thesaurus,* which is published in a variety of editions. When you choose a word from a thesaurus, always check your dictionary as well to be sure that the word has the connotations that you want. For example, you may find *fluent, voluble, glib,* and *flippant* listed as synonyms, but while speakers may thank you for calling them fluent, they will not be pleased if you call them voluble, and they will be offended by *glib* or *flippant.*

The many synonyms and connotations of English give us a choice of levels on which to write and speak, from the very formal to the very informal, as the four examples at the beginning of this chapter demonstrate. **Standard English,** or **standard edited English,** is the name for the word choice and kind of sentence structure writers use for more serious publications intended for the general reader—newspapers like the *New York Times, San Francisco Chronicle,* and *Chicago Tribune;* magazines like *Time* and the *Atlantic Monthly;* business documents; and most college textbooks, especially those intended for introductory courses.

Scholarly and technical English is more formal and uses whatever specialized words and phrases are appropriate to the subject, ordinarily a high proportion of words of Greek and Latin origin. The sentences have the same basic structures as those of standard English, but they are often much longer.

Colloquial English is informal—the level most people use when writing and speaking to their friends. The word choice and sentence structure are somewhat simpler than those of standard English and may include many contractions, some slang, some regional and dialect words, and fragmentary sentences. Your college dictionary will tell you if a word is colloquial, dialect, or slang and therefore perhaps inappropriate in a formal paper.

Avoid "officialese," the use of scholarly or technical

terms to make something sound more important than it is. Some branches of government and some businesses now try to simplify their writing, but they still have a long way to go. Colleges, too, are often guilty of inflated language. One art department, discovering that other departments did not think "Freehand Drawing" could be a serious course, renamed it "Fundamentals of Graphic Expression."

Choose simple, familiar words whenever they will give your meaning as clearly as longer or more complicated ones. Why write "It is my considered opinion that the team achieved victory in the game due to the fact that they really exerted an enormous effort," when you can write "I think that the team won because they tried hard." If your assignment requires more words, find more examples or details to support your ideas. Added support will strengthen your writing; extra words will only dilute it.

Good English is appropriate English—right for the occasion, the purpose, and the listeners or readers. For most of your writing, in college and later, "standard English" will be appropriate.

EXERCISES

A. In the following groups, some words differ in denotation, others in connotation. Check your dictionary for all the denotations, etymologies, and information on their connotations.

1. wise, clever, knowledgeable, sagacious
2. love, fondness, partiality, devotion
3. stumble, stagger, falter, trip
4. quake, quiver, tremble, wobble

5. stupid, unintelligent, fatuous, backward
6. misfortune, catastrophe, tragedy, ruin
7. dame, lady, woman, madam

B. Choose one of the word groups listed in Exercise A and compose a short paragraph using the four words so that the distinctions among them are clear. The shorter your paragraph, the more it will emphasize contrasts among the words and the more challenging the exercise will be. For example, this paragraph shows the distinctions among *horse, equine, nag,* and *steed:*

The advertisement had shown a beautiful girl taking her powerful *steed* over a six-foot fence, and the sign at the gate said "*Equine* Academy." We expected to find an elegant training school for *horses* but we saw only three old knock-kneed *nags* that could barely stand up.

C. Translate the following paragraph into simple, direct English. In the process you should be able to shorten it by at least 50% with no loss of meaning.

A perusal of the evidence submitted on the perpetration of this criminal act may induce the scrutinizers to arrive at the conclusion that the said criminal act is identifiable as one of premeditated homicide. Moreover, in addition to this, it is the considered opinion of those members of the legal profession who have had extensive experience in the course of their professional activities with cases bearing some similarity to the one under discussion that the perpetrator of an act of premeditated homicide such as that referred to in the preceding sentence should be brought to trial with all due and appropriate speed.

13

2 ◆ SPELLING

A spell is a magic formula that gives one power over something, and spelling, which comes from *spell*, may sometimes seem to require magical ability. English is a difficult language to spell because of its mixed origins and because its pronunciation continued to change after the invention of printing stopped most spelling changes. Learning to spell correctly, however, will help you to see how English words are related to each other, to older forms of English, and to other languages. It will increase your vocabulary and help you to choose words with the precise meanings and associations you want.

Word processing programs and electronic typewriters that have "spellcheckers" can detect misspellings that create nonexistent words, but they cannot help you to know whether to write *stationary* or *stationery*, *flaunt* or *flout*, or *to, too,* or *two* because all of these are legitimate words. If spelling is a serious problem for you, these electronic aids can save time. Remember, however, that you will often be writing in circumstances where you cannot use a spellchecker; in any case, this device cannot catch many of the most common misspellings. Do not despair. The suggestions and rules that follow will help you to become a better speller. Be sure to use them all—they reinforce one another.

1. **Pronounce each syllable very slowly and carefully** so that you hear every sound in the correct order. Careful pronunciation will help you to avoid the four main types of spelling error:

a. Do not add extra letters for sounds that are not really there—for example, in *athletics, disastrous, laundry, mischievous, umbrella.*

b. Do not omit letters for sounds that are slurred over—for example, in *accidentally, government, library, quantity, strength, surprise, temperature.*

c. Do not confuse the correct sequence of letters— for example, in *environment, irrelevant, perform, tragedy.*

d. Do not confuse words that have the same or very similar sounds but different meanings—for example, *except* and *accept, effect* and *affect, instance* and *instants.*

2. **See all the letters in each word.** Every day, take a small index card and print three or four words on it in large letters. Leave plenty of space around each word so that you can see all the words at a glance. Carry the card with you all day and take it out as often as possible, staring hard at the letters in each word. Say the letters to yourself slowly. If no one is listening, say them out loud. Spend only a few seconds on the process, but keep repeating it in your free moments— while you are waiting for a class to begin or standing in line at the cafeteria—even when you are caught in traffic. The more often you look hard at the letters in each word, the better your visual memory of it will be.

3. **Play games with words.** For example, look for the *iron* in *environment, a rat* in *separate,* and *age* in *tragedy.* You already know how to spell the short word, and it contains the same sequence of letters as does the word you want to learn.

You can also make a game of looking for repeated patterns. For example, the troublesome part of *embarrass* has two *a*'s, two *r*'s, and two *s*'s.

2a Spelling rules

A few rules will help you to remember the sequence of letters in a large number of words that cause problems:

RULE 1 The most famous spelling rule is the old rhyme that covers most of the problems of whether *i* or *e* comes first. Almost everyone remembers the beginning, but the whole rhyme is useful because it covers many words:

> Write *i* before *e,* except after *c*
> Or when sounded like *a*
> As in n*ei*ghbor and w*ei*gh,
> But *ei*ther, n*ei*ther, l*ei*sure, and s*ei*ze
> Are four exceptions, if you please.

Of course, *seized, seizing,* and *seizure* are like *seize.* The rhyme does not cover words in which *i* and *e* are pronounced separately, as in *science,* or words in which *c* is pronounced *sh,* as in *ancient.* There are only eight exceptions not mentioned in the rhyme: *counterfeit, financier, foreign, heifer, height, sheik,* and *weird.*

RULE 2 Of all the words of two or more syllables whose last syllable rhymes with *seed,* only one ends with *sede: supersede.* Three end in *ceed: exceed, proceed,* and *succeed.* All the others end in *cede*—for example, *concede, precede, intercede,* and *recede.*

RULE 3 In a word of *one* syllable ending in *one* consonant that is preceded by only *one* vowel, *double the final consonant* when adding an ending that begins with a vowel. This is often called "the rule of one-one-one," a good way to remember it.

bat + ing = batting   net + ed = netted
mud + y = muddy

In a word of more than one syllable, the one-one-one rule applies if the final syllable ends in one consonant preceded by one vowel and if it receives the stress both before and after adding the ending:

admit + ed = admitted
refer + ing = referring
commit + ee = committee
occur + ence = occurrence

If the stress is not on the final syllable, or if it shifts when the ending is added, do *not* double the final consonant:

limit + ed = limited
refer + ence = reference
refer + ee = referee

RULE 4 If a word ends with a consonant and you add an ending beginning with the same consonant, *keep both consonants:*

final + ly = finally
green + ness = greenness

RULE 5 If a word ends in a silent (unpronounced) *e* and you add an ending that begins with a vowel, *drop the silent e:*

love + ing = loving   love + able = lovable

EXCEPTIONS: Keep the *e* in words ending in *oe,* such as *canoeing* and *shoeing.* Keep the *e* in words ending in *ge* or *ce* if the addition begins with *a* or *o,* as in *courageous* and *serviceable,* to keep the *g* or *c* soft.

RULE 6 If a word ends in *y* preceded by a consonant, *change the y to i* when adding an ending that does not also begin with *i*:

> glory + ous = glorious   happy + ly = happily

EXCEPTIONS: Most one-syllable words keep the *y: shyness, dryly.*

CAUTION: To add an *s* ending for the plural of words that end in *y,* follow the *"y* to *i"* rule; but to add an *s* for the possessive, do *not* follow the rule:

> Each society's (singular possessive) customs may be affected by those of neighboring societies (plural).

RULE 7 To add a syllable that ends in a consonant to the beginning of a word that starts with a consonant, *keep both consonants:*

> mis + spell = misspell
> un + necessary = unnecessary

If a word begins with a vowel, do not double a consonant at the end of the addition:

> dis + appear = disappear
> un + imaginable = unimaginable

2b Homonyms and homophones

Homonyms (from Greek *homos* = same + *onyma* = name) are words that are spelled alike but differ in meaning, for example, *tear* (= a drop of liquid from the eye) and *tear* (= rip). Homophones (from Greek *homos*

= same + *phone* = sound) are words that sound alike but differ in both meaning and spelling, for example, *alter* and *altar*. Homophones are a problem in spelling. Check the full dictionary entries on homophones; their different etymologies often make the spelling easier to remember. Common homophones are:

accept, except
access, excess
affect, effect
air, heir
aisle, isle
allowed, aloud
allusion, illusion
altar, alter
bare, bear
born, borne
bridal, bridle
capital, capitol
cast, caste
cite, sight, site
coarse, course
complement,
    compliment
core, corps
council, counsel
descent, dissent
dew, do, due
discreet, discrete
dual, duel
dyeing, dying
eminent, imminent
fair, fare

forbear, forebear
foregoing, forgoing
forth, fourth
grate, great
hear, here
holy, wholly
hurdle, hurtle
incidence, incidents
instance, instants
ladder, latter
lead, led
lessen, lesson
lightening, lightning
loath, loathe
medal, meddle, metal,
    mettle
passed, past
peace, piece
pedal, peddle, petal
plain, plane
pole, poll
precede, proceed
presence, presents
principal, principle
profit, prophet
prophecy, prophesy

rack, wrack
rap, wrap
right, rite, write
role, roll
rung, wrung
scents, sense
shudder, shutter
stationary, stationery

straight, strait
than, then
threw, through
to, too, two
waiver, waver
wear, were, where
weather, whether
yoke, yolk

2c Words frequently misspelled

academic
accommodation
acknowledge
across
adequate
amateur
anxiety
apparatus
around
audience
awkward
bachelor
calendar
campaign
cemetery
challenge
coliseum
column
committee
competition

complexion
conscientious
criticism
critize
dealt
desperate
disease
divide
eligible
embarrass
environment
exaggerate
excellent
exercise
fascinate
fiery
forty
fundamental
gauge
grammar

grandeur
guarantee
huge
indispensable
infinite
innocuous
inoculate
inquiry
instructor
intercede
interfere
irresistible
laboratory
library
license
loneliness
medical
memento
mountain
muscle

musician	privilege	sacrilegious
mysterious	probably	sandwich
occasion	professor	schedule
odor	pronunciation	separate
pamphlet	psychology	similar
parallel	questionnaire	skeptical
pastime	recommend	specimen
permissible	rehearsal	susceptible
persuade	religious	threshold
phenomenon	reminiscence	until
physician	repetition	villain
physiology	restaurant	visible
pneumonia	rhythm	Wednesday
prejudice	sacrifice	writing

2d Compound words

We combine two or more words to form a compound word either by writing the combination as one word or by using hyphens. Compounds like the following are written as single words:

grandmother	bathtub	toothache
however	moreover	furthermore
nevertheless	whereas	tablecloth

We write combinations of *all, any, every, no,* and *some* with *body, one,* and *thing* as one word or two depending on what we mean:

The doctor examined every body *(all the bodies)* in the morgue while everybody *(all the people)* on the staff watched.

We were all ready *(all of us)* by four o'clock, but the plane had already *(before that time)* left.

NOTE: When we combine *all* with *ready, together,* and *ways,* we drop one *l: already, altogether, always.* In formal English, *all right* is always spelled as two words, but you will often see it spelled as one word in advertisements that are meant to seem informal.

We use hyphens to make the following kinds of compounds:

1. All compound numbers under one hundred when they are spelled out, such as *thirty-one* and *fifty-six*
2. All compounds with *great* and *in-law* that express family relationships, such as *great-grandmother, great-uncle,* and *sister-in-law*
3. All compounds with *self* and most of those with *half,* such as *self-interest, self-motivated, half-baked*
4. All fractions when they are spelled out, such as *three-fifths*
5. All compounds formed with a cardinal number (*one, two, three,* and so on) and a unit of measurement, such as *two-inch nail* and *six-foot pole*
6. Compounds of two or more nouns, such as *actor-playwright* and *toaster-oven* when the two words are intended to have equal importance
7. Compounds with *odd,* such as *forty-odd students*
8. Compounds with all, such as *all-powerful* and *all-out*
9. Compounds of two or more words describing a following word, such as *three-year-old* and *never-to-be-forgotten moment* (but omit the hyphens when the combination follows the word it describes, as in "The moment was never to be forgotten")
10. Compounds with *well, ill, better, best, little, lesser,*

and so on, and a past participle, as in *little-known facts* and *better-trained athletes*, when they precede the words they describe (when they follow those words, omit the hyphens)

11. Compounds of some prefixes and suffixes with nouns, such as *ex-football player* and *president-elect*

12. Compounds of a participle and its object when they precede the words they describe, such as *attention-getting remark*

13. Compounds of a verb and a modifier when they act as a noun, such as *drive-in* and *mix-up*

14. Compounds of letters and words, such as *U-turn*, *S-curve*, and *I-beam*

NOTE: Use suspension hyphens when parts of a compound word are understood, as in "The box contained two-, three-, and four-inch nails," or "The cast includes both well- and little-known actors."

We also use hyphens to avoid ambiguity in the pronunciation of a word, as in *anti-intellectual*, in which the hyphen separates the two *i*'s, and to avoid ambiguity in meaning, as in *re-covering chairs*, in which the hyphen distinguishes *re-covering* from *recovering*, as in "recovering lost property."

3 ◆ WORDS IN ACTION:
SENTENCE ESSENTIALS

We can discuss how sentences are constructed and analyze what makes one version of a sentence more effective than another if we know what roles the words in them are playing. The dictionary entry for a word names the roles that the word can play: *n* = noun, *v* = verb, *adj* = adjective, *adv* = adverb, *pn* = pronoun, *prep* = preposition, *conj* = conjunction, and *interj* = interjection. These roles are called the eight parts of speech.

All words in English can act in more than one role. For example, in "Several companies make cars," *make* acts as a verb, but in "This is a new make of car," *make* acts as a noun. We can even construct a sentence in which one word acts as a different part of speech each time it appears:

> noun
> The *up* in the stock market yesterday was good,
> adverb
> and if the market goes *up* again today, our neighbors
> adjective   verb
> will be in an *up* mood and may *up* their offer to buy
> preposition
> land *up* the river.

We can determine which role each word is playing in a particular sentence by looking at the basic structure of the sentence.

Every sentence is like a miniature drama, with the words as actors. Just as a drama needs characters and a plot, so two elements are essential for a sentence, a **subject** and a **predicate**. The subject (from Latin *subjectus* = proposed, presented) tells us what person, place, thing, or idea the sentence is about. The predicate (from Latin *praedictum* = that which is declared, announced) tells us what that subject does, is, or seems, or what is done to it. The predicate always contains a word or word group acting as a **verb** (for discussion of verbs, see **6**). We can construct many complete sentences containing only two words, one as the subject and one as the predicate. For example: *Birds fly. Children play. Snow fell. Cars skidded.*

Usually, the predicate contains more information, as in *Birds fly through the trees* or *Children play games in the park.* Any words that complete the meaning of the verb by showing who or what is affected by the verb are part of the predicate and are called the **complement** of the verb (not compli*ment* but comple*ment*, from Latin *complementum* = that which fills up or completes).

Using only a subject and a predicate, we can construct the seven basic sentence patterns. Notice that each has a subject and a predicate, but the first example has only a verb in the predicate, while the others have complements as well.

Subject	Predicate	
	Verb	**Complement**
Bands	play.	
Bands	play	tunes.
Bands	play	us tunes.
Bands	are	successes.
Bands	are	successful.
Bands	make	tunes hits.
Bands	make	tunes popular.

25

We classify each complement according to its function in relation to the subject and verb. It may act as a direct object, an indirect object, a subject complement, or an object complement. These are the classifications for the complements in the sentences just given:

	Subject	Verb	Indirect Object	Direct Object	Subject Complement	Object Complement
1.	Bands	play.				
2.	Bands	play		tunes.		
3.	Bands	play	us	tunes.		
4.	Bands	are			successes.	
5.	Bands	are			successful.	
6.	Bands	make		tunes		hits.
7.	Bands	make		tunes		popular.

A **direct object** is a word or group of words that tells us who or what directly receives the action indicated by the verb, as in

   S   V   DO
Dogs chase cats.

Verbs that take direct objects are called transitive verbs.

An **indirect object** is a word or group of words that tells us who or what receives the direct object, as in

   S   V   IO   DO
The guard threw the forward the ball.

26

or

The chef cooked us dinner.
$$\overset{\text{S}}{\text{The chef}} \overset{\text{V}}{\text{cooked}} \overset{\text{IO}}{\text{us}} \overset{\text{DO}}{\text{dinner.}}$$

The indirect object usually stands between the verb and direct object as in these examples, but we can also express the same thought by using *to* or *for,* as in "The guard threw the ball to the forward" and "The chef cooked dinner for us." (See prepositional phrases in **11a.3**.)

A **subject complement** may rename the subject with another noun, often called a predicate noun, as in

$$\overset{\text{S}}{\text{The trees}} \overset{\text{V}}{\text{are}} \overset{\text{SC}}{\text{oaks.}}$$

or it may describe the subject with an adjective, often called a predicate adjective, as in

$$\overset{\text{S}}{\text{The trees}} \overset{\text{V}}{\text{are}} \overset{\text{SC}}{\text{tall.}}$$

It is called a subject complement because it completes the description of the subject and appears after the verb without receiving any action indicated by the verb. (See the discussion of nouns in **4** and of adjectives in **7a**.) In sentences with subject complements, the verb acts only as a link to connect the subject complement to the subject and is therefore called a *linking verb.* Common examples of linking verbs are *seem, become, appear,* and all forms of *be,* such as *are, is, am, was, were,* and *have been.*

An **object complement** renames or describes a direct object to show the effect on it of the action indicated by the verb. It may rename the object with another noun, as in

$$\overset{\text{S}}{\text{The voters}} \overset{\text{V}}{\text{elected}} \overset{\text{DO}}{\text{Chris}} \overset{\text{OC}}{\text{mayor.}}$$

or it may describe the object with an adjective, as in

        S   V   DO   OC
The music made the children happy.

In either case, the object complement shows how the direct object has been affected by the action indicated by the verb.

Sentence types The examples of basic sentences just given are all called **declarative** because they make a statement of fact or opinion. Most of the sentences that we write and speak are declarative. In their simplest form, declarative sentences begin with their subject and conclude with their predicate, but three variations can alter the order of the subject and the predicate.

    In the most common variation, the word *there* appears where we expect the subject, and the real subject comes after the verb:

There are two bands in the amusement park.

Because *there* fills in for the subject, it is called an *expletive* (from Latin *ex* = out + *plere* = to fill). Similarly, when a descriptive word or group of words begins the sentence, the verb may sometimes precede the subject:

Then rose the moon.

Happy is the person who has friends.

At the end of a long driveway stood the house.

On rare occasions, for special emphasis or to indicate a strong wish, the verb may begin the sentence:

Came the dawn.

May the best team win.

The second variation, also common, helps us to simplify a subject composed of several words or to emphasize the subject by delaying its appearance in the sentence:

It is obvious that the band is successful.

It is a safe bet that they will win the game.

In this variation, *it* is an *anticipatory subject*—it comes before the real subject and so anticipates it. The real subject is in the subject complement position and is called the *delayed subject*.

In the third variation, a rare one used only for special emphasis, the direct object precedes the subject and the verb:

Money he has, but not happiness.

Nature I loved, and next to Nature, Art.

Although declarative sentences are the most common type, we have two other types, **imperative** and **interrogative**.

Imperative sentences give commands:

Play tunes.   Give me a chance.
Be a success.   Go!

Imperative sentences contain only a predicate because the subject of the verb is *understood* and has been omitted. The understood subject is usually *you,* because most imperative sentences address commands directly to someone to do or be something.

Interrogative sentences ask questions. The special characteristic of one type of interrogative sentence is that the verb or a part of the verb called an *auxiliary* precedes the subject (for discussion of auxiliaries, see **6c** and **g**):

Are you happy?   Would you lend me a dollar?
Has the show started?   Did the baby cry?

We can also construct interrogative sentences by beginning them with an interrogative pronoun *(who, whom,
whose, which, what)* or an interrogative adverb *(how,
when, where, why):*

Who is the bandleader?
Which band plays tonight?
Where has the band played?
When will the show start?

Although we have only these choices for basic sentence structure, we can create endless variety by using
modifiers. Modifiers are words or word groups that change
or add to our understanding of any element in the subject
or predicate. We can construct modifiers in many ways,
placing them in many different positions within our sentences. For example, we can expand the three-word sentence "Bands play tunes" to seventy-six words by adding
modifiers:

Traditionally, every Fourth of July at the amusement park, two large high school bands, one wearing
uniforms composed of red jackets and black trousers
and the other wearing uniforms composed of blue jackets and white trousers, play, with great vigor and at a
great volume, the marching tunes that, over the years,
their teacher has found to be most popular with holiday
crowds, which range in age from babies in strollers to
senior citizens in wheelchairs.

Although the modifiers greatly change the meaning of the
sentence, the basic structure of subject, verb, and object
remains the same.

To discuss sentence structure a knowledge of grammatical terms is not a necessity, but it is a convenience, just as knowing standard names for parts of a car engine will help you to tell a mechanic about repairs to your car. Traditional grammar begins with eight terms that we call the *parts of speech:* nouns, pronouns, verbs, adjectives, adverbs, prepositions, conjunctions, and interjections.

4 ◆ NOUNS

Nouns (from Latin *nomen* = name) name persons, places, and things. What they name may be concrete and tangible *(person, city, book, knife, apple)* or abstract and intangible *(truth, democracy, beauty, happiness).* All of these are examples of **common nouns. Proper nouns** name specific persons, places, and things (George Washington, Chicago, Coca-Cola). **Collective nouns** name groups of persons, places, or things *(army, committee,* and the word *group* itself). **Compound nouns** are composed of two or more words treated as one *(baseball, tablecloth, brother-in-law, Stratford-upon-Avon, high school, stock market).*

In every sentence, the words or groups of words playing the roles of the subject, direct object, and indirect object are acting as nouns. Nouns can act as subject complements, as in "Bands are successes," and as object complements, as in "Bands make tunes hits." Nouns can also act as appositives (see **11a.2**), as the objects of prepositions (see **11a.3**), and as the subjects, direct objects, indirect objects, and object complements of gerunds, participles, and infinitives (see **11b**).

4a Plurals

Nouns take a special ending, usually *s,* to distinguish the plural from the singular:

Singular: The tourist made a plan to visit North and South Dakota.

Plural: The tourist*s* made plan*s* to visit the Dakota*s*.

Compound nouns and titles composed of two or more words take the plural *s* on the part most important for identification, as in *passers-by, attorneys general, sisters-in-law, grants-in-aid.*

If the singular form of a noun ends in *s, z, x,* or a cluster of consonants that would be unpronounceable with an added *s,* we add *es:*

Several moss*es* grew in patch*es* by the lake.

The Morris and Perez families, five Morris*es* and four Perez*es,* visited the Brown*s.*

Most words ending in *o* take *s* in the plural, for example, *radios, zoos,* and *Eskimos;* but some take *es,* for example, *tomatoes, potatoes, embargoes,* and *heroes.* Check your dictionary when you are in doubt.

Some words ending in *fe* or *f* change the *f* to *v* and take *es* in the plural, for example, *wives* and *halves;* but many do not, for example, *proofs* and *beliefs.* A few take either form, for example, *scarfs* and *scarves, hoofs* and *hooves.* Check your dictionary when you are in doubt.

Ten words have kept their Old English forms in the plural: *feet, teeth, geese, brethren, children, men, oxen, women, lice,* and *mice.* A few words are the same in the singular and plural, for example, *sheep, deer, trout,* and *moose.* Some words that end in *s* are always treated as singular, for example, *mathematics, measles,* and *billiards;* but *politics* may be either singular or plural. A few words that name a single object are treated as plurals because the objects are plainly formed of two parts, for example, *scissors, trousers,* and *eyeglasses.*

To form the plurals of words referred to as words, letters of the alphabet, numerals, and abbreviations that contain periods, we add an apostrophe and an *s:*

The preceding sentence has five *of*'s and two *to*'s.

On some typewriters we must use l's to make 1's.

Jim and Linda have B.A.'s from the same college.

Traditionally, an apostrophe was used with an *s* to indicate the years forming a decade, as in "They remember the 1960's," but modern usage now omits the apostrophe, as in "1960s."

For the plurals of most foreign words that we have adopted into English, we use the *s* ending, not the form of the original language—*areas,* not *areae,* and *campuses,* not *campi.* But we have kept the original plurals for some, for example:

stimulus—stimuli
alumnus—alumni (men, or both sexes)
alumna—alumnae (women)

alga—algae
addendum—addenda
phenomenon —phenomena
criterion—criteria

With other words we add *s* in ordinary usage but keep the original plural in scholarly and scientific writing, for example:

nebula—nebulas *or* nebulae

formula—formulas *or* formulae

antenna—antennas *or* antennae

appendix—appendixes *or* appendices

radius—radiuses *or* radii

curriculum—curriculums *or* curricula

Most Greek nouns ending in *is* form their plurals with *es,* as in *thesis—theses, analysis—analyses,* and *crisis—crises.*

Two words have caused recent debate: *data* and *media.* In Latin, these are the plural forms of *datum* and *medium.* In formal English, *data* may serve as singular or plural, but *media* requires a plural verb and must be referred to as *they,* not *it.*

The current data *is* complete, and we have *it* on file.

or

The current data *are* complete, and we have *them* on file.

but

The media *are* covering the trial, but the judge has warned *them* against overdramatizing the case.

EXERCISES

A.   Which of the following words are singular, which are plural, and which could be either? Using your dictionary, list all the plural and singular forms you find for each word:

arena, larva, agenda, impedimenta, memento, matrix, chassis, locus, memorandum, cherubim

B. Follow the instructions for exercise A with these foreign words:

memorabilia, axis, milieu, index, chateau, kibbutz, oases, aquarium, genus, crux

4b Possessives

All nouns have a *possessive case,* a form to indicate that the person, place, or thing they name possesses something or someone named by another word in the sentence. We form the possessive of almost all singular nouns by adding *'s:*

the child's toy   a book's title   a witch's cat

This rule also applies to words that end in *s* or *ss* in the singular:

the boss's office   the princess's crown

NOTE: We may use only an apostrophe after the possessive singular of nouns ending in *s* or *ss* if they are followed by a word beginning with an *s* sound, as in "for goodness' sake." We also add only an apostrophe to make the possessive forms of ancient Greek and Roman names that have more than one syllable and end in *es,* as in "Sophocles' plays." Opinions vary on forming the possessive of other names ending in *s.* In general, add *'s* if the result will be easy to say, as in "James's novels"; however, if it would be difficult to say, add only an apostrophe, as in "Bridges' poems."

For nouns in the plural with an *s* or *es* ending, we add only an apostrophe after the ending (*not* a second *s*):

     the books' titles   the princesses' crowns
     the witches' cats

For compound nouns that do not form the plural with *s* on the last word, such as *sisters-in-law* and *attorneys general,* use "belonging to" or "of" to indicate possession, as in "the car belonging to my sister-in-law" or "the office of the attorney general." In speech and in informal writing, the possessive *'s* is added to the end of such compounds when they are in the singular, as in "my sister-in-law's car" or "the attorney general's office."

For the few nouns whose plural is not formed by adding *s* or *es,* we add *'s* to make the possessive case, as in "women's coats," "men's gloves," "children's toys," and so on.

In all these examples, the nouns in the possessive case act as *adjectives* because they modify another noun, telling us who or what "possesses" it: the women possess the coats, the men possess the gloves, and so on. Nouns in the possessive case can also act as *nouns* when the word indicating what is possessed is understood from information already given, as in "Our lawyer wrote my uncle's will, but not my aunt's," in which we understand the word "will" after "aunt's."

REMINDER: We use the *s* ending for three completely different purposes: to mark the third person *singular* of the present tense of verbs (see **6c**), to mark the *possessive* of all nouns in the singular, and to mark the *plural* of almost all nouns (see **4a**), as in "The driver wipe*s* the car*'s* window*s.*"

EXERCISE We can shorten many modifiers that begin with *of* by using possessive case nouns. For example, we can shorten "The instructor read the essay of each student" to "The instructor read each student's essay." In the following sentences, replace the modifiers in italics with a possessive case noun.

1. They sent the uniforms *of the girls* to the cleaners.
2. The trail *of the deer* led into the forest.
3. The jackets *of the man* hung in the closet.
4. The plans *of the women* were approved.
5. The jackets *of the boys* hung in the closet.

4c Nouns as appositives

Nouns also act as modifiers when they are appositives (from Latin *appositus: ad* = to, at, near + *positus* = placed, put). An appositive modifies another noun by renaming it. An appositive usually comes immediately after the noun it modifies:

The first car, *a sedan,* struck the second one, *a limousine.*

We sent postcards from Miami to our neighbors, *the Browns.*

(For discussion of punctuation with appositives, see **18,** rule 4.)

4d Verb forms as nouns

Three verb forms can act as nouns: infinitives, gerunds, and past participles. These are formed from the principal parts of verbs (see **6a**).

1.   Infinitives are usually marked by *to:*

   > They learned *to skate.* (infinitive as direct object)

2.   Gerunds always end in *ing:*

   > *Pitching* requires coordination. (gerund as subject)

   Gerunds may take an *s* to indicate the plural:

   > We watched the *comings* and *goings* of the holiday shoppers.

3.   Past participles usually end in *ed* or *d;* when they act as nouns they take the same form in the plural as in the singular:

   > We helped the *wounded.* (past participle as direct object)

5 ◆ PRONOUNS

Pronouns (from Latin *pro* = in the place of + *nomen* = name) take the place of nouns. Without pronouns, we might be forced to compose awkward sentences like this one:

> The customers called the manager when the waiter gave the customers the customers' bill because the customers claimed that the bill contained an error.

By using pronouns, we can avoid the awkward repetitions:

> The customers called the manager when the waiter gave *them their* bill because *they* claimed that *it* contained an error.

In the revised version, *customers* is the **antecedent** of the pronouns *them, their,* and *they,* and *bill* is the antecedent of *it*. An antecedent (from Latin *ante* = before + *cedere* = to go) is the noun that a pronoun replaces in the sentence. Antecedents usually precede the pronouns that refer to them, as in the example, but sometimes a pronoun comes before its antecedent, as in "While *they* were in Colorado, *the Browns* learned to ski."

We have six types of pronouns, which are named either for their functions or for the kinds of nouns they replace: **personal, reflexive, interrogative, relative, demonstrative,** and **indefinite.**

5a Personal pronouns

We use the **personal** pronouns most often. We describe the different forms of the personal pronouns in terms of *person* (first, second, or third), *number* (singular or plural), and *case* (subjective, objective, or possessive). The *first-person* pronouns refer to ourselves when we speak or write: *I* (singular) and *we* (plural). The *second-person* pronouns refer to anyone listening to what we say or reading what we write: *you* (singular and plural). The *third-person* pronouns refer to everyone and everything else that we name: *he, she, it* (singular), and *they* (plural). Unlike nouns, the personal pronouns have two forms in the possessive case, one that acts as a noun in the sentence and one that acts as an adjective. Personal pronouns also have an objective case, whose forms can act as objects of any kind.

5a Pronouns

SINGULAR

Person	Subjective Case	Objective Case	Possessive Case as Adjective	Possessive Case as Noun
first	I	me	my	mine
second	you	you	your	yours
	thou*	thee*	thy*	thine*
third	he	him	his	his
	she	her	her	hers
	it	it	its	its

PLURAL

first	we	us	our	ours
second	you	you	your	yours
	ye*	ye*	your	yours
third	they	them	their	theirs

*These are archaic (early) forms for the second person, now used only in some dialects and religious texts.

I (you, he, she, it, we, you, they) called the coach.

The coach called me (you, him, her, it, us, you, them).

The coach called my (your, his, her, its, our, your, their) name.

These books are mine (yours, his, hers, its, ours, yours, theirs).

IMPORTANT: There is **no** apostrophe in *hers, its, ours, yours,* or *theirs.* The personal pronouns are the only words that do **not** use an apostrophe in the possessive case. Remember that *it's* is not a possessive form; it is the contraction of *it is.*

40

5b Pronoun cases

For each pronoun you must choose the case—subjective, objective, or possessive—that is appropriate for the pronoun's role in the grammar of the sentence. Be especially careful with pronouns in a list that includes proper nouns.

1. Use the *subjective* case when a pronoun acts as the subject of a verb:

    He, she, and *I* went to the movies last night. In the doorway stood Betty, Jim, and *I.*

2. Use the *subjective* case when a pronoun acts as the complement after a linking verb:

    To our surprise, it was *he* who came to the door.

3. Use the *objective* case when a pronoun acts as the object of a verb, verbal (infinitive, gerund, participle), or preposition:

    We saw *them* at the party, and they saw *him* and *her.* We hope to beat *you* and *them* in the tennis match. We enjoy watching *them* on the tennis court. They stood on the court, waving *us* good-bye. They could not come home *with* us.

NOTE: In informal English, we accept such constructions as "It must be them at the door" or "That's me in this snapshot." In formal English, however, we use the subjective case with linking verbs: "It must be they at the door," and "That is I in this snapshot." If you are unsure of the pronoun cases in such sentences, imagine reversing the subject and its complement: *"They* must be it" and *"I* am that" show clearly which case the pronoun should take.

4. Use the *possessive* case (adjective form) when a pronoun replaces a noun in the possessive case:

   The team earned *their* victory. (their = the team's)

5. Use the *possessive* case (adjective form) when a pronoun shows who or what is performing the action named by a gerund (a verb form ending with *ing* that is used as a noun; see **6b**):

   We enjoyed *their* playing.

6. Use the *possessive* case (noun form) when a pronoun replaces a combination of a possessive pronoun and a noun:

   The victory was *theirs.* (theirs = their + victory)

EXERCISES

A. Choose the correct form of the pronoun in parentheses.

  1. I hope you will vote for her and (I, me).
  2. The voters know that it is you and (they, them) who have worked hardest.
  3. Voters will be angry if Bob and (she, her) refuse to debate.
  4. The election resulted in a tie between Pat and (I, me).
  5. All of (us, we) students will have to vote again.
  6. Pat will receive more votes in the run-off than (I, me).

B. Choose the correct form of the pronoun in parentheses.

1. Will you vote for (he, him) or (she, her)?
2. A number of (we, us) voters are not sure whether (he, him) or (she, her) will win the election.
3. (We, us) voters have only two candidates to choose from because Ann and (he, him) will drop out of the race.
4. Running for election gives Pat and (I, me) experience in local politics.
5. If we get more votes than (they, them), it will show that the public trusts us more than (they, them).

5c Reflexive and intensive pronouns

Reflexive pronouns (from Latin *re* = back + *flexus* = bending) indicate that their antecedents are doing something to themselves—their actions are "bending back" on them, as in "I helped *myself* to the turkey" or "The Browns gave *themselves* a vacation."

Person	Singular	Plural
first	myself	ourselves
second	thyself, yourself	yourselves
third	himself, herself, itself	themselves

Using reflexive pronouns to avoid the problem of choosing pronoun cases creates awkward sentences like "The secret is between Betty and myself," instead of "The secret is between Betty and me." Substituting reflexive for personal pronouns suggests that the writer is afraid to choose pronoun cases.

43

Intensive pronouns have the same forms as reflexive pronouns, but we use them to emphasize their antecedents:

The drivers *themselves* pushed their cars.

The drivers pushed their cars *themselves*.

5d Demonstrative and interrogative pronouns

Demonstrative pronouns—*this* and *that* (singular), and *these* and *those* (plural)—call attention to a nearby word or word group acting as a noun:

This is the best restaurant in town.

A holiday in Puerto Rico—they dreamed of *that* all winter.

Interrogative pronouns—*who, which,* and *what* (singular and plural)—substitute for nouns in questions. *Who* has three forms: *who* (subjective), *whom* (objective), and *whose* (possessive). (Remember that *who's* is the contraction of *who is* or *who has.*) *Which* and *what* have the same form in all three cases. Ordinarily, we use *who, whom,* and *whose* to refer to people and *which* and *what* to refer to anything else.

Who is the new student?

Whom did you meet at the party?

This coat is mine, but *whose* is this?

Which is their car? *Which* do you prefer?

What happened? *What* have you eaten?

Like all nouns in the possessive case, *whose* can act as an adjective, and so can *which* and *what*. Use *which* when choosing within a known group, but use *what* when choosing among an unknown number:

Whose coat is this?

Which coats on this rack are waterproof?

What foods disagree with you?

CAUTION: The choice between *who* and *whom* can be difficult. We usually place these pronouns at the beginning of a question, where we expect the subject, so we tend to use *who* automatically. In informal English, many people now use *who* as both a subject and an object; in standard, formal English, *whom* is still the appropriate form for the object.

If you are unsure whether to use *who* or *whom* in a question, turn the question into a statement. Then ask yourself whether *he, she,* or *they* would make sense for the pronoun or *him, her,* or *them.* If *he, she,* or *they* would make sense, use *who;* if *him, her,* or *them* would make sense, use *whom.* For example, we can be sure that formal usage requires *whom* in "Whom will you meet at the party?" because the question turns into the statement "You will meet him, her, or them at the party."

5e Relative pronouns

The **relative** pronouns are *who, whom, whose, which, what,* and *that* (the first five are the same words as the interrogative pronouns). Relative pronouns, as their name implies, can relate one group of words to another. With a relative pronoun, we can merge two or more sentences into one. For example, we can merge:

The customer wanted a refund.

The customer called the manager.

Together, they become either

The customer *who* wanted a refund called the manager.

or

The customer *who* called the manager wanted a refund.

The basis for choosing *who* or *whom* is the same as in questions. Use *who* if *he, she,* or *they* would make sense in the original sentence; use *whom* if *him, her,* or *them* would make sense:

My family likes the man *who* is marrying my sister.

This sentence combines "My family likes the man" and "He is marrying my sister," so *who* replaces *he.*

My family likes the man *whom* my sister is marrying.

This sentence combines "My family likes the man" and "My sister is marrying him," so *whom* replaces *him.*

We add the ending *ever* to the relative and interrogative pronouns to mean "anyone who" or "anything which," as in *whoever* and *whichever.* Choose between *whoever* and *whomever* on the same basis as you choose between *who* and *whom:*

The crowd praised *whoever* won the races.

This sentence combines "The crowd praised someone" and "He, she, or they won the races," so *whoever* replaces *he, she,* or *they.*

The crowd praised *whomever* they liked.

This sentence combines "The crowd praised someone" with "They liked him, her, or them," so *whomever* replaces *him, her,* or *them.*

EXERCISE Choose the correct form of the pronoun in parentheses:

1. (Who, Whom) do you think will win the next election?
2. (Who, Whom) do you think you will vote for in the election?
3. I will vote for (whoever, whomever) will lower taxes.
4. They will vote for (whoever, whomever) they like.
5. The voters want a leader (who, whom) they can trust.

5f Indefinite pronouns

Indefinite pronouns have no specific antecedents because they do not refer to a particular person, place, or thing. With them we can express number or quantity with respect to people, places, and things. The common indefinite pronouns refer to:

1. *Two or more* individuals or groups:

    many   several   others

    Tourists crowded into the bus. *Many* carried suitcases, *several* had small children, and *others* had backpacks.

2. *Only two* individuals or groups:

> either   neither   both

The menu offers ham and chicken. *Neither* is expensive, *both* look appetizing, and we think *either* is a good choice.

3. *One or more* individuals or groups:

> all   any   most   more   some

Pat ate *some (most, all)* of the cake, but Chris did not want *any*. (refers to a single thing—the cake)

Pat ate *some (most, all)* of the cookies, but Chris did not want *any*. (refers to more than one thing—the cookies)

4. *Only one* individual or group:

> one   none   other   another   each
> someone   somebody   something
> anyone   anybody   anything
> no one   nobody   nothing
> everyone   everybody   everything

Everybody cheers the players as *each* comes on the field, but *no one* is predicting who will win.

Many of the indefinite pronouns can also act as adjectives:

Chris had *one* cookie, but Pat had *some* cake.

5g Indefinite pronouns—special problems

Indefinite pronouns can create special problems of agreement and reference. They are singular, as the endings *body, one,* and *thing* show; but because we often use them with more than one person or thing in mind, we are tempted to refer to them with *they, them,* or *their.* A plural after any of these pronouns is accepted in informal writing but not in strictly formal writing:

Formal: Nobody wants his or her efforts to be wasted. Everybody says that he or she is ready to work.

Informal: Nobody wants their efforts to be wasted. Everybody says that they are ready to work.

NOTE: When we use *none* to mean "no persons" or "no things," we may use a plural pronoun and verb in formal writing:

None of our friends want their efforts to be wasted.

One is the traditional pronoun to refer formally to people in general, but it often sounds awkward when repeated several times:

One has many options in choosing one's career if one gives careful thought to one's alternatives.

To avoid this awkwardness, use forms of *we* when you are including yourself with your readers:

We have many options in choosing our careers if we give careful thought to our alternatives.

Avoid the vague use of *you* to mean "people in general," "anyone," or "everyone":

Vague reference: Everyone needs a vacation because you may grow stale on your job.

In such sentences, *you* would refer to the reader, who might not agree with the opinions. More acceptable versions are:

Most people need vacations because they may grow stale on their jobs.

We need vacations because we may grow stale on our jobs.

CAUTION: Be consistent. If you begin by addressing your readers as *you* because you are giving advice, continue to use *you* and do not switch to *one* or *anyone*.

EXERCISE Revise sentences that have vague or inappropriate pronoun references.

1. They used to draft you into the army before you were old enough to vote, but they changed the law.
2. If everyone got what they wanted, we would all be happy.
3. One has to plan ahead, or you won't have time for all the things you want to do in life.
4. Nobody who buys a computer will regret their decision.
5. If you really want to, anyone can find a job after they go to college.

5h Pronouns and sexism

Pronouns can cause another problem—with gender. Some writers continue the old custom of using *he, him,* or *his* in referring to a person who may be of either gender. Many readers criticize this custom because it may suggest that everyone referred to is male. We have several ways to solve the problem:

Everyone must sign an application form. (This solution is preferable when personal possession is not the issue.)

Everyone must sign their application form. (This solution is colloquial and not appropriate in formal writing.)

Everyone must sign his/her application form. (This solution is often used in technical writing and on official forms.)

Everyone must sign his or her application form. (This solution is accurate, but awkward when used often.)

Everyone's application form must be signed. (This solution uses the pronoun in its possessive form with the verb in the passive, which weakens the force of the sentence.)

All students must sign their application forms. (This solution replaces the pronoun with a plural noun.)

Replacing the pronoun with a plural noun makes the smoothest construction, and a specific word, such as *students,* makes a clearer statement than an indefinite word such as *everyone.*

EXERCISE   In the following paragraph, the plural *workers* makes it possible to avoid problems with gender. Rewrite the paragraph in *four* versions, first, changing *the workers* to *every woman;* second, to *every man;* third, to *everyone,* used formally; and fourth, to *everyone,* used informally. Make any other changes necessary so that each version will be consistent.

In the company where Chris worked, the workers wanted their salaries increased. They thought that they deserved more money. They also wanted their working conditions improved. The workers said that their poor conditions made them less efficient and that they were tired of being tired.

6 ◆ VERBS

What is your first reaction when you read the following?

Two cars, a gray stretch limousine and a blue two-door compact, on a four-lane highway in the rain on October 3rd at 9:00 A.M.

Did you ask "What happened?" or "What did the cars do?" In spite of the details given, we need one more word to make sense out of the rest—for example, *crashed, stopped, passed,* or simply *were.* The word we need is a **verb**.

Verbs are words that express action or state of being. This traditional definition may not be helpful if we think of it as applying to words like *decision, alive, happy,* and *peace,* which cannot act as verbs. To learn about verbs, we must examine their forms and their functions.

6a Principal parts

The principal parts of a verb are the basic forms we use to indicate time, number, voice, and mood. The principal parts of *to play,* our sample verb, are *play, played, played, playing.*

1. **Present**   This part is often called the *verb base* or *stem.* It is the form by which the verb is listed in dictionaries and the one we use for the present tense, as in "Children *play* games." We also use the present stem to form the present infinitive, as in "to *play*" (see verbals, **6b**).

2. **Simple past**   For most verbs, we form this part by adding a *d* or *ed* ending to the present stem, as in "Children *played* games."

3. **Past participle**   This part is called a participle (from Latin *pars* = part + *capere* = to take) because it takes part in the nature of both verbs and adjectives. We form the past participle of most verbs by adding a *d* or *ed* ending to the present stem. We use the past participle in all the perfect tenses, as in "They have *played* games," and in the passive voice, as in "Games are *played.*" Past participles can also act as nouns and adjectives (see verbals, **6b**).

4. **Present participle**   For all verbs, we form the present participle by adding *ing* to the present stem, as in *playing.* We use the present participle in all the progressive forms of the verb tenses, as in "They are *playing* games." Technically, the present participle is not a principal part because it was not included as one in Latin grammar, but it is so essential in forming verb

tenses that we include it here with the principal parts. Present participles can also act as nouns and adjectives (see verbals, **6b**).

The great majority of English verbs have the same pattern as *play, played, played, playing* for their principal parts, and we therefore call them **regular verbs**, for example:

call   called   called   calling
seem   seemed   seemed   seeming

About 200 verbs are *irregular,* among them some that we use often, for example, *break, broke, broken, breaking;* or *run, ran, run, running;* or *hit, hit, hit, hitting.* (See **6j** for a list of the principal parts of common irregular verbs.) Dictionaries give the principal parts for irregular verbs; for regular verbs, they give only the first principal part—unless spelling rules cause a change, such as dropping the final *e* of *glide* to form *gliding* or doubling the final consonant of *omit* to form *omitted* and *omitting*.

6b Verbals

Infinitives, present and past participles, and gerunds are often called *verbals* because they derive from verbs, but they cannot act as the verb in a sentence. They can act as other parts of speech—nouns, adjectives, and adverbs—but like verbs they have tense and voice. The forms of the infinitive and the participles are discussed as principal parts in **6a**. The form of the gerund is the same as the present participle, but its function is different.

The **infinitive** (from Latin *in* = not + *finitus* = ended, limited) is not limited by person or number. The infinitive is formed from the first principal part, the present stem, and it is usually introduced by *to*. It can act as a noun, adjective, or adverb:

They like to swim. (infinitive as noun, direct object of the verb *like*)

They could not find a place to park. (infinitive as adjective, modifying the noun *place*)

We struggled to escape. (infinitive as adverb, modifying the verb *struggle*)

The **present participle** always ends in *ing* and always acts as an adjective:

The smiling hosts welcomed their guests. (present participle as adjective, modifying the noun *hosts*)

The **past participle** of regular verbs ends in *ed,* but the past participles of irregular verbs vary—for example, *gotten, slept, swum.* The past participle can act as a noun or adjective:

Our family eats *stuffed* turkey on Thanksgiving. (past participle as adjective, modifying the noun *turkey*)

In some adventure stories, the hunters become the *hunted.* (past participle as noun, the subject complement of the noun *hunters*)

The **gerund** always ends in *ing* and always acts as a noun: *Swimming* builds muscles. (gerund as noun, subject of the verb *builds*)

6c Tense

Any word acting as a verb changes in form to indicate a relation to time—past, present, or future. We call these changes **tenses** (from Latin *tempus* = time). We have six tenses in English. In the first two, the verb is a single word:

PRESENT TENSE:
verb base (base + *s* for third-person singular)

Person	Singular	Plural
first	I play games	we play games
second	you play games	you play games
third	he, she, *or* it plays games	they play games

REMINDER: In the present tense, we add an *s* ending to the third person singular for *all* verbs. Do not confuse this *s* with the two other *s* endings in English—the plural and the possessive forms of words acting as nouns; see **4a** and **4b** on nouns.

PAST TENSE:
verb base + *d* or *ed* ending

Person	Singular	Plural
first	I played games	we played games
second	you played games	you played games
third	he, she, *or* it played games	they played games

To make the other four tenses, we combine one of the principal parts of the verb with one or more **auxiliary** verbs (from Latin *auxiliaris* = helpful), also called "helping verbs."

FUTURE TENSE:
auxiliaries *will* or *shall* + verb base

Person	**Singular**	**Plural**
first	I shall *or* will play games	we will play games
second	you will play games	you will play games
third	he, she, *or* it will play games	they will play games

NOTE: In formal English, in the future tenses the first person uses *shall* and the second and third persons use *will,* as in "Tomorrow, we *shall* play soccer, but they *will* play tennis." To show determination or insistence in formal English, however, the use of *shall* and *will* is reversed, as in "I *will* play soccer, no matter what my doctor says," and "You *shall* play tennis today; you may not be excused." This use of *shall* is also standard in defining legal obligation, as in "The defendant *shall* pay the damages." Informal usage does not follow this distinction, and formal modern usage often ignores it.

To make the perfect tenses (from Latin *perfectus* = completed, finished), we combine the past participle of a verb with the verb *have* as an auxiliary (*have, had, had, having;* the third-person singular in the present tense is *has*):

PRESENT PERFECT:
auxiliaries *have* or *has*
+ past participle

Person	Singular	Plural
first	I have played games	we have played games
second	you have played games	you have played games
third	he, she, *or* it has played games	they have played games

PAST PERFECT (*or* pluperfect):
auxiliary *had*
+ past participle

Person	Singular	Plural
first	I had played games	we had played games
second	you had played games	you had played games
third	he, she, *or* it had played games	they had played games

FUTURE PERFECT:
auxiliary *will* or *shall*
+ past participle

Person	Singular
first	I shall *or* will have played games
second	you will have played games
third	he, she, *or* it will have played games

Person	Plural
first	we shall *or* will have played games
second	you will have played games
third	they will have played games

Progressive forms emphasize that an action or state of being continues in time. To make the progressive forms, we combine the present participle with an appropriate tense of the verb *be*. *Be (be, was, been, being)* is so irregular in the present and past tenses that some forms look completely different from the others:

PRESENT TENSE:

Person	Singular	Plural
first	I am	we are
second	you are	you are
third	he, she, *or* it is	they are

PAST TENSE:

Person	Singular	Plural
first	I was	we were
second	you were	you were
third	he, she, *or* it was	they were

PRESENT PROGRESSIVE:
auxiliary *am, is,* or *are*
+ present participle

Person	Singular	Plural
first	I am playing games	we are playing games
second	you are playing games	you are playing games

Person	Singular	Plural
third	he, she, *or* it is playing games	they are playing games

PAST PROGRESSIVE:
auxiliary *was* or *were*
+ present participle

Person	Singular	Plural
first	I was playing games	we were playing games
second	you were playing games	you were playing games
third	he, she, *or* it was playing games	they were playing games

FUTURE PROGRESSIVE:
auxiliary *will be* or *shall be*
+ present participle

Person	Singular
first	I will *or* shall be playing games
second	you will be playing games
third	he, she, *or* it will be playing games

Person	Plural
first	we will *or* shall be playing games
second	you will be playing games
third	they will be playing games

PRESENT PERFECT PROGRESSIVE:
auxiliary *have been* or *has been*
+ present participle

Person	Singular
first	I have been playing games
second	you have been playing games
third	he, she, *or* it has been playing games

Person	Plural
first	we have been playing games
second	you have been playing games
third	they have been playing games

PAST PERFECT PROGRESSIVE:
auxiliary *had been*
+ present participle

Person	Singular
first	I had been playing games
second	you had been playing games
third	he, she, *or* it had been playing games

Person	Plural
first	we had been playing games
second	you had been playing games
third	they had been playing games

FUTURE PERFECT PROGRESSIVE:
auxiliary *will have been* or *shall have been*
+ present participle

Person	Singular
first	I will *or* shall have been playing games
second	you will have been playing games
third	he, she, *or* it will have been playing games

Person	Plural
first	we will *or* shall have been playing games
second	you will have been playing games
third	they will have been playing games

TENSES OF THE INFINITIVE:

	Simple	Progressive
present	to play	to be playing
perfect	to have played	to have been playing

TENSES OF THE PARTICIPLE:

	Simple	Progressive
present	playing	playing
perfect	having played	having been playing

NOTE: In precise terms, what we call "perfect tenses" are not actually separate tenses at all. They are forms that show a particular *aspect* (from Latin *aspectus* = a viewing, a looking at) or way of looking at time. There are three aspects: the *simple* *aspect,* which views an action in a time period; the *perfect aspect,* which views an action as already completed before a time period; and the *progressive aspect,* which views an action as continuing within a time period. For example, in "They play games" (simple aspect), we view an action in the present time; in "They have played games" (perfect aspect), we view an action as already completed in relation to the present time; and in "They are playing games" (progressive aspect), we view an action as continuing in the present time. Ordinarily, however, we simplify this precise terminology by treating the perfect aspect as a set of different tenses and the progressive aspect as a set of different forms.

6d Voice

All the examples of verbs that we have examined so far are in the *active voice*— the subject of the verb is performing the action, as in "Bands play." Most verbs can be put in the *passive voice* (from Latin *passus* = having endured, having undergone) to show that the subjects are receiving the action instead of performing it, as in "Tunes are played" or "Logs are burned." We form the passive voice by combining the auxiliary *be* in the appropriate person, number, and tense with the past participle:

PASSIVE FORMS OF THE TENSES

present	tunes are played
past	tunes were played
future	tunes will be played
present perfect	tunes have been played
past perfect	tunes had been played
future perfect	tunes will have been played

Just as the active voice has progressive forms, so does the passive voice. We form the passive progressives by combining the auxiliary *be* in the appropriate tense, the present participle *being,* and the past participle of the verb: "Tunes are being played" (present), "Tunes were being played" (past), and so on.

Infinitives and participles also have passive forms:

PASSIVE FORMS OF THE INFINITIVE

	Simple	**Progressive**
present	to be played	to be being played
present perfect	to have been played	to have been being played

PASSIVE FORMS OF THE PARTICIPLE

	Simple	**Progressive**
present	being played	being played
present perfect	having been played	having been being played

CAUTION: The passive voice is less forceful than the active voice. For effective sentences, eliminate passive-voice verbs wherever possible. For example, change "Tunes were played by the band" to "The band played tunes."

EXERCISE Wherever possible, change each passive verb to the active voice and each active verb to the passive voice.

1. The weather report predicts sunshine for next week, so our picnic will be held on Tuesday.
2. If you are asked by our friends to bring something to the picnic, what will you bring?
3. I will make potato salad because it can be made a day in advance and kept in the refrigerator.
4. If the forks are left behind, we will use spoons instead.
5. Last year our picnic was spoiled by the rain, but this year we expect clear skies and warm weather.

6e Transitive and intransitive verbs

We call verbs that can take direct objects **transitive** (from Latin *transitus* = passed across) because the action expressed by the verb is passed on to affect someone or something directly. In "Bands play tunes," *tunes* are directly affected by the band's action of playing.

Some verbs are **intransitive**—a direct object would make no sense with them because they do not indicate that any action is passed on to anything else. For example, *glow* is an intransitive verb. "The fire glows" makes sense as a sentence, but "The fire is glowed" does not. In contrast, "The fire burns," "The fire burns the log," and "The log is burned" make sense because *burn* can be either transitive or intransitive. *All linking verbs are intransitive*—they cannot take direct objects. (For discussion of three pairs of problem verbs—*sit, set; lie, lay; rise, raise*—see **6i**.)

The dictionary labels every verb either *vt*, meaning "verb transitive"; *vi*, meaning "verb intransitive"; or both *vi* and *vt* if the verb is like *play* and *burn* and may be used with or without a direct object. Transitive verbs also have a passive voice, but intransitive verbs do not (see **6d**). If you are unsure whether a verb is transitive, intransitive, or both, check your dictionary.

6f Mood

We can use verb forms to indicate *mood* (from Latin *modus* = manner; way of acting, doing, or being). We have three moods for verbs in English: **indicative, imperative,** and **subjunctive**.

We use the **indicative mood** whenever we make a statement, as in "Bands played tunes" or "Children like games."

We use the **imperative mood** to give a command or make an urgent request. In most sentences with verbs in the imperative mood, the subject is in the second person *(you),* whoever is being addressed. To form an imperative of this type, use the first principal part, the verb base, and omit the subject, which is understood to be "you," as in "Go home," or "Drive carefully," or "Please hurry." Occasionally you may wish to use the imperative in the first or third person. To do this, use *let* with the appropriate pronoun in the objective case—*me, him, her, it, us,* or *them*—with the verb base, as in "That way madness lies; let me shun that" (Shakespeare, *King Lear*), "Let us love one another," "Let's go," or "Let him speak now or forever hold his peace." In these examples, *let* is not a command to "you" to permit something. It is instead a command to "me," "us," or "him."

We use the **subjunctive mood** for three purposes: to make certain set phrases, to express a strong intention or wish, and to indicate a condition that is hypothetical or contrary to fact. The subjunctive has only two tenses, present and past. The present subjunctive, like the imperative, uses the first principal part, the verb base, for all three persons, singular and plural.

Uses of the present subjunctive We use the present subjunctive in certain exclamations and set phrases:

Long *live* the king!

Suffice it to say that they paid the bill.

Far *be* it from me to argue over ten cents.

We also use the present subjunctive to express a strong intention or wish, for example:

The audience insists that the song *be played*.

The audience urged that the band *play*.

Compare these with "The audience hears that the song *is played*" and "The audience learned that the band *played*."

The law required that this criminal *be punished*.

Compare this with "The newspaper reported that this criminal *was punished*."

Uses of the past subjunctive The past subjunctive of the verb *be* is *were*. For all other verbs, the past subjunctive is the same in form as the past tense (the second principal part). In formal English, the past subjunctive indicates a *hypothetical condition* or one *contrary to fact* and is usually introduced by *if* or *as though*—for example:

If I *were* you, I would ask for a raise.

This is a statement contrary to fact—"I" am not "you." Compare this statement to "If I am the winner, I shall celebrate."

If he *were* failing, everyone would be shocked.

This is a hypothetical condition; in reality, "he" is not failing. Compare this sentence to "If he is failing, everyone will be shocked," which expresses uncertainty—it is not known whether he is failing.

6g Modal auxiliaries

We have ten modal auxiliaries: *can, could, may, might, should, would, must, ought to,* and, in certain constructions, *shall* and *will.* We use them to indicate the *mode*—the manner or way of acting, doing, or being—expressed by the verb.

Can   To indicate the ability or permission to do something:

> They can play tennis very well.

> Can we have more pie? ("May we have more pie" is more formal or polite.)

To indicate theoretical possibility:

> Even a fool can be wise sometimes.

To indicate factual possibility:

> This coat can be altered to fit you.

Could   To indicate a past ability:

> Last summer we could sleep late every day.

To indicate present or future permission:

> Could we leave the party now?

To indicate present possibility:

> We could reach Topeka by midnight if we hurry.

To indicate a hypothetical situation:

> If we were younger, we could ride the train free.

May   To indicate permission:

> You may leave whenever you are ready.

To indicate a real possibility:

> The weather may change tomorrow.

Might   To indicate permission (rare usage):

> Might we have more pie?

To indicate possibility, theoretical or factual:

> We might go to Dallas today if the weather is good.
>
> This movie might amuse my parents.

Should   To indicate obligation and logical necessity (alternative to *ought to*):

The children should clean up their rooms.

To indicate an opinion after certain expressions:

It is strange that they should be so rude to us.

To indicate a real condition (formal usage):

If you should decide to go, call us tomorrow.

or Should you decide to go, call us tomorrow.

Would To indicate willingness:

Would you please pass the sugar?

To indicate insistence (with *would* stressed):

They *would* stay out late last night, and now they will miss breakfast.

To indicate characteristic or habitual activity in the past:

My grandfather would take a nap before dinner.

To indicate a possibility dependent upon a condition stated in an "if" clause:

If they learned Spanish, they would enjoy their trip to Mexico more.

To indicate probability:

> That coat would be more useful on your trip than this one.

Must To indicate present obligation (alternative to *have to*):

> I must return this book to the library today. (for past obligation we use *had to:* I had to return this book yesterday.)

To indicate logical necessity:

> That clock must be wrong. My watch says it's ten.

Ought to To indicate obligation and logical necessity (alternative to *should*):

> We ought to call the Browns to say thank you. They must be lost because they ought to have arrived by now.

Shall To indicate willingness:

> You shall sleep as late as you wish here.

To indicate intention in the first person:

> We shall overcome our difficulties.

To indicate insistence or requirement in the second and third persons (standard legal usage):

> The landlord shall maintain the hallways and lobby.

Will   To indicate willingness in polite requests:

Will you please call me later?

To indicate intention (usually contracted):

We'll help them whenever we can.

To indicate insistence (with *will* stressed):

He *will* stuff himself, no matter what the doctor tells him.

To indicate prediction (often contracted):

They'll never be ready in five minutes.

To indicate habitual action:

Our neighbors will complain about anything.

To indicate timeless action:

Wherever you are on this planet, the sun will rise in the east.

We have three additional auxiliaries to indicate distinctions in time or to indicate a future action or intention not only as seen in the present but also as it was seen in the past.

Used to   To indicate habitual actions in the past that do not continue in the present:

They used to live here, but they moved away.

Be + going to To indicate an action somewhere in the future (with *am, is,* or *are + going to +* verb base):

> They are going to take a vacation in Miami.

To indicate an action intended in the past but not completed (with *was* or *were + going to +* verb base):

> They were going to visit Miami, but their uncle died.

Be + about to To indicate an action in the immediate future (with *am, is,* or *are + about to +* verb base):

> They are about to take a vacation in Miami.

To indicate an action intended in the past but not completed (with *was* or *were + about to +* verb base):

> We were about to go out the door when the phone rang.

The irregular verb *do (do, did, done, doing)* can also act as an auxiliary. We use it to form **negative** statements in the present and past tenses, as in "The band did not arrive on time," and to form questions in the present and past tenses, as in "Does the band play here every week?" We also use it to emphasize a verb, as in "We never thought we would see them again, but they did come to the wedding," or to indicate a contradiction by emphasizing the verb, as in "You are mistaken. The band did play yesterday." We also use it to avoid repetition, as in "The band played well yesterday, as it always does."

6h Contractions

A contraction is the omission of one or more letters from a word. In speech and informal writing, we often contract *am, are, is, have, has, shall, will,* and *would,* combining them with the word acting as the subject. Use an apostrophe to mark the place in each word where you have omitted one or more letters.

We*'d* like to leave because we*'re* ready, but he*'s* late.

When the program*'s* over, they*'ll* leave, but I*'m* staying.

Similarly, we may contract *not,* combining it with forms of *be, have,* and *do;* with the auxiliaries *can, could, should, would, may, might, must,* and *ought;* or with the verb *need.*

They couldn*'t* leave because he wasn*'t* ready and they didn*'t* have a car, but you needn*'t* worry about them.

NOTE: When the auxiliary *can* is followed by *not,* we usually spell the combination as one word: *cannot.* When the auxiliaries *can, shall,* and *will* are combined with *not,* they contract irregularly: *can't, shan't,* and *won't.* The contraction *ain't,* which is often used in informal speech for *am not, are not,* and *is not,* is not used in standard, formal English.

Because contractions are informal, they are not appropriate in most college and business writing. When you do use them, do not forget the apostrophe; without it, *we're* looks like *were*, *he'll* looks like *hell*, and so on. Remember also that *it's* is the contraction of *it is* or *it has*, but *its* is the possessive of *it*.

EXERCISE   In the following sentences, replace the contractions with the full words that they represent.

1.   You can't use the telephone until I've finished.
2.   I'd like to know who's going to stop me.
3.   You needn't be so selfish when you're using my telephone.
4.   Now the telephone's not working, and it's all your fault.
5.   Don't blame me if it's broken; you're the one who's been using it.

6i Three pairs of problem verbs

Three verbs that are usually transitive look confusingly like three other verbs that are usually intransitive.

1.   *set, sit*

set   set   set   setting   (almost always *transitive*)

sit   sat   sat   sitting   (almost always *intransitive*)

The waiter *set* down the soup, and the guests *sat* down. Please *set* the table before you *sit* down.

NOTE: When *set* is transitive, it means *arrange* or *place*. When it is intransitive, it means *disappear below the horizon*, as in

"The sun sets in the west"; *settle down,* as in "The hen sets on her eggs"; or *harden,* as in "Glue sets quickly in dry air."

2. *raise, rise*

| raise | raised | raised | raising | *(transitive)* |
| rise | rose | risen | rising | *(intransitive)* |

We *raised* the windows as the sun *rose* over the mountains.

3. *lay, lie*

| lay | laid | laid | laying | *(transitive)* |
| lie | lay | lain | lying | *(intransitive)* |

The children *laid* pillows on the floor and *lay* down to watch television.

If we *lay* pillows on the floor, we can *lie* down comfortably.

This pair is especially confusing because *lay* is a principal part of both verbs. The confusion is made greater by another intransitive verb, *lie, lied, lied, lying,* meaning "to tell a falsehood." Wherever *place, placed, placed, placing* makes sense, use *lay, lay, laid, laying.* Wherever *recline, reclined, reclined, reclining* makes sense, use *lie, lay, lain, lying.*

6j Principal parts of common irregular verbs

arise—arose—arise
awake—awaked—awaked
   (*or* awake—awoke
   —awoken)
be—was—been
beat—beat—beaten

become—became—
   become
begin—began—begun
behold—beheld—beheld
bend—bent—bent
bet—bet—bet

bid—bade—bidden
  (*or* bid—bad—bid)
bind—bound—bound
bite—bit—bitten
bleed—bled—bled
blow—blew—blown
break—broke—broken
breed—bred—bred
bring—brought—
  brought
build—built—built
burst—burst—burst
buy—bought—bought
cast—cast—cast
catch—caught—caught
choose—chose—chosen
cling—clung—clung
come—came—come
cost—cost—cost
creep—crept—crept
cut—cut—cut
deal—dealt—dealt
dig—dug—dug
dive—dived
  (*or* dove)—dived
do—did—done
draw—drew—drawn
drink—drank—drunk
drive—drove—
  driven
eat—ate—eaten
fall—fell—fallen
feed—fed—fed
feel—felt—felt

fight—fought—fought
find—found—found
flee—fled—fled
fling—flung—flung
fly—flew—flown
forbid—forbade (*or*
  forbad)—forbidden
forget—forgot—forgotten
forgive—forgave—
  forgiven
forsake—forsook—
  forsaken
freeze—froze—frozen
get—got—got (*or* gotten)
go—went—gone
grind—ground—ground
grow—grew—grown
hang—hung—hung (*but*
  hang—hanged—
  hanged *for* "execute")
have—had—had
hear—heard—heard
hide—hid—hidden
hit—hit—hit
hold—held—held
keep—kept—kept
kneel—kneeled
  (*or* knelt)—kneeled
  (*or* knelt)
know—knew—known
lead—led—led
leave—left—left
lend—lent—lent
let—let—let

lie—lay—lain
light—lit (*or* lighted)—lit
  (*or* lighted)
lose—lost—lost
make—made—made
mean—meant—meant
meet—met—met
mistake—mistook—
  mistaken
put—put—put
read—read—read
rid—rid—rid
ride—rode—ridden
ring—rang—rung
rise—rose—risen
run—ran—run
see—saw—seen
seek—sought—sought
sell—sold—sold
send—sent—sent
set—set—set
shake—shook—shaken
shed—shed—shed
shine—shone—shone
  (*but* shine—shined
  —shined *for* "polish")
shoot—shot—shot
show—showed—shown
  (*or* showed)
shrink—shrank—shrunk
shut—shut—shut
sing—sang—sung
sink—sank—sunk

sit—sat—sat
slay—slew—slain
sleep—slept—slept
slide—slid—slid
sling—slung—slung
slink—slunk—slunk
slit—slit—slit
speak—spoke—spoken
spend—spent—spent
spin—spun—spun
spit—spit—spit
  (*or* spit—spat—spat)
split—split—split
spread—spread—spread
spring—sprang—sprung
stand—stood—stood
steal—stole—stolen
stick—stuck—stuck
sting—stung—stung
stink—stank (*or* stunk)
  —stunk
stride—strode—stridden
strike—struck—struck
  (*or* stricken)
string—strung—strung
strive—strove—striven
  (*or* strive—strived—
  strived)
swear—swore—sworn
sweep—swept—swept
swell—swelled—swollen
  (*or* swelled)
swim—swam—swum

swing—swung—swung
take—took—taken
teach—taught—taught
tear—tore—torn
tell—told—told
think—thought—thought
throw—threw—thrown
thrust—thrust—thrust
tread—trod—trodden (or trod)
wake—waked—waked
(or wake—woke—woken)
wear—wore—worn
weave—wove—woven (or weave—weaved—weaved, *depending on sense*)
weep—wept—wept
win—won—won
wind—wound—wound
wring—wrung—wrung
write—wrote—written

EXERCISE Test yourself on irregular verbs. Without looking at the list of principal parts, change the italicized verbs from the simple present tense to the simple past tense. Then check the list to see if you have remembered the standard forms.

When the courthouse clock *strikes* ten, guards *throw* open the doors. Men and women *burst* into the lobby and *tear* along the corridors. As they *go*, they *wear* concerned expressions and *hold* official forms. They *choose* different paths to the second floor: some *stride* up the marble steps; some *take* the creaky elevators. When the clerks *hear* people coming, they *hide* their coffee cups. As one clerk *reads* out names, another *writes* them down. The crowding applicants *get* in lines and *cling* to the guide ropes, but their spirits *sink* as the lines *grow* longer. They *stand* impatiently and *speak* softly. They *begin* to lose confidence as the lines *keep* growing. They *strike* different poses as they *fight* off boredom. At last, they *break* into smiles as they *see* the lines move forward.

6k Subject-verb agreement

   A subject and its verb must agree in number. To "agree in number" means that if the subject is singular, its verb must be singular, and if the subject is plural, its verb must be plural.

Singular subject and verb: The band plays.

Plural subject and verb: The bands play.

RULE 1 A subject in the third person **singular** takes a verb with an *s* ending when the verb is in one of these tenses:

PRESENT

	Active	Passive
simple	The band play*s*.	The tune i*s* played.
progressive	The band i*s* playing.	The tune i*s* being played.

PAST

	Active	Passive
simple	The band played.	The tune wa*s* played.
progressive	The band wa*s* playing.	The tune wa*s* being played.

PRESENT PERFECT

	Active	Passive
simple	The band ha*s* played.	The tune ha*s* been played.
progressive	The band ha*s* been playing.	The tune ha*s* been being played.

This rule also applies when the verb has two or more subjects, each in the singular, that are joined by *or, either . . . or,* or *neither . . . nor:*

No coffee or soda wa*s* offered.

Either coffee or soda i*s* being offered.

Neither coffee nor soda ha*s* been offered.

If the last subject named is in the plural, however, then the verb is in the plural:

Neither coffee nor sodas *were* being served.

If one subject is plural but the others are singular, try to place the plural subject last to avoid a clumsy sentence like "No sodas or coffee is served."

RULE 2 If two or more singular subjects are joined by *and,* they act together as a plural subject and take a plural verb:

The mare and her foal *are* in the pasture.

EXCEPTION: If the elements of such a subject refer to the same person or thing, they take the singular form of the verb:

81

The owner and operator of the vehicle *is* responsible for this accident. (The owner is the operator.)

The owner and operator of the vehicle *are* responsible for this accident. (The owner and operator are two people.)

RULE 3 If *every* or *each* precedes two or more singular subjects joined by *and,* then the subjects take a singular verb because each subject is considered separately:

Each (*or* every) student and teacher in the school *was* present at the graduation.

CAUTION: Connecting phrases such as *in addition to, as well as,* and *accompanied by* are not coordinating conjunctions (see **8**); therefore the words they connect to the subject do not act as additional subjects. Compare these sentences:

The driver, as well as the passengers, *was* injured.

The driver and the passenger *were* injured.

RULE 4 If *each* follows a plural subject or two or more subjects joined by *and,* then the verb is usually plural:

The ten racing drivers each *have* two mechanics.

RULE 5 The pronouns *everybody, somebody, anybody, nobody, either, neither, everyone, someone, anyone, no one,* and *one* are singular, so they take verbs in the singular:

Everybody *has* arrived.   Neither *was* injured.

NOTE: Remember that plural words describing these pronouns do **not** make the pronouns plural, as in "Everyone on the two teams *has* a new uniform" or "Neither of the players *was* injured."

RULE 6 The pronouns *all, any, most,* and *some,* and the fractions *half, quarter, third,* and so on, take a verb in the singular when they refer to a single person or thing:

Some (most, half, a third, all) of the milk *was* sour.

They take a plural verb when they refer to more than one:

Some (most, half, a third, all) of the bottles *were* full.

RULE 7 The pronoun *none* can take either a singular or a plural verb, but in formal English, *none* usually takes a singular verb:

Formal: None of the bottles *is* full.

Informal: None of the bottles *are* full.

RULE 8 The pronouns *who, which,* and *that* take a singular verb when their antecedent is singular and a plural verb when their antecedent is plural:

The guest who *is* coming for dinner is an old friend.

The guests who *are* coming for dinner are old friends.

RULE 9 Nouns coming between the subject and the verb do not affect the number of the subject:

The reading list of fifty books for the three courses *was* impressive. (*List* is singular, even though fifty books and three courses are mentioned.)

The lists for the course *were* impressive. (*Lists* is plural, even though only one course is mentioned.)

RULE 10 Several nouns that end in *s* are treated as singular—for example, *news, mathematics, physics, electronics, measles:*

Measles *has been* a common disease for centuries.

Mathematics *is* fundamental to all the sciences.

Some nouns ending in *ics,* such as *athletics, politics,* and *statistics,* are singular when they name a unified body of knowledge but plural when they name assorted facts or activities:

International politics *is* my major.

My neighbor's politics *are* confusing.

RULE 11 A *collective noun* takes a singular verb when the group it names acts as a unit but a plural verb when the group members are considered individually:

The jury *has* agreed on a verdict.

The jury *are* arguing among themselves.

Three-quarters of the field *is* planted in corn.

Three quarters of the field *are* flooded. (Notice the hyphen in the first use of *three-quarters,* which makes the fraction a single unit. Without the hyphen, each quarter is being considered as a separate part.)

Ten minutes *is* enough time for the job.

The ten minutes *were* passing slowly.

RULE 12 In sentences with linking verbs and subject complements, like "Bands are successes," a subject in the singular takes a singular verb, even when the subject complement is plural:

Their chief amusement *is* video games.

RULE 13 Any word discussed as a word, whether it is singular or plural, takes a singular verb:

"Cookies" *was* the first word the baby learned to say.

RULE 14 The title of a literary work, a work of art, or a musical composition always takes a verb in the singular and is referred to by a singular pronoun:

Wuthering Heights is a novel that was made into a movie.

NOTE: Remember that a verb may come before its subject in some sentences, but it must still agree with the subject:

Here *is* the result of the investigation.

but

Here *are* the results of the investigation.

Down the hills and into the valleys *roars* the wind.

but

Down the hills and into the valleys *roar* the winds.

EXERCISES

A. Make the subjects agree with their verbs by choosing *is, are, was,* or *were* to fill the blanks.

1. "Goldilocks and the Three Bears" _____ a familiar children's story.
2. *Star Wars, The Empire Strikes Back,* and *Return of the Jedi* _____ a popular science fiction trilogy.
3. The president, in addition to the members of the Senate, _____ responsible for foreign policy decisions.
4. Each of the members _____ required to donate one hour a week.
5. Politics _____ everybody's business.

B. Correct any verbs that do not agree with their subjects. Write *C* over any verbs that are correct.

1. The ringing of bells are used to signal the beginning and end of classes.
2. There is ten-minute breaks between classes.
3. Into the hallways and down the stairwells rushes all of the students.
4. Twelve weeks of summer vacation gives many students time to earn money for the new school year.
5. There are fifty-two weeks in a year.

7 ◆ MODIFIERS

Modifiers are words that act as *adjectives* or *adverbs.* They modify—describe, make more definite—another word or word group in the sentence. Modifiers may be added almost anywhere within the basic subject-verb-object structure of the sentence.

7a Adjectives

Adjectives modify a word or word group that acts as a noun. They tell us *which* or *what kind* of person, place, or thing is named by a noun. For example, compare these two sentences:

Children watched balloons.

The neighbors' three small, disappointed, weeping, red-eyed children watched their shriveling, bright green balloons.

All the added words are adjectives. We can see the relationships between the adjectives and nouns in this arrangement:

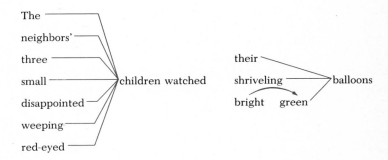

These adjectives are examples of the six types we use frequently.

1. **Common adjectives** *Small* almost always acts as an adjective, as do descriptive words such as *large, pretty, ugly, grand, sick, hot, tall, honest,* and *certain.* We

form many common adjectives by adding endings to nouns and verbs, for example:

health—healthy	hope—hopeless
beauty—beautiful	glory—glorious
honor—honorable	impress—impressive
base—basic	radiate—radiant
terrify—terrific	fool—foolish
type—typical	friend—friendly

2. **Articles**   The adjectives we use most often are the two articles: the definite article *the* and the indefinite article *a* (spelled *an* when the word following it begins with a vowel or a silent *h*, as in "an apple" and "an honor").

3. **Participles**   *Disappointed, eyed, weeping,* and *shriveling* are participles acting as adjectives. *Disappointed* and *eyed* are the past participles of *disappoint* and *eye; weeping* and *shriveling* are the present participles of *weep* and *shrivel.*

4. **Nouns**   *Three, red,* and *green* act as adjectives in the example, but these words often act as nouns, as do all words for color and number. Most common nouns can also act as adjectives—for example, *floor cover, machine language, football field, apple pie,* and *army blanket.* Proper names, which are always nouns, often act as adjectives—for example, *Ford pickups* or the *Omaha schools.*

5. **Nouns and pronouns in the possessive case**   The noun *neighbors'* is in the possessive case and modifies *children.* The pronoun *their,* which is also possessive, modifies *balloons.* When a noun acts as an adjective, it may still have an adjective modifier of its own—in the example, *bright* modifies *green.*

6. **Compound adjectives** Two or more words working together as a unit form a compound. Usually, we hyphenate compound adjectives when they precede the nouns they modify, as in *red-eyed,* in which *red* modifies *eyed* and the two words together modify *children.*

7. **Infinitives** A less common type of adjective is not illustrated in the sentence example. The infinitive can act as an adjective, as in "They have the right to vote." Here, *to vote* modifies the noun *right.* (For more information on infinitives, see **6a–b.**)

We usually place adjectives before the nouns they modify, but for emphasis we may place them after the nouns:

> The neighbors' three small children, disappointed, weeping, and red-eyed, watched their balloons, bright green but shriveling.

Adjectives that act as complements normally follow the verb, as in "Bands are successful" or "She felt happy."

EXERCISE In the following sentences, replace the underlined adjectives by choosing appropriate adjectives of your own.

1. The winter wind was biting and damp.
2. As the evening sky grew dark, the last tired group left.
3. Several students wore down jackets and long wool scarves.
4. Thick, slushy snow clung to the students' boots.
5. One minute later, the snow-covered campus looked deserted.

7b Adverbs

An **adverb** (from Latin *ad* = to, towards + *verbum* = word, verb) modifies a word or word group in the sentence that acts as a verb, adjective, or adverb. Adverbs tell us *how, when, where,* or *to what extent* something or someone is or does something:

The team ran slowly. (*how* they ran)

The team ran yesterday. (*when* they ran)

The team ran here. (*where* they ran)

The team ran very slowly. (*to what extent* they ran slowly)

Occasionally, an adverb may modify a whole sentence, as in *"Fortunately,* the weather was good on our vacation." It is then called a sentence adverb.

We form most adverbs by adding the ending *ly* to adjectives, as in *quickly, clearly, beautifully, enormously,* and *amazingly.* Some common adverbs do not end in *ly*—for example, *very, somewhat, soon, here, ever, yet, always, too,* and *even.* A few words may act either as adjectives or as adverbs—for example, *fast, late, long, hard, slow, early, quick, well,* and *only.*

Infinitives can also act as adverbs. Besides telling how, when, where, or to what extent, infinitives can also tell *why* and *to what purpose,* as in "They hurried *to meet* the deadline."

EXERCISE In the following sentences, replace the underlined adverbs by choosing appropriate adverbs of your own.

1. The captain <u>awkwardly</u> rushes <u>forward,</u> <u>sharply</u> kicks the ball, and <u>eagerly</u> runs after it.
2. The spectators <u>always</u> lean <u>very</u> <u>intently</u> toward the players struggling <u>fiercely</u> near the goal.
3. <u>Hoarsely</u> yelling, the crowd tries <u>hard</u> to encourage the team.
4. <u>Here</u> and <u>there</u>, loyal alumni <u>madly</u> wave banners.
5. The whole school <u>desperately</u> hopes for a victory today.

7c Comparison

Adjectives and adverbs have three different forms, called degrees: the *positive,* the *comparative,* and the *superlative.* The *positive degree* is the form we use to describe something. We use the *comparative degree* when comparing two things, and the *superlative degree* when comparing more than two things.

With all one-syllable adjectives and adverbs we add *er* as an ending for the comparative degree and *est* for the superlative degree, as in *great, greater, greatest,* or *fast, faster, fastest.* We also add *er* and *est* to many two-syllable modifiers whose second syllable is unstressed, as in *happy, happier, happiest* or *pleasant, pleasanter, pleasantest.* With all other adjectives and adverbs we add *more* and *most* before the modifier.

The first typist is *quick* and *efficient* and types *accurately;* the second is *quicker* and *more efficient* and types *more accurately;* but the third is the *quickest* and *most efficient* of all and types *most accurately.*

To indicate that something has less or least of what the modifier describes, we add *less* and *least* before the modifier.

The first typist is *less efficient* and types *less accurately* than the second, but the third typist is the *least efficient* of all and types *least accurately*.

REMINDER: Some adjectives and adverbs cannot logically have comparative and superlative degrees. Although you may hear something described as "most unique," *unique* means "one of a kind." Something cannot be more "one of a kind" than something else that is also "one of a kind"; substitute "most unusual." Similarly, one action cannot be "more impossible" or "more unforgettable" than another; it can, however, be "more difficult" or "more memorable."

EXERCISE Provide the comparative and superlative forms for each of the following adjectives and adverbs.

1.	large	4.	piercing	7.	early	10.	broadly
2.	delicate	5.	fast	8.	hard		
3.	grimy	6.	carefully	9.	pretty		

7d Irregular comparison

Several adjectives and adverbs have irregular forms for the comparative and superlative degrees:

IRREGULAR ADJECTIVES

Positive	Comparative	Superlative
bad, ill	worse	worst
far	farther, further	farthest, furthest
good, well	better	best
little	less, lesser	least
much, many	more	most

IRREGULAR ADVERBS

Positive	Comparative	Superlative
well	better	best
ill, badly	worse	worst
much	more	most
far	farther, further	farthest, furthest

NOTE: As an adjective, *well* means "healthy." In formal English, if you are referring to someone's health, expressions such as "You seem well" and "They looked well" are preferable to "You seem good" or "They looked good."

8 ◆ CONJUNCTIONS

A conjunction (from Latin *con* = with + *junctus* = joined) connects words or word groups. We have three kinds of conjunctions: **coordinating, subordinating,** and correlative. In addition, **conjunctive adverbs** can show a relationship between statements, but they do not connect grammatical structures.

Coordinating conjunctions connect words or word groups of equal importance. The coordinating conjunctions are *and, but, for* (meaning "because"), *or,* and *nor;* in addition, we can use *so* (meaning "as a result") and *yet* (meaning "but").

We studied French, *and* they studied Spanish.

You studied German, *but* they did not.

You will study French, *for* you are going to Paris.

Did you study Greek *or* Latin?

I have not studied German, *nor* have they.

She studied Italian, *so* she wants to visit Rome.

They were going to Paris, *yet* they studied Spanish.

Subordinating conjunctions connect modifiers to the words they modify. We have many subordinating conjunctions—for example, *although, as, because, if, so* (meaning "in order that"), *than, when, whenever, where, wherever, whether,* and *while.* Several prepositions (see 9) can also act as subordinating conjunctions—for example, *after, before, since,* and *until.* Some subordinating conjunctions are compounds—for example, *as far as, as if, as long as, as much as, as though, except that, in case, in order that, provided that, rather than, sooner than,* and *so that.*

Although you studied French, they studied Spanish.

We learned German *because* we were going to Berlin.

If we are going to Rome, shouldn't we study Italian?

When you studied Spanish, did you go to Madrid?

Until we studied Arabic, we did not want to visit Egypt.

She studied Russian *rather than* Spanish.

He will study Spanish *in case* he is sent to Peru.

Correlative conjunctions are conjunctions used in pairs—for example, *as . . . as, both . . . and, either . . . or, neither . . . nor, not only . . . but also,* and *whether . . . or.*

Both French *and* Spanish are spoken in North America.

We studied *not only* Spanish *but also* French.

Conjunctive adverbs show a relationship of thought between words or word groups—for example, *accordingly, besides, furthermore, however, indeed, instead, likewise, moreover, nevertheless, otherwise,* and *therefore*—but they do not connect them grammatically.

Columbus hoped to find a new route to the East Indies; *instead,* he found the West Indies.

His sailors grew discouraged; *however,* Columbus sailed on.

Columbus believed he had reached the East Indies; *accordingly,* he called the native inhabitants Indians.

He claimed vast territories for Spain; *nevertheless,* he died a poor man.

EXERCISE Join these sentences by using subordinating conjunctions.

1. Paul is usually a careful driver. He had an accident yesterday. The brakes on his car failed.
2. Paul took the car to a body shop to be fixed. The repairman had to replace both front fenders.
3. The work was being done. Paul had to walk to school.
4. The repairs were finally completed. Paul had to wait another week. He earned the money to pay the bill.
5. Paul takes his car in for regular tune-ups. He may be able to avoid another accident.

9 ◆ PREPOSITIONS

A **preposition** (from Latin *prae* = before + *positus* = placed) connects a word acting as a noun to another word in the sentence. In "We drove through the center of the town," the preposition *through* connects the noun "center" to the verb "drove," and the preposition *of* connects the noun "town" to the noun "center." The preposition and its noun (*through* + center; *of* + town) form a **prepositional phrase** that acts as an adjective or adverb; the noun in the phrase is called the **object** of the preposition. (For discussion of prepositional phrases, see **11a.3.**)

The most common prepositions in English are:

aboard	along	behind	beyond
about	amid	below	but
above	among	beneath	(meaning
across	around	beside	"except")
after	at	besides	by
against	before	between	concerning

despite	into	through	unto
down	like	throughout	up
during	near	till	upon
except	of	to	with
for	off	toward	within
from	on	towards	without
in	over	under	
including	past	underneath	
inside	since	until	

Some prepositions are composed of two or more words—for example, *according to, as compared with, as for, aside from, as to, because of, in addition to, in spite of, out of, on account of, owing to, with reference to.*

Prepositional adverbs are prepositions that act as adverbs to modify verbs—for example, *up, down, in, out, on, off.* They may create different meanings for a verb:

The general called the reserves.

The general called the reserves *up.*
(*or* The general called *up* the reserves.)

The general called the reserves *out.*
(*or* The general called *out* the reserves.)

The general called the reserves *in.*
(*or* The general called *in* the reserves.)

At first glance, "up the reserves," "out the reserves," and "in the reserves" may appear to be prepositional phrases, but looking more closely you can see that *reserves* is the direct object of *called,* not the object of *up, out,* or *in.* In each case, the prepositional adverb tells us *how* the general called the reserves.

CAUTION: Avoid unnecessary prepositional adverbs. For example, *up* adds no meaning in "They connected up the wires."

EXERCISE In the following sentences, which prepositions function as adverbs? Which ones form phrases with nouns?

1. Lost *in* the mountains, the explorers ate *up* their supplies.
2. Although their water was giving *out,* they did not give *up* hope.
3. They filled *up* their canteens *with* snow melted *over* the fire.
4. The cold wore them *down,* but they struggled *on* day *after* day.
5. *At* last, a party *of* rescuers tracked them *down.*

10 ◆ INTERJECTIONS

An **interjection** (from Latin *interjectus* = thrown between) is a word that expresses emotion but is not part of any grammatical structure. Interjections are usually exclamations showing feelings such as anger, surprise, or excitement.

Ah! What a pleasure to see you again.

Ouch! You're stepping on my foot.

Yea team! Go for the touchdown!

11 ◆ PHRASES

A **phrase** (from Greek *phrasis* = speech, wording) is any group of words that functions as a unit and does not have a subject and predicate. We can use phrases to make our sentences more informative and compact and therefore more effective. Consider these two versions of a student's sentence:

First draft

Bryan Trottier is an outstanding hockey player. He uses great finesse and physical strength. Often, he bottles up the opposing team. They cannot leave their zone. As a result, they make risky passes.

Final draft

Bryan Trottier, an outstanding hockey player, uses great finesse and physical strength to bottle up the opposing team in their zone, forcing them to make risky passes.

The rough draft is wordy and awkward; it contains 5 sentences and 33 words. The revision is 20% shorter. It is a single sentence of 27 words, but it contains all the information just as clearly. The difference between the two versions is in the use of *phrases.*

We may loosely divide phrases into two categories, depending on the key elements that they contain. In one category, the key elements are nouns; in the other, verb forms.

11a Phrases with nouns

We construct three kinds of phrases with nouns: *noun phrases, appositive phrases,* and *prepositional phrases.*

11a(1) Noun phrases

A **noun phrase** consists of a noun and its modifiers. It may play any role in the sentence that a noun can play:

> *A fat, green frog* crossed *the shallow pond.* (The first phrase acts as the subject of the sentence, the second as the direct object.)

> *Their cousin's farm* is in *southern Illinois.* (The first phrase acts as the subject of the sentence; the second phrase acts as the object of the preposition *in.*)

11a(2) Appositive phrases

An **appositive phrase** (from Latin *appositus* = placed next to) consists of a noun and its modifiers. Any word or word group that can act as a noun can also act as an appositive or appositive phrase, including participles, gerunds, infinitives, verbal phrases, and noun clauses. Appositive phrases usually stand next to the nouns they modify, giving more identification of the person or thing named by the noun. They play essentially the same role in the sentence as the nouns they modify:

Everest, *the tallest mountain in the world,* is in Asia.

John Adams, *our fourth president,* was born in Virginia.

NOTE: For a discussion of punctuation with appositive phrases, see **18**, rule 4.

Personal pronouns in appositive phrases have the same case as the nouns they modify:

Our group, *Ann, Bob, and I,* attended the concert. ("Group" acts as the subject of the sentence, so the pronoun is in the subjective case.)

They seated our group, *Ann, Bob, and me,* in the balcony. ("Group" acts as the direct object, so the pronoun is in the objective case.)

11a (3) Prepositional phrases

A **prepositional phrase** consists of a preposition with a noun or noun phrase as its object. (For a discussion of prepositions, see **9**.) Prepositional phrases can act as adjectives or adverbs. One sentence may contain a variety of prepositional phrases:

On our tour of Washington we walked down the Mall
    with our friends from Chicago for a look at the Capi-
    itol.

On our tour acts as an adverb, telling *when* "we
walked";

of Washington acts as an adjective, telling *what kind* of
tour;

down the Mall acts as an adverb, telling *where* "we
walked";

with our friends acts as an adverb, telling *how* "we
walked";

from Chicago acts as an adjective, telling *which* of "our
friends";

for a look acts as an adverb, telling *why* "we walked";

at the Capitol acts as an adjective, telling *what kind* of
"look."

11b Phrases with verb forms

We can construct different kinds of phrases with different verb forms. Using verbs and auxiliaries, we can
construct *verb phrases.* Using verbals, we can construct
verbal phrases, which are named separately according to
the verbal they contain *(participial phrases, gerund
phrases, infinitive phrases)* or their grammatical relationship to the rest of the sentence *(absolute phrases).* (For a
discussion of verbs and verbals, see 6 a–g.)

11b(1) Verb phrases

A **verb phrase** consists of a principal part of a verb and whatever auxiliaries are needed to indicate the tense, voice, and mood of the verb. It acts as the verb in a predicate:

They *must have walked* more than ten miles today.

11b(2) Participial phrases

The **participial phrase** is the most common kind of verbal phrase. It consists of a participle with whatever subject, object, and modifiers complete the meaning of the participle, and it acts as an adjective:

Discussing the test and *groaning over their mistakes,* the students strolled to the cafeteria.

Both participial phrases modify *students,* the subject of the sentence. *Discussing* has *test* as its object, and *groaning* is modified by the prepositional phrase *over their mistakes.*

Both participles are in the present tense, so they indicate simultaneous action: the students were discussing and groaning while they were strolling. To indicate that the students had discussed and groaned before strolling, we can use the present perfect participle (*having* + the past participle of the verb):

Having discussed the test and groaned over their mistakes, the students strolled to the cafeteria.

We can also indicate a time relationship by using a subordinating conjunction, such as *while, after,* or *before:*

*After **discussing** the test and **groaning** over their mistakes,* the students strolled to the cafeteria.

Three positions are available in a sentence for a participial phrase that modifies the subject of the sentence:

1. Immediately before the noun that the phrase modifies, as in the examples given.
2. Immediately after the noun:

   The students, discussing the test and groaning over their mistakes, strolled to the cafeteria.

3. In the predicate, if readers will easily see which noun or nouns the phrase modifies:

   The students strolled to the cafeteria, discussing the test and groaning over their mistakes.

This flexibility in placing participles gives you valuable choices in constructing effective sentences. (See **30**.)

Beware of misplaced participles—ones that are too far from the noun that they modify for readers to be sure of the connection. For example, consider this sentence:

The students left the teacher, discussing the test and groaning over their mistakes, and strolled to the cafeteria.

The phrases are misplaced; they seem to modify *teacher* because it is the closest noun. They should appear as close to *students* as possible, as in the earlier examples.

Beware of dangling participles—ones in sentences that do not include the words the participles should modify:

> *Seated next to the fireplace,* their cold hands were warmed by the flames.

This sentence seems to say that "their hands" were seated next to the fireplace. We can correct the problem only by adding a noun or pronoun that the participle can modify and by adjusting the rest of the sentence accordingly, as in

> *Seated next to the fireplace,* the guests warmed their cold hands at the flames.

Some misplaced or dangling participles may not confuse readers but may inspire a laugh the writer did not intend, as in "They heard the telephone, buttoning their coats," or "Flying overhead and honking, they watched the wild geese."

11b(3) Gerund phrases

A **gerund phrase** consists of a gerund and whatever object and modifiers complete the meaning of the gerund. Gerund phrases, like gerunds, always act as nouns and can play any role that a noun can play in the sentence. For example, "playing songs on the piano" acts as a gerund phrase in each of the following sentences:

1. *Playing songs on the piano* amused the guests. (subject)
2. The guests enjoyed *playing songs on the piano.* (direct object)
3. The guests gave *playing songs on the piano* their attention. (indirect object)

4. The guests devoted their time to *playing songs on the piano*. (object of the preposition *to*)
5. The guests had a favorite pastime, *playing songs on the piano*. (appositive of *pastime*)

Notice that *playing* has *songs* as its object and that *playing* is modified by the prepositional phrase *on the piano*.

Use the **possessive case** for a noun or pronoun to indicate who or what is performing the action named by a gerund:

The guests' *playing songs* woke the neighbors.

NOTE: Because it uses the possessive case, this sentence does **not** have the same meaning as "The guests playing songs on the piano woke the neighbors." In the first version, *playing songs* is the subject, and *guests'* acts as an adjective to modify it. In the second version, *guests* is the subject, and *playing songs* is a participial phrase acting as an adjective to describe *guests*.

EXERCISE Underline each gerund phrase and indicate what role it plays in the sentence:

1. Watching television has replaced reading books as America's favorite pastime.
2. Many people prefer renting a house to owning one.
3. His job, stapling insulation in the attic, lasted for weeks.
4. Children enjoy driving bumper cars at the amusement park.
5. Your leaving the company will be a great loss to us all.

11b(4) Infinitive phrases

Infinitive phrases consist of an infinitive and whatever subject, object, and modifiers complete the meaning of the infinitive. They can act as nouns, adjectives, or adverbs. For example, "to play the piano well" acts as an infinitive phrase in each of the following sentences:

1. *To play the piano well* requires practice. (subject)
2. By June, they hope *to play the piano well.* (direct object)
3. The only student *to play the piano well* was hired. (adjective)
4. They practiced *to play the piano well.* (adverb)
5. They achieved their goal, *to play the piano well.* (appositive)

Sometimes an infinitive that is in the active voice and that is being used as an adjective may have a passive meaning:

The show *to watch on television tonight* is a new comedy. (The meaning is that the show is to be watched.)

Three verbs—*have* (when meaning "see to it" or "cause"), *let*, and *make*— take "bare" infinitives, ones not marked by *to:*

The supervisors { make / have / let } the staff work on weekends.

Compare that sentence to "The supervisors ask the staff *to work on weekends,*" in which the infinitive is marked by *to.*

Several verbs indicating sensory perception—*feel,*

hear, notice, see, smell, and *watch*—when in the active voice may take a bare infinitive that has its own subject in the phrase:

We watched *the workers **paint** the house.*

When a pronoun is the subject of an infinitive, the pronoun is in the objective case:

We watched *them **paint** the house.*

The jury thought *him **to be** guilty.*

The *to* has the same relationship to the infinitive as the *ing* and *ed* endings have to a participle. It is part of the infinitive, even though we write it as a separate word. Avoid splitting the *to* from an infinitive:

Split: We hoped *to* quickly and quietly ***solve** the problem.*

Revised: We hoped ***to solve** the problem* quickly and quietly.

EXERCISE In the following sentences, indicate what role (noun, adjective, or adverb) each infinitive phrase is playing.

1. To know them is to love them.
2. Do you want to say something?
3. The best time to find sales is in January.
4. The train stopped to take on passengers.
5. They realized their ambition, to dance in a Broadway show.

11b (5) Absolute phrases

An **absolute phrase** (from Latin *absolutus* = loosened, untied from) is composed of a participle and the subject of the participle along with their complements and modifiers. An absolute phrase is not tied to any other word in the sentence; indeed, we can turn it into a separate sentence simply by changing the participle to a verb.

An absolute phrase modifies the whole sentence, playing the role of a sentence adverb. It can be placed before the subject, between the subject and the verb, or after the verb, unlike the participial phrase, which always acts as an adjective and must be close to the noun it modifies. An absolute phrase is always set off by punctuation, as in these examples:

*The weather **being** hot,* we went to the lake for a swim.

We left in a hurry, *a violent thunderstorm **having broken** directly overhead.*

The lake, *its water **churned into whitecaps*** and *the nearby trees **bent** double by the wind,* was a dramatic sight.

EXERCISE Create two separate sentences from each one below by changing the participles in the absolute phrases to verbs.

1. No one being home, the mailman left the package on the porch.
2. The new cars sit in the dealer's lot, their freshly waxed bodies dazzling in the bright sunlight.

3. A sudden thought coming to mind, she paused at the door.
4. The baby carriage, the child having outgrown it, was stored in a corner of the garage.
5. All the spaces having been taken by visitors, the employees had to park their cars in the back alley.

12 ◆ CLAUSES

Every sentence has at least one clause (from Latin *clausus* = closed, limited). Clauses are so named because each has its own subject and predicate, so it encloses a thought. Each of these sentences is composed of one clause:

The band marched in parades.

The band played popular tunes.

The band practiced all year.

Many sentences, however, consist of more than one clause. We can use a *coordinating conjunction* (such as *and, but, for, or, nor)* to combine two sentences into one, for example:

The band marched in parades, and it played popular tunes.

The band practiced all year, and it marched in parades. (To avoid awkward repetition, *it* replaces *the band.)*

Our original sentences are now *independent clauses* in the new sentences. They are "independent" because each can still make sense standing alone as a separate sentence.

We can also combine two sentences into one by using a *subordinating conjunction* (such as *when, if, because*) or a *relative pronoun* (such as *who, which, that*):

> When the band marched in parades, it played popular tunes.

> The band, which played popular tunes, marched in parades.

In each of these examples, one of the original sentences has become a *dependent clause.* "When the band marched in parades" and "which played popular tunes" do not make sense alone. Each needs an independent clause to complete its meaning. We classify dependent clauses according to their function; they can act as adverbs, adjectives, or nouns.

12a Adverb clauses

Adverb clauses, like adverbs, answer *how, when, where, why,* or *to what extent* about the words they modify. An adverb clause begins with a subordinating conjunction that indicates the relation between the dependent clause and the rest of the sentence. Common subordinating conjunctions include *after, as, because, before, if, since, than, that, then, unless, until, when, while,* and such phrases as *as soon as, except that, in order that, in that, so that,* and *whether or not.* We divide some phrases that act as subordinating conjunctions, such as *no sooner*

. . . *than* and *such . . . that,* placing the first part near the words that the dependent clause modifies and the second part at the beginning of the dependent clause.

> Our neighbors sometimes block our driveway *because they park their car carelessly.*

> *As soon as we arrived home,* we called the Browns.

> We had *no sooner* arrived home *than we called the Browns.*

> The car made *such* odd noises *that we knew the engine needed repairs.*

CAUTION: Place adverbial clauses close to the verbs they modify.

> We think that Harrison will win the election because the polls have predicted victory.

Have the polls affected Harrison's winning or our thinking? In the example, "because the polls have predicted victory" must modify "Harrison will win"; the adverb clause is closer to "will win" than to "think." If, however, we wish the clause to modify "we think," then the word order should be:

> Because the polls have predicted victory, we think that Harrison will win the election.

or

> We think, because the polls have predicted victory, that Harrison will win the election.

NOTE: *As, since,* and *while* may sometimes confuse your readers:

The driver stopped the car *as* the storm was increasing.

Did the driver stop *when* the storm was increasing or *because* the storm was increasing? Either meaning is possible. In such sentences, use *when* or *because* to make your meaning clear.

Since they wrote to us, we have sent them a card.

Did we send a card *because* they wrote or *after* they wrote? In such sentences, use *because* or *after* to make your meaning clear.

The Browns always go to Florida in the winter, while the Smiths ski in Utah.

Do the Browns go to Florida only *when* the Smiths are in Utah, or is the writer making a *contrast* between the Browns and the Smiths? In such sentences, use *when* or *but* to make your meaning clear.

12b Adjective clauses

An **adjective clause,** like an adjective, answers *which* or *what kind* about the words it modifies. Usually, it begins with a relative pronoun—*who, whom, which, what, whoever, whomever, whichever, whatever,* or *that*—to relate it to the word it modifies.

Our neighbors' car, *which is a huge old sedan,* often blocks our driveway.

Our neighbors, *who are careless drivers,* often block our driveway with their car.

Our neighbors, *whom we called twice,* finally moved their car yesterday.

Our neighbors, *to whom we complained*, apologized.

The car *that was blocking our driveway yesterday* is there again today.

NOTE: For punctuation with adjective clauses, see **18**, rule 4.

In informal writing, when a relative pronoun is the object of a preposition, the preposition may follow the verb instead of preceding the pronoun, as in "Our neighbors, whom we complained to, apologized." In formal and informal writing, the relative pronoun is often omitted when it acts as the object of a verb: "The visit *(that)* we made to the Grand Canyon inspired us with awe."

Occasionally, adjective clauses begin with a subordinating conjunction, such as *when, where,* or *why:*

The time *when the show begins* is eight o'clock.

The street *where we live* is narrow.

You know the reason *why we are here.*

12c Noun clauses

Noun clauses, like nouns, can act as subjects, objects, and appositives. They commonly begin with *that* as a subordinating conjunction:

We think *that our neighbors park carelessly.*

Frequently *that* is omitted, as in "We think *our neighbors park carelessly.*"

Noun clauses may begin with any of the other subordinating conjunctions or relative pronouns:

Our neighbors knew *why we called.* (direct object)

How our neighbors park is a problem for us. (subject)

Our problem, *where they park,* has been solved. (appositive)

Whoever parks carelessly is a nuisance. (subject)

We criticized *whoever parked carelessly.* (direct object)

We complained to *whoever would listen.* (object of the preposition *to*)

REMINDER: A relative pronoun takes its case from the role it plays in its own clause, *not* from the role that the clause plays in the sentence. In the last two examples, the pronoun is *whoever,* not *whomever,* because in each sentence the relative pronoun is acting as the subject of the verb in the dependent clause. In both examples, the noun clauses act as objects—in the first as the direct object of the verb *criticized* and in the second as the object of the preposition *to.*

EXERCISE   In the following sentences, label each dependent clause as a noun clause, an adjective clause, or an adverb clause.

1.   Sir Edmund Hillary said that he climbed Mount Everest "because it was there."
2.   You are what you eat.
3.   If children are raised in a bilingual home, they learn both of the languages that are used; but they usually learn to speak later than children raised in monolingual homes.

115

4. We all know people who think burping is funny.
5. When Pete Rose, who had already matched Ty Cobb's record, got up to bat, the fans were ready to stage a demonstration the moment that he hit the ball.

12d Pronoun reference—clear connections

Check your sentences to make sure that readers will be able to connect pronouns and antecedents easily. Remember that you, as the writer, know what you want each sentence to mean, but your readers have only your words to guide them, and they may be confused. Murphy's Law—"Anything that can go wrong will go wrong"—applies here: if readers can misread a sentence, they will.

RULE 1 **Make the reference of each pronoun clear.** Take advantage of sentence structure and word order, and, in extreme cases, the repetition of the noun itself to clarify pronoun references.

Confusing: The Smiths explained to the Browns that they were invited to a barbecue.

Were the Smiths explaining that they were invited, or were they explaining that the Browns were invited? If the Smiths were invited, we may write:

Clearer: As they explained to the Browns, the Smiths were invited to a barbecue.

If the Browns were invited, we may write:

Clearer: As the Smiths explained, the Browns were invited to a barbecue.

Confusing: The manager told Jim that his schedule had changed.

Whose schedule had changed, the manager's or Jim's? If we mean the manager's schedule, we may write:

Clearer: Speaking about his own schedule, the manager told Jim it had changed.

    or: The manager told Jim, "My schedule has changed."

If we mean Jim's schedule, we may write:

Clearer: The manager told Jim that Jim's schedule had changed.

    or: The manager told Jim, "Your schedule has changed."

Confusing: Jenny called Mrs. Roberts while she was having lunch.

Who was having lunch, Jenny or Mrs. Roberts? If Jenny was having lunch, then we may write:

Clearer: While having lunch, Jenny called Mrs. Roberts.

    or: While Jenny was having lunch, she called Mrs. Roberts.

If Mrs. Roberts was having lunch, we may write:

Clearer: Mrs. Roberts was having lunch when Jenny called her.

    or: Jenny called when Mrs. Roberts was having lunch.

RULE 2 **Make sure that the antecedent for *which* is nearby and specific** so that readers will make the connection easily.

Confusing: The hot dogs were cold and greasy, which we disliked.

What exactly did we dislike? Any of three revisions will make the reference specific:

We disliked the hot dogs, which were cold and greasy.

We disliked the fact that the hot dogs were cold and greasy.

We disliked the cold, greasy hot dogs.

RULE 3 **Make sure your readers will know what each *it* is.** We use *it* without a specific antecedent in conventional statements about the weather and the time, as in "It's cold outside" and "It's late"; however, in other kinds of sentences, *it* needs a clear reference. In the following sentence, for example, *it* makes no sense:

In the newspaper it says that Parks may win the election.

A more precise version would be:

The newspaper says that Parks may win the election.

or

A report in the newspaper says that Parks may win the election.

Because we use *it* so often, we may confuse readers by placing one *it* too close to another *it* when they have different references.

Confusing: We bought a new car last summer. It has a sun roof, and when it's hot, we like having it open.

Clearer: Last summer we bought a new car with a sun roof, which we like having open in hot weather.

RULE 4 **Make sure your readers will know who *you* and *they* are.** In conversation we often use *you* or *they* to refer to people in general. In writing we should be more precise in our references so that readers will be sure of our meaning. For example, what does *they* mean in this sentence?

In this college, they demand a lot from you.

Does *they* mean the faculty? a department? the college administrators? the student organizations? Similarly, who is *you*? The interpretation depends on who the writer is and how much the reader knows about the writer. To clarify the meaning, *they* and *you* should be replaced by specific nouns, for example: "In this college, the faculty demands a lot from the students."

12d (1) Relative pronouns and verb agreement

Make sure that a verb whose subject is a relative pronoun agrees with the antecedent of the relative pronoun.

It is John and Mary who *are* not going bowling tonight. (*who* refers to *John and Mary*)

Tina Turner is one of the popular singers who *have* made extraordinary comebacks. *(who* refers to *singers,* not to *Tina Turner)*

Ours is the only office in these three buildings that *has* a view of the lake. *(that* refers to *office)*

12d (2) Relative pronouns and case

To determine whether to use *who* or *whom* in a relative clause, first mentally convert the clause into a separate sentence and then follow the method described at the end of 5c. For example, use *who* in "The waiter who was asked for the check has disappeared" because the relative clause, when converted into a sentence, becomes *"He* was asked for the check." Similarly, we use *whom* in "The waiter whom we asked for the check has disappeared" because the relative clause, when converted into a sentence, becomes "We asked *him* for the check."

Clauses inserted as side comments, such as *we think* or *it seems,* do not affect the grammar of the sentence. In "The waiter who, we think, was asked for the check has disappeared," the pronoun must be *who* because it is the subject of *was asked*—*"he* was asked." However, in "The waiter whom, we believe, we asked for the check has disappeared," the pronoun must be *whom* because it is the object of *asked*—"we asked *him."*

EXERCISE In the following sentences, fill in the blanks with *who, whom, whose, who's, whoever,* or *whomever.*

1. _____ wrote this essay?

2. The friend from _____ we learned about the accident saw it happen.

3. Everyone _____ witnessed the accident may be called to testify in court.

4. The friend _____ we heard describe the accident knew both drivers.

5. The friend _____ , we learned, saw the accident knew both drivers.

6. The reporters interviewed _____ they could find at the scene.

7. _____ going to pay for this sandwich?

8. _____ coat is on the chair?

9. _____ taken my coat?

10. A friend _____ car has broken down needs a ride.

Part Two

SENTENCES

13 ◆ SENTENCE COMPLETENESS

How many complete sentences are in this description?

Two old men in our neighborhood share a small apartment. With their five cats, three canaries, and six goldfish. They take a walk every day.

At a quick glance, most readers, seeing three periods and three capital letters, will say that the paragraph contains three sentences. After a closer look, however, they will probably notice that "With five cats, three canaries, and six goldfish" has no subject or verb and is therefore not a complete sentence. It is a sentence fragment. Writers who are inexperienced or merely careless may confuse phrases and dependent clauses with complete sentences and, as a result, may puzzle their readers.

Recognizing verbs and complete sentences   Before experimenting with sentence structure and punctuation, make sure that you can recognize the words that are acting as verbs and tell whether a group of words forms a complete sentence.

Test yourself with the following paragraph. Underline the words acting as verbs. Mark the beginning of each sentence by capitalizing the first letter of the first word, and mark the end of each by adding a period.

a smiling crowd in formal evening wear was moving toward the ticket-takers who were dressed in bright red uniforms people passing by paused in hopes of glimpsing the movie stars who had come to the opening night of the show guards stood at attention by barriers holding back the public however their authority was challenged by one gate-crasher who tried to sneak past them into the theater

Check your accuracy by reading the corrected paragraph on page 127.

If you had trouble recognizing the verbs or the ends of any of the sentences or if you have sometimes been unsure where your own sentences end, the following procedures will help you. They may at first seem clumsy and roundabout, but they will help you to find not only the verbs but also their subjects and to know whether you have constructed a complete sentence or only a fragment.

First, find all the words acting as verbs. Begin by looking for these ten words: *will, would, shall, should, can, could, may, might, must, ought.* Then look for these eleven forms of *be, have,* and *do: am, is, are, was, were, have, has, had, do, does, did.* Wherever these words appear, they are almost certain to be acting as verbs or auxiliaries of verbs.

To find other words that are acting as verbs, look for words that you can emphasize by using *do, does,* or *did,* as in this sentence from the test paragraph:

> Guards stood/did stand at attention by barriers holding back the public.

NOTE: To add *do, does,* or *did,* we must change the verb to its base form, *stand,* by which it is listed in the dictionary.

With this method we can identify all the verbs in the test paragraph. We can also be sure that the following words that can act as verbs or as parts of verbs in other sentences are not doing so here: *smiling, crowd, evening, wear, passing, hopes, glimpsing, stars, opening, show, guards, holding, back, sneak.* For example, a sentence such as "A smiling crowd in formal evening do wear was moving toward the ticket-takers" or "Guards stood at attention by barriers do hold back the public" makes no sense.

Next, determine which are verbs in complete sentences. Every complete sentence must have at least one verb, but not all groups of words that contain verbs are complete sentences. "Guards stood at attention" and "However, their authority was challenged" can act as complete sentences, but "who were dressed in bright red uniforms" and "who had come to the opening night of the show" cannot because each of them depends on something else to complete its meaning.

To find out if a group of words forms a sentence, try to turn the group of words into a question that can be answered by "yes" or "no." If you can make such a question without omitting any words, it is a complete sentence. For example, "Guards stood at attention" and "However, their authority was challenged" can become "yes" or "no" questions: "Did the guards stand at attention?" and "However, was their authority challenged?" But "Who were dressed in bright red uniforms?" and "Who had come to the opening of the show?" require more than a "yes" or "no" answer.

When you have found the words that are acting as verbs, you can also identify their subjects. Make a question by placing "Who or what" in front of each verb. The word or words that will answer the question will be the subject. "Who or what stood at attention?"—*guards.* "Who or what was challenged?"—*their authority.* "Who or what had come?"—*who,* substituting for *stars* as the subject.

Any group of words that does not form a complete sentence must be attached to a group that does. In the version of the test paragraph that follows, with verb and sentence ends marked, notice that "dressed in bright red uniforms" is attached to "A smiling crowd in formal evening wear was moving toward the ticket-takers" and that "who had come to the opening night of the show" is attached to "People passing by paused in hopes of glimpsing the movie stars."

Answer to the test paragraph

A smiling crowd in formal evening wear was moving toward the ticket-takers, who were dressed in bright red uniforms. People passing by paused in hopes of glimpsing the movie stars who had come to the opening night of the show. Guards stood at attention by barriers holding back the public. However, their authority was challenged by one gate-crasher who tried to sneak past them into the theater.

NOTE: Commas have been added after *ticket-takers* and *However* because conventional punctuation requires them, but they are not part of the test.

EXERCISES

A. In the following sentences, underline all the words acting as verbs and circle all the subjects. Remember that words acting as subjects tell us *who* or *what* performs the action or is in the state of being described by the verb.

1. People who are learning to drive often have trouble with parallel parking.
2. If a space is small, parking a large car in it may require a considerable amount of maneuvering by the driver.
3. The driving instructor did not teach parallel parking until the students had learned how to use reverse.
4. The class, which had practiced parking, demonstrated great skill.
5. The instructor, pleased with the students' skill, nevertheless made them repeat the demonstration.
6. The students took turns parking the car.
7. They readjust the seat and the rearview mirror whenever they exchange places at the wheel.
8. Before road practice comes a film showing basic techniques.
9. There are films that use diagrams as well as live scenes.
10. When a driver has to park, it is always a test of skill.
11. Many drivers work hard to park their cars neatly.
12. They park their cars neatly with hard work.
13. Because of their hard work, many drivers park neatly.
14. Does anyone forget to use the hand brake?

B. Turn each of the sentences in exercise A into a "yes" or "no" question. Then make a list of the verbs that make the sentences complete—these are the verbs that you moved or to which you added *do, does,* or *did* to make a question.

C. In the following paragraph, underline all the words acting as verbs and circle all the subjects. Remember that words acting as subjects tell us *who* or *what* performs the action or is in the state of being described by the verb.

The Johnsons camp at a stream near their house. They dive and swim with skill. They always dive from the same tree trunk. Often, leaves float on the water. The Johnsons gather sticks and branches and take turns building a campfire. They also put up a tent. Visitors always praise the stream and the campsite. They deserve praise.

D. Study this sentence: "When he *leaves* with his *rake*, we must *rake* the *leaves* that he *left* on the *left* side of the driveway." All the words in the following list are like *rake*, *left*, and *leaves* in the example: they can play the role of a verb or of a subject or object, and they have different meanings in different roles. Some even have more than one meaning for the same role. Compose ten short sentences in each of which you use one or more of the words in the following list at least twice, with a different meaning for each use. The more listed words you use in a short space, the more challenging you will make the exercise. (Add an *s*, *d*, or *ed* ending whenever necessary for your meaning.)

bear	block	peer	bat	bank	lie	lap
board	hide	roll	batter	rock	type	sense
ring	fare	brood	might	sign	tire	sink
last	row	train	trip	run	flow	slice

14 ◆ SENTENCE FRAGMENTS

A **sentence fragment** is a group of words that is punctuated to look like a sentence but that lacks an essential part. Most fragments are really phrases or dependent clauses.

Prepositional phrases punctuated as if they were complete sentences create a choppy effect and may confuse readers. For example, in the description at the beginning of **13**, does the prepositional phrase "with five cats, three canaries, and six goldfish" describe how the old men live or how they take a walk every day? The first guess seems more logical, but the second is possible; as a result, readers cannot be sure of the meaning. By removing the period after "apartment," we can clarify the relationships among the pieces of information:

> Two old men in our neighborhood share a small apartment with five cats, three canaries, and six goldfish. They take a walk every day.

Verbal phrases punctuated as if they were complete sentences are also likely to confuse readers:

> The two old men take a walk every day, rain or shine. Their shoulders squared, their backs held straight, their eyes looking straight ahead. The neighbors always watch them with amazement.

Here, "squared," "held," and "looking" are all verbals, not verbs. Since the three phrases are punctuated as if they formed a sentence, readers cannot be sure whether the phrases modify *men* or *neighbors*. A comma after *shine* would make the phrases modify what precedes them. A comma after *ahead* would make the phrases modify what follows them.

Appositives punctuated as if they were complete sentences can also be confusing:

> The two old men march down the street side by side. Former army officers, each with a chestful of decorations, and each intensely proud of his record. The policemen at the precinct house always salute the old men respectfully.

Who wears the decorations and who is proud of his record, each of the two old men or each of the policemen? Again, a comma instead of the first period would make the appositives modify "old men," whereas a comma after "record" would make them modify "policemen."

A **compound predicate** divided and punctuated as if it were two complete sentences can also be confusing:

> The two old men always cross the highway at a steady pace, even in heavy traffic when the drivers honk angrily. And then turn down a side road into the park.

Who turn down the side road, the drivers or the two old men? A comma instead of the period after *angrily* would indicate that "even in heavy traffic when the drivers honk angrily" is a non-restrictive modifier set off from the rest of the sentence by a pair of commas and that "and then turn" refers to "two old men."

Dependent clauses punctuated as if they were complete sentences may confuse readers:

> On their daily walks the two old men always carry their umbrellas. Even when the weather is sunny and

the skies are blue. They swing the umbrellas to and fro steadily.

"When" is a subordinating conjunction; therefore, any clause that it introduces cannot be independent. Since the clause is punctuated as if it were a sentence, readers cannot tell whether it modifies what precedes it, telling us when the men carry the umbrellas, or what follows it, telling us when the men swing them.

The problem can be solved by using a comma instead of one of the periods. A comma after *umbrellas* would make the clause modify what precedes it:

> On their daily walks the two old men always carry their umbrellas, even when the weather is sunny and the skies are blue.

A comma after *blue* would make the clause modify what follows:

> Even when the weather is sunny and the skies are blue, they swing the umbrellas to and fro steadily.

Writers are particularly likely to forget that *because* is a subordinating conjunction and should introduce only dependent clauses and phrases:

> Although the two old men are over eighty, both are healthy and full of energy. Because they eat simple food and exercise regularly. They are our neighborhood characters.

Are they full of energy because of their food and exercise? or characters because of their food and exercise? The problem can be solved by using a comma instead of one of the periods. A comma after *energy* would make the clause modify what precedes it; a comma after *regularly* would make it modify what follows it.

Some fragments are not confusing—common sense may make only one interpretation possible—but readers expect to find an independent clause in whatever is punctuated as a sentence and may be annoyed and frustrated when they do not find one. Also, fragments create a choppy effect, so that the writing may seem to bump along like a car with a flat tire.

Not all fragments are bad. Sometimes they can emphasize words and phrases effectively, and you will see them often in advertisements and in fiction. In most formal writing, however, they are unsuitable. Save your use of fragments for very special purposes.

EXERCISES

A. In this exercise, some of the items contain one or two complete sentences; others contain sentence fragments. On a numbered sheet of paper, write *C* for each item that consists of complete sentences. If an item contains fragments, rewrite it to incorporate any fragments in the sentence.

1. That steam could do mechanical work was recognized more than 2,000 years ago. When it was used to operate simple toys.

2. In the 18th century, when such inventors as James Watt developed steam engines sufficiently to make them practical and inexpensive. Owners of coal mines in England began to use them to pump water out of coal shafts.

3. But using steam to move ships and railroads had to wait. Until the early years of the 19th century.

4. Americans recognize Robert Fulton as the father of the steam age in transportation. Despite British claims that William Symington's experiment in 1802 was the first steamboat.

5. Fulton steamed up the Hudson River in 1807. From New York to Albany took 32 hours.

6. Born in Pennsylvania in 1765, Fulton was actually a painter by occupation. Trying his hand first at submarines and torpedoes, in France and England, without much success.

7. His paddle-wheel steamboat, the *Clermont,* gained him immediate and widespread fame. Substituting steam power for the age-old dependence on the inconstant winds, a more dramatic change than the first use of the atom to power submarines.

8. From that time on, however, it was no longer the winds that decided a ship's course and speed. It was the ship's captain.

9. Of course, more developments were to come. Before the modern propeller would replace the paddle-wheel. And before boilers could use high pressures safely and economically.

10. By the time of his death in 1815, Fulton had built the first steam-powered warship for the United States Navy. A forty-four-gun vessel called the *Fulton.*

B. In this exercise, follow the instructions for exercise A.

1. Edward Jenner, an 18th century Englishman, was a man of many talents. Primarily a physician, but also a good musician, a poet, a hot-air balloonist, and an ornithologist.

2. He was employed in London in 1771 as a naturalist. Arranging the zoological specimens collected by Captain Cook on his famous first voyage to the South Seas. Work that impressed Cook so much that he invited Jenner along on his next voyage.

3. Fortunately, Jenner turned down the offer. And returned to the routine of his medical practice.

4. That simple decision changed human history. By contributing to the health of hundreds of millions of humans since then.

5. At home, Jenner scientifically pursued a popular local belief. That a human infected with an animal disease, cowpox, would be immune against the deadly human disease of smallpox.

6. His research convinced him to experiment. Inoculating his eight-year-old son with cells from cowpox blisters on a milkmaid's hands. Then, two months later, inoculating the child with real smallpox without producing the disease.

7. Jenner repeated the experiment in 1798. And he was again successful.

8. He proved that injecting cowpox creates immunity to smallpox for five to seven years. Sometimes longer.

9. Later, the same method succeeded in preventing typhoid fever, diphtheria, rabies, cholera, typhus, and yellow fever. The vaccine being created from dead or weakened organisms.

10. Jenner could have sailed off to the South Seas with Captain Cook, no doubt returning with interesting animal specimens. But staying at home brought him immortality. And to medical science a new and powerful way to fight disease.

15 ◆ COMMA SPLICES AND RUN-ONS

A **comma splice** (also called a **comma fault**) occurs when a comma divides two independent clauses with no conjunction joining them:

> Regardless of the weather, the two old men enjoyed a walk in the park every day, they liked to visit the duck pond and feed the ducks.

REMEMBER: A comma divides; it does not connect.

A **run-on sentence** (also called a **fused sentence**) occurs when two independent clauses have no punctuation to divide them and no conjunction to connect them:

> Regardless of the weather, the two old men enjoyed a walk in the park every day they liked to visit the duck pond and feed the ducks.

We have two ways to correct comma splices and run-ons. We must either *separate* the independent clauses to form complete sentences or *join* the independent clauses to form one sentence. To separate the clauses, we use a *period:*

> Regardless of the weather, the two old men enjoyed a walk in the park every day. They liked to visit the duck pond and feed the ducks.

To join the clauses, we have four choices:

1. We can add a *comma* at the end of the first clause and a *coordinating conjunction* to begin the second clause—*and, but, or, nor, for, yet,* or *so:*

136

Regardless of the weather, the two old men enjoyed a walk in the park every day, and they liked to visit the duck pond and feed the ducks.

2. Instead of a comma, we can use a *semicolon,* which will indicate that the first clause gives the main point of the sentence and the second offers additional information or that the two clauses are equal in importance:

Regardless of the weather, the two old men enjoyed a walk in the park every day; they liked to visit the duck pond and feed the ducks.

3. A *colon* after the first clause will indicate that it is introductory and that the second gives the main point of the sentence:

Regardless of the weather, the two old men enjoyed a walk in the park every day: they liked to visit the duck pond and feed the ducks.

4. A *subordinating conjunction* or *relative pronoun* at the beginning of one clause will make it dependent on the other:

Regardless of the weather, the two old men enjoyed a walk in the park every day because they liked to visit the duck pond and feed the ducks.

or

Regardless of the weather, the two old men, who liked to visit the duck pond and feed the ducks, enjoyed a walk in the park every day.

REMINDER: Conjunctive adverbs, such as *instead, moreover, therefore,* and *nevertheless,* cannot join two independent clauses to form a single sentence; they show a

137

connection between ideas, but they do **not** join grammatical structures. To join the clauses, use a semicolon or add a coordinating conjunction:

> Yesterday was cold and rainy; nevertheless, the two old men went for a walk.

> Today, the weather forecast predicted rain, but instead, the sun is shining.

EXERCISE In this exercise, each item contains a comma splice. On a numbered sheet of paper, copy the last word before the comma splice in each item and the first few words after it, and then indicate your correction for each one. You may use a comma and a coordinating conjunction, a semicolon, a semicolon and a conjunctive adverb, or a period and a capital letter, but do not use the same solution for every case.

1. The concept of a ship able to move under water rather than on it goes back to ancient times, in the Renaissance, Leonardo da Vinci toyed with the idea of underwater ships for warfare.

2. A Dutchman named Drebbel, in the service of King James I of England, tested the first practical submarine in 1620, twelve men propelled a modified rowboat, which was covered with leather, about 15 feet below the surface of the Thames River.

3. The first American attempt to use a submarine was a failure, in 1776 the *Turtle* tried to attack a British ship in the harbor of New York.

4. American sailors wanted to attach a time bomb to the enemy warship, they were not able to force screws through the warship's metal-plated hull, so they gave up the project.

5. The first "kill" made by a submarine occurred on the night of February 17, 1864, in Charleston harbor, the Confederate submarine *David* exploded a torpedo next to a Union ship, the *Housatonic,* which was blockading the Southern port.

6. Ironically, the *David,* having shot its "Goliath," also sank, it was flooded with water pouring through an open hatch.

7. With increasing mechanical improvements like the periscope and long-range torpedoes, these ships took on new importance, by World War I, German submarines, called U-boats, had grown so deadly that they almost won the war for Germany.

8. In four years of combat, the U-boats sank more than 5,400 ships, the Germans lost only 203 submarines.

9. In World War II, the Allies and neutral nations lost over 21 million tons of shipping to submarine attacks, American submarines in the Pacific compensated for much of the loss by destroying most of the Japanese merchant fleet.

10. Further improvements in speed, range, and depth performance have made submarines even more important, they can also serve now as launching pads for nuclear weapons.

16 ◆ SENTENCE STRUCTURE

We classify every sentence according to the kinds of clauses that it contains. A sentence may be simple, compound, complex, or compound-complex.

16a Simple sentences

A simple sentence has one independent clause and no dependent clauses. In its most basic form, a simple sentence has one subject, one verb, and, if necessary to complete the meaning, one object, as in *Bands play* and *Bands play tunes*.

More often, however, a simple sentence has words or phrases acting as modifiers. Some sentences that we classify grammatically as simple may seem long and rather complicated, for example:

> With much singing of old songs and shouting of high school cheers, the neighbors in the house to the west of us, the house with the large backyard, gave a Fourth of July barbecue party for all of the members of their high school class still living in the vicinity to celebrate the twentieth anniversary of their graduation.

A simple sentence may have a compound subject, a compound predicate, or both. *Compound subjects* are composed of two or more subjects that share the same predicate, and *compound predicates* are composed of two or more predicates that share the same subject. The following example is a simple sentence that has both a compound subject and a compound predicate:

> Our neighbors and several old high school classmates had a backyard barbecue yesterday, sang old rock songs, and reminisced about their high school days.

16b Compound sentences

A compound sentence has two or more independent clauses. The divisions between the clauses may be marked by (1) a **comma followed by a coordinating conjunction** *(and, but, or, nor, for, yet,* and *so),* (2) a **semicolon,** or (3) a **colon,** as these examples show:

1   For the reunion, our neighbors made a big barbecue, their guests helped to cook and clean up, and everyone had a wonderful time.

A *comma* marks the division between the clauses, and a *conjunction* indicates the thought relationship. In a sentence like the example with a series of three or more clauses, the conjunction is necessary only between the last two.

2   Students must show their ID cards to enter the library stacks; several books have been stolen recently by outsiders posing as students.

A *semicolon* indicates that the first of two independent clauses contains the important point and that the second clause adds information, *or* it may indicate that two or more clauses are equally important and form a kind of series, as in "Students must show their ID cards to enter the stacks; alumni must show proof of their degrees; all others must obtain permission from the supervisor." A semicolon is particularly useful between independent clauses that contain one or more commas.

3   The library announced a new policy: starting Monday, all students must show their ID cards to enter the stacks.

A *colon* indicates that the first of the two clauses is preparatory and that the second contains the important idea of the sentence.

16c Complex sentences

A complex sentence has one main clause and at least one dependent clause.

> When the neighbors gave a big barbecue, their guests helped to cook and clean up.

NOTE: In some complex sentences, the independent clause may be shorter than the dependent clause and may seem merely introductory rather than truly independent. This is especially characteristic of sentences in which a noun clause is the object of a such verbs as *say, think, report,* and *see* or where it completes the meaning of such constructions as "it is clear that" or "there is no way that":

> Our neighbors said that they planned to give a big barbecue to celebrate the twentieth anniversary of their high school graduation.

> Unfortunately, there is no way that everyone will be able to attend.

16d Compound-complex sentences

A compound-complex sentence has two or more independent clauses at least one of which contains a dependent clause. As its name implies, the compound-complex sentence is a combination of the two preceding types of sentences:

> Although our neighbors planned a barbecue to celebrate their class reunion, they feared that the

weather might be bad, so they included a "rain date" on the invitations that they sent out.

EXERCISES

A. Mark the independent and dependent clauses in each of the sentences in the following paragraph; then label each sentence according to type—simple, compound, complex, or compound-complex.

In the 1840s, people began to dream of a railroad that would cross the United States from one coast to another, but the need for such a transcontinental rail link was not pressing until the gold rush of 1849 greatly increased the population of California. For another decade, the possible route for such a railroad was fiercely debated because the North wanted a path through Chicago to the Pacific Northwest, while the South was in favor of a path through New Orleans and Texas to southern California. Many land surveys were made for both of the possible routes, but the dispute did not end until the Civil War. When the Confederacy seceded from the rest of the country, the Northerners in control of the Union were at last able to dictate the path that the railroad would take. In 1862 Congress passed the Pacific Railway Bill. In effect, this legislation joined two railroads, the Union Pacific and the Central Pacific, and set them the task of spanning the nation. The Union Pacific began building westward from Council Bluffs, Iowa; the Central Pacific began building eastward from California. Seven years later, on May 10, 1869, a gold spike was driven into the last piece of track in Promontory Point, Utah, at a great celebration honoring the junction of the two great engineering efforts.

B. Combine each of the following pairs of sentences to form a single complex sentence. To do this, convert one of the sentences into a dependent clause, either adjective or adverb, by using a subordinating conjunction, such as *because, if, when, that, so that,* or *unless* (see **8**), or a relative pronoun, such as *who, whom, whose,* or *that* (see **5e**).

   At least two combinations are possible for each pair. Compose as many as you can to explore different possibilities in thought relationships. For examples, look again at the combinations of sentences in **5e**.

1. Bruce Springsteen is America's most popular male rock star.
   Bruce Springsteen is the lead singer and guitarist of the E Street Band.
2. Florida has become home to a growing number of retired people.
   The climate is mild all year long.
3. The economy is improving.
   Many college graduates are still having trouble finding jobs.
4. By nine o'clock the beach was already crowded with people.
   People had spread out blankets and towels and put umbrellas everywhere.
5. The Traffic Commissioner missed the meeting.
   The Traffic Commissioner was caught in a traffic jam.

C. Combine each of the following groups of sentences to form a single complex sentence. To do so, convert two of the sentences into dependent clauses, either adjective or adverb clauses or one of each, by using a subordinating conjunction, such as *because, if, when, that, so that,* or *unless* (see **8**), or a relative pronoun, such as *who, whom, whose,* or *that* (see **5e**).

At least two combinations are possible for each pair. Compose as many as you can to explore different possibilities for relating the thoughts. For examples, look again at the combinations of sentences in **5e**.

1. A new law has been passed.
   The new law will improve the quality of the air.
   People can no longer burn leaves in their yards.
2. American wine consumption is increasing.
   Grape growers in many states have huge surpluses.
   Imported wines are popular.
3. It is raining hard.
   We will have to postpone the softball game.
   The baseball diamond dries out.
4. Manatees are water animals.
   Elephants are land animals.
   Manatees and elephants are closely related.
5. Opals are unusual stones.
   Opals have water trapped in their crystals.
   Water makes opals iridescent.

D. Combine each of the following pairs to form one complex sentence, eliminating *someone* or *something*. To do so, convert one sentence into a noun clause by using a relative pronoun, such as *who, whom, what, whoever,* or *whatever,* or a subordinating conjunction, such as *how, when, where, why, whether,* or *that,* to introduce it. Most pairs can form many combinations, so explore as many possibilities as you can. Omit

145

any words that the combined sentence makes unnecessary.

1. The car battery was dead.
   They discovered something yesterday.
2. Something is a big problem.
   They have no money.
3. They owe their success to something.
   They have studied something.
4. They will buy something.
   They will like something.
5. They should take the test.
   Something is an open question.
6. Someone won the race.
   The judges gave a prize to someone.
7. The judges gave a prize to someone.
   The judges admired someone.
8. Do they know something?
   Pat went to Bermuda.
9. Something was announced.
   The flight was delayed.
10. Someone wins the race.
    Someone wins the prize.

Part Three
PUNCTUATION AND MECHANICS

17 ◆ TERMINAL PUNCTUATION

Punctuation and mechanics are a system of written signals. Like road signs, punctuation marks help readers to stay on the right track in sentences, so that they will see the connections and divisions in the thought. We mark the ends of sentences, questions, and exclamations with **terminal** punctuation.

RULE 1 **End every declarative sentence** with a period. In a declarative sentence, the writer states a fact or opinion:

We elect a president every four years.

We think that our team will win the game.

RULE 2 **End every direct question** with a question mark. In a direct question, the writer asks for an answer:

Can our team win the game?

How often do we hold presidential elections?

RULE 3 **End every indirect question** with a period. In an indirect question, the writer reports that someone has asked a question but does not actually quote the words of the question:

The judge asked the jury what they had decided.

I wondered where I was.

Compare these indirect questions with direct versions:

148

The judge asked the jury, "What have you decided?"

I wondered, "Where am I?"

RULE 4 **End a rhetorical question** with a question mark or a period, depending on the emphasis you wish to give the question. In such a question, the writer is not really asking a question, but rather making a statement; the writer assumes the answer is obvious:

How can anyone be so insensitive? (question emphasized)

Why settle for second best when the best is available. (question not emphasized)

RULE 5 **End an exclamation** with an exclamation point:

Have courage!

What an impressive sight!

CAUTION: In most of your writing for college and for your career, exclamations will not be appropriate.

EXERCISE Add terminal punctuation to these sentences.

The first time I saw someone throw a pinch of salt over his left shoulder, I could not believe my eyes What a strange thing to do Apparently it is a common superstition that goes back to the Romans They thought—can you imagine this—that spilling salt was an unlucky omen They believed that evil could be avoided if the person who spilled the salt threw a little of it over his left shoulder with his right hand The Jews, as well as the Greeks and Romans, used salt in performing sacrifices Do you think it became a symbol of purity because of its preservative quality Many serious scholars think so In the Middle Ages it was not uncommon to put salt into a coffin, for it was said that Satan hates salt I have read that it was customary to throw a handful of salt into the vats when brewing beer in order to keep the witches away Did you know that Judas Iscariot can be recognized in Leonardo da Vinci's *Last Supper* by the saltcellar knocked over accidentally by his arm I do not have much faith in such superstitions Do you

18 ◆ COMMAS

The **comma** is the most difficult punctuation mark to define because we use it in many ways and because it is optional in some kinds of sentences.

REMEMBER: A comma *divides* parts of a sentence; it does not join them.

RULE 1 **Compound sentences** Use a comma to divide the independent clauses of a compound sentence when they are joined by a coordinating conjunction *(and, but, or, nor, for, yet,* and *so).* See **16b** on compound sentences.

The Browns spent a week in Florida, and the Smiths visited cousins in Denver.

The Browns went to Florida, the Smiths visited cousins in Denver, and we went to Houston.

IMPORTANT: *Be sure to include a coordinating conjunction* when you punctuate a compound sentence with a comma. Failure to include a conjunction is an error called a comma splice (see **15**), which may cause readers to misread the sentence completely. (For other ways to punctuate compound sentences, see **16b**).

NOTE: Some writers omit the comma between two independent clauses joined by a coordinating conjunction if at least one of the clauses is very short and no other commas are needed in the sentence. It is wise, however, always to use the comma so that your readers will understand the structure of the sentence easily.

RULE 2 **Items in a series**   Use commas to divide the items in a series composed of three or more words, phrases, or clauses.

They entered the bright, crowded, noisy room.

We bought apples, pears, and peaches.

We enjoyed swimming in the lake, hiking in the mountains, and playing tennis at the club last summer.

CAUTION: Many writers omit the comma between the last two items in a series if they are connected by a coordinating conjunction. Be cautious in doing this; the omission may cause confusion:

The dessert menu offered apple pie, walnut cake, ice cream and peaches.

Punctuated this way, the sentence indicates that ice cream and peaches together form a single dessert. If, however, the ice cream and peaches are two separate desserts, a comma must divide them: "ice cream, and peaches."

Use a comma to divide the parts of a compound predicate containing a series of *three or more verbs* with their complements:

> On our vacation last summer we swam in the lake, hiked on the mountain trails, played tennis at the club, and visited several historical sites.

NOTE: Many writers omit the comma between the last two divisions of a compound predicate if they are connected by a coordinating conjunction. To make sure that your readers will understand the structure of your sentence easily, it is better to include the comma as shown in the example.

When a compound predicate contains only *two* verbs joined by a coordinating conjunction, do *not* separate them with a comma:

> On our vacation last summer we swam in the lake and hiked on the mountain trails.

RULE 3 **Coordinate adjectives** Use commas to divide coordinate adjectives. Coordinate adjectives are ones that can be arranged in any order the writer wishes to use:

> A sleepy, sleek cat lay curled in the chair.

> The bored, lonely, mischievous child teased the cat.

Notice that we could as easily write "A sleek, sleepy cat" or "The mischievous, lonely, bored child," whichever sequence we prefer, because the adjectives are co-ordinate.

EXCEPTION: Do **not** use commas to divide a series of *cumulative adjectives.* A cumulative adjective modifies the combination of the noun and the other adjectives coming between it and the noun, so the sequence cannot be rearranged:

A young brown Irish hunting dog ran in the field.

The house stood in a narrow Boston street.

No one familiar with English would write "a brown hunting Irish young dog" or "a Boston narrow street."

RULE 4 **Non-restrictive modifiers** Set off all non-restrictive modifiers (appositives, phrases, and clauses) with commas wherever they appear in the sentence. A non-restrictive modifier describes a thing, person, or event, but it does not pinpoint (restrict) its identity. For example, in the following sentences, the modifiers describe Rome and the Tiber, but they do not identify them because only one city called Rome and one river called the Tiber are being considered:

Rome, *the capital of Italy,* is on the Tiber River. (non-restrictive appositive)

Rome, *situated on the Tiber,* is the capital of Italy. (non-restrictive verbal phrase)

The Tiber River, *flowing westward,* empties into the Tyrrhenian Sea. (non-restrictive verbal phrase)

Rome is on the Tiber River, which flows westward to the sea. (non-restrictive adjective clause)

Compare those non-restrictive modifiers with the following examples of restrictive modifiers. Notice how the restrictive modifiers pinpoint the identity of whatever they modify:

> The name *Tiber* is "Tevere" in Italian. (restrictive appositive)
>
> An ancient city *situated on a river* usually became a center for trade. (restrictive verbal phrase)
>
> A river *flowing westward in Italy* will empty into the Tyrrhenian Sea. (restrictive verbal phrase)
>
> A river that flows westward in Italy will empty into the Tyrrhenian Sea. (restrictive adjective clause)

All the examples just given are adjective modifiers. Most adverbial modifiers are restrictive because they pinpoint *how, when, where,* or *why* something happens. They are not, therefore, set off by commas unless they are introductory:

> The river grew muddy after the heavy rain. (prepositional phrase as adverb)
>
> The river grew muddy whenever it rained. (adverb clause)
>
> The river grew muddy because the rain was heavy. (adverb clause)

RULE 5 **Introductory modifiers**   Set off all introductory modifiers with a comma, whether they are restrictive or non-restrictive:

> *Situated on a river,* an ancient city could develop trade.

Flowing westward in Italy, rivers empty into the Tyrrhenian Sea.

Because the rain was heavy, the river grew muddy.

EXCEPTION: Many writers omit the comma after a short
introductory modifier that cannot confuse readers:

On Tuesday the weather changed abruptly.

It is safer as a habit, however, to include the comma: "On
Tuesday, the weather changed abruptly."

RULE 6 **Transitions** Set off transitional expressions,
such as *moreover, meanwhile, for instance, in contrast,*
and *as we have seen,* with commas wherever they appear
in a sentence:

Many ancient cities, *as we have seen,* were built on
rivers.

Rome, *for example,* is on the Tiber and, *as a result,* has
access to the sea.

The Romans adopted most of the Greek gods; *however,*
they made changes in many Greek myths.

NOTE: When *however* acts as a subordinating conjunction
meaning "in whatever manner," it is not set off with commas.
Compare:

They will lose *however hard they try.* (conjunction)

They will lose. *However,* they will try hard. (transitional
expression)

RULE 7 **Parenthetical expressions** Set off parenthetical expressions with commas. Parenthetical expressions

offer side comments or pieces of information that are not part of the sentence structure. Parenthetical expressions may be of any length, from a single word to a complete clause.

> The lawyer, *naturally,* was being very cautious.

> Their case, *of course,* was worth the risk.

> The clients, *it was obvious,* were determined to proceed with the case.

> The problem, *the lawyer explained at some length,* was the risk of a countersuit.

To set off a long parenthetical expression that has one or more commas within it, most writers prefer to use dashes or parentheses (see **21** and **22**).

RULE 8 **Interruptions in normal word order** Use commas to set off adverbial clauses that come between a subject and verb or a verb and its complement:

> The people saw, *after a storm,* that the river grew muddy.

> The people, *after a storm,* saw that the river grew muddy.

Notice the difference in meaning between those sentences and this:

> The people saw that the river grew muddy after a storm.

In the first two examples, *after the storm* modifies *saw;* in the third it modifies *grew.* In a sentence with two or more verbs, place each adverbial modifier near the verb it modifies to avoid ambiguity.

RULE 9 **Names and titles in direct address**   Set off the names and titles of persons you are addressing:

> We want to thank you, *Chris,* for your work as treasurer.

> I am writing, *Mr. President,* to urge you to veto the bill.

RULE 10 **Dates and addresses**   Separate parts of exact dates and addresses with commas:

> On Tuesday, June 6, 1944, American troops landed in France.

> The White House is at 1600 Pennsylvania Avenue, Washington, D.C.

NOTE: When only the month and year appear, no comma is necessary: The building was dedicated in January 1983.

EXERCISES

A.   Add commas where they are necessary in the following sentences.

1. He used to live at 131 Mackey Road Rockland Oregon.
2. On April 4 1983 he married his high school sweetheart and they bought a small farm in Idaho.
3. Now they are thinking of moving again but this time they are going to choose a sunnier climate.
4. They are reluctant to leave the small fertile friendly valley where they have been living yet they feel that they must find an area where they can both work at better-paying jobs before they start having a family.
5. Although their little farm has given them tranquillity

privacy and a feeling of closeness to nature they know that their few acres will never be very profitable.

6. Until they have built up a sufficient nest egg they are postponing the financial responsibilities of children.

7. Together they have gone camping in California New Mexico and Arizona always searching for a new place to settle.

8. Should they choose a rural area like the ones where they have lived or should they settle in a suburban community one with greater job opportunities?

9. From the rugged California coastline near San Francisco to the wide-open Arizona desert near Phoenix they have sampled the richly varied temptingly beautiful landscapes of the Southwest.

10. They both want to be certain however of making the right choice so they are not rushing their decision.

11. To be sure they are approaching the problem as logically as possible but they are also hoping they admit that the right place will somehow announce itself to them when they find it.

12. They are enjoying the process of choosing which is a luxury they can afford to indulge in for at least another year.

13. They both come from families that did not have so much freedom of choice and they wish to make the most of their opportunities.

14. Once they have started having children it will be more difficult for them to move.

15. Of course if they are like the statistically average American family they will move every six or seven years but they are trying not to think in those terms.

B. Add commas where they are necessary in the following sentences.

1. Shakespeare immortalized the scene that took place in the Roman Senate on March 15 44 B.C.
2. On that day known as the ides of March in the Roman calendar Julius Caesar was assassinated by a group of conspirators.
3. Breathing his last Caesar reproached a friend who had joined with the conspirators: "You too Brutus!"
4. Because it exemplifies a struggle still going on in our world this scene remains a vivid image for us but it was not really a decisive moment in Roman history.
5. The conspirators believed in the old republican ideal of Rome and they opposed putting all power in the hands of one man.
6. By depicting Caesar as a dangerous tyrant the conspirators made his murder seem like a worthy deed but it was actually a political crime.
7. They were afraid that Caesar who was already an immensely successful military leader was going to make himself an emperor and a god.
8. That was however the path on which Rome had already embarked and Caesar's death did nothing to change matters.
9. Eventually Caesar's heir Augustus did become both an emperor and a god although he was not deified until after his death.
10. In history Julius Caesar's place as a great general is secure because of his campaigns in Germany Spain Asia and Britain.
11. Caesar himself wrote stirring accounts of his wars in

Gaul which have remained unsurpassed as models of clear writing.

12. In only four years as dictator Julius Caesar restored peace to the city of Rome which had been repeatedly torn apart by civil wars improved the government of the provinces and instituted measures to benefit both business and agriculture.

13. Caesar an administrator of obvious genius surely intended to extend the frontiers of the Roman Empire but his successors did that quite well without him.

14. During his rise to power and while he ruled Caesar aroused popular support with showy expensive circuses and he always considered himself an ally of the "people's party."

15. Even though it is impossible to know what would have happened if Caesar had not been killed in the Senate it is unlikely that the history of the world would have been greatly changed had he lived.

C. Add commas where they are necessary in the following sentences.

1. Mohammed and Abu Bekr his disciple and afterwards successor fled on camelback from Mecca in A.D. 622.

2. Their 200-mile ride to Medina known as the Hegira marked the beginning of the Mohammedan calendar and it was the start of Islam as a world force.

3. Mohammed himself was already fifty-two at the time but revelation of his destiny as a prophet had come to him a dozen years earlier.

4. Before he took on his religious role Mohammed had been a shepherd and a shopkeeper.

5. After the Angel Gabriel appeared to him while he

was praying on Mount Hira near Mecca Mohammed began to make converts but it was slow work—only forty accepted him as the Prophet after four years of his preaching.

6. Having written verses that would become the basis of the sacred Koran Mohammed began to attract a wider following.

7. When the rulers in Mecca feared that his new religion would threaten their power they plotted against Mohammed's life.

8. They broke into his house but Mohammed and Abu Bekr had already fled to the safety of Medina.

9. The reverse of their journey the pilgrimage to Mecca became a central part of the Moslem creed which every male believer tries to carry out in his lifetime.

10. Although Mohammed thought of himself as simply the last in a series of inspired prophets that included Adam Moses and Jesus and though his teachings were similar in many respects to those of Judaism and Christianity the Western impression of Islam is of a fanatically warlike philosophy.

11. As a matter of fact Mohammed's early followers had to depend on caravan raids for a living and the success of these raids attracted fighters to the faith.

12. Later the military weakness of the Eastern Roman Empire which was in serious decline invited even stronger attacks.

13. As Islam grew its power spread as far as Constantinople which was captured in 1453.

14. The leaders who followed Mohammed spread their conquests to amazing lengths—through Spain for example and to India even to the borders of China.

15. While successors to Mohammed struggled to extend their empire the Arabic word *Islam* kept its original

meaning "submission to the will of God" and it still means that for almost a half billion people in India the Near East and North Africa.

D. Add commas where they are necessary in the following sentences.

1. Languages undergo different kinds of changes in different parts of the world even those that have originally come from a single parent language.
2. If the changes are strengthened by such factors as geographic isolation political rivalry or economic differences they will steadily build on each other first producing different dialects then creating genuinely different languages.
3. The language of the Romans was of course Latin which was at first used only in a very small part of central Italy.
4. As the Romans expanded their control they soon made Latin the dominant language of the Italian peninsula.
5. The Romans conquered more and more of their neighbors incorporated more and more territory into their empire and extended the frontiers of their civilization and language.
6. When the Roman Empire finally crumbled under the attacks of Germanic tribes from the north and east the provinces that had made up the empire were separated from one another and cut off from Rome itself.
7. Because of their geographic separation each province developed its own distinct dialect of Latin and these dialects continued to change until they became the modern languages that we call French Italian Portuguese Spanish and Romanian.

8. We call this group the Romance languages because they are descended from the language of the Romans but today they are quite different from one another.

9. The early colonists in our own country used many different dialects of English for they had come from many different parts of their native country.

10. In addition to the colonists who came from Great Britain there were settlers from other parts of Europe as well.

11. Scots settled in Georgia Swedes in New Jersey Germans in Pennsylvania Dutch in New York French in Louisiana and Spaniards in Florida and they all added fresh elements to American English.

12. In the 19th century new waves of immigration brought large numbers of people from Mexico Ireland and Italy.

13. America famous as a "melting pot" of nationalities has also been a "melting pot" of languages.

14. Little by little the English used in America has changed from the language used in England and we have developed our own dialect American English.

15. Furthermore the development of our dialect has not stopped; new forces like television for example are now altering our accents adding to our vocabulary and modifying our language.

19 ◆ SUPERFLUOUS COMMAS

RULE 1 Do *not* separate the subject and verb or the verb and complement of any clause with a *single* comma. Use a *pair* of commas to set off non-restrictive clauses and phrases that come between the subject and verb or the verb and complement:

not

> The players who had worked hard for the team , were praised by the coach.

but

> The players who had worked hard for the team were praised by the coach. (restrictive)

or

> The players, who had worked hard for the team, were praised by the coach.

RULE 2 Do *not* use a comma to divide two words, phrases, or subordinate clauses that are joined by a coordinating conjunction *(and, but, or, nor, for, yet, so):*

> The horses galloped across the pasture, kicking up their heels⊙ and racing each other to the stream.

(Here "and" joins two participial phrases.)

RULE 3 Do *not* use a single comma between a coordinating conjunction and the words it joins to the sentence:

> They should have been happy, but⊙ their luck ran out.

(If emphasis on the coordinating conjunction is important, use a dash before it, as in "They should have been happy—but their luck ran out," or insert a non-restrictive modifier immediately after the conjunction so that a comma will be correct, as in "They should have been happy, but, sad to say, their luck ran out.")

RULE 4 Do *not* use commas around restrictive modifiers:

The children⊚ who had taken a nap⊚ were full of energy.

(If the "who" clause is pinpointing which children were full of energy, not simply describing the children, do not use commas.)

RULE 5 Do *not* use a comma after *like, such,* or *such as* when they introduce examples:

This law firm specializes in cases involving major crimes, such as⊚ murder, grand larceny, and rape.

RULE 6 Do *not* use a comma before words enclosed in parentheses. **After the closing parenthesis mark, use whatever punctuation would be appropriate if the parenthesized words were omitted.** Compare:

The date of the next meeting (Tuesday, July 17)⊚ was chosen by the committee.

The chairman made a note of the next meeting (Tuesday, July 17), the committee having agreed on the date.

RULE 7 Do *not* use commas to divide cumulative adjectives, ones arranged in an order that cannot logically be changed:

They wore new⊚ brown⊚ exercise suits.

RULE 8 Do *not* use commas to divide an adverb from an adjective that it modifies:

They entered a very₍₎ large, brightly₍₎ lit room.

RULE 9 Do *not* use a comma after a period, question mark, exclamation point, or dash:

He shouted, "Who's there?"₍₎ as she rattled the doorknob.

EXERCISE In the following sentences, delete the commas that are not correct.

1. Only students, who have accumulated sixty credits, may take advanced courses, so we will have to wait another semester.
2. When the restaurant offered free french fries with their hamburgers, business picked up, but, the restaurant lost so much money, that they went out of business.
3. The dark, night sky was suddenly lit up by an explosion at a factory, which was manufacturing fireworks, but fortunately no one was injured.
4. We sat through the long, travel film, and decided that if an ocean cruise was as boring as it looked on the screen, we would be better off staying home, and going to the beach this summer.
5. Have you ever dreamed of going to faraway places like, China, Australia, or, Argentina? Maybe you should try writing away for travel brochures, which can help you plan such a trip, and it would probably help to speak to people, who have traveled there already.

20 ◆ SEMICOLONS AND COLONS

Semicolons and colons are alternatives to commas and periods. You can write correct sentences all your life without ever using a semicolon or a colon, but they can create more precise relationships between thoughts than commas and periods can.

RULE 1 Use a **semicolon** between the independent clauses of a compound sentence that are *not* joined by a coordinating conjunction. The semicolon indicates either that the clauses are of roughly equal importance *or* that the second clause summarizes the first or gives additional information about it:

Florida residents learn to expect hurricanes and prepare for them; northerners are often taken by surprise.

The early settlers in North America were often dependent on the Indians for survival; they needed help in learning how to grow unfamiliar vegetables and in trapping game.

RULE 2 Use **semicolons** between independent clauses that are joined by coordinating conjunctions if one or more clauses contain several commas; the semicolons will show readers where the most important divisions in the sentence occur:

During the American Revolution, Yale College, which became Yale University, was closed; so was King's College, which became Columbia University; and

167

even twenty years after the Revolution, the entire Harvard faculty consisted of the president, three professors, and four tutors.

RULE 3 Use **semicolons** to divide the items in a series if the items themselves require commas:

They have skied in Colorado at Aspen, Vail, and Boulder; in Switzerland at Gstaad, St. Moritz, and Zermatt; in Austria at St. Anton and Kitzbühel; and in Vermont at Woodstock, Killington, and Stowe.

RULE 4 Use a **colon** at the end of an independent clause to indicate that it serves as an introduction and that the important words in the sentence will follow. What follows a colon may be as short as a single word or as long as an independent clause with modifiers, but it should serve as a climax for the sentence:

In the long months of famine, the thoughts of the starving people were reduced to a single point: food.

When they returned from vacation, they had an ugly shock: their house had been ransacked from top to bottom.

RULE 5 Use a **colon** after a formal introduction to a quotation:

The opening sentence of *Moby Dick,* Herman Melville's best-known novel, is famous: "Call me Ishmael."

RULE 6 Use a **colon** after an independent clause introducing a long list of any kind:

The store stocks a variety of footwear: walking shoes, dress shoes, jogging shoes, tennis shoes, hiking boots, and even ballet slippers.

RULE 7   Use a **colon** after an independent clause introducing a list of any length in which the items themselves require punctuation:

They narrowed their vacation plans to two possibilities: a cruise down the Mississippi on a paddle-wheel steamboat, stopping at Vicksburg, Natchez, Baton Rouge, and New Orleans, or a big-spenders' three-day weekend in Las Vegas, all expenses paid.

REMINDER: A **semicolon** tells readers to look back because the beginning of the sentence is more important *or* at least as important as what follows the semicolon. A **colon** tells readers to look forward because what follows the colon is more important.

EXERCISE   Replace incorrect commas with semicolons or colons.

1. In high school, I had no interest in classical music, however, a course in music appreciation has changed my listening habits.
2. I thought the history of music was simple, in the beginning there were the Beatles, now there is Bruce Springsteen.
3. Little by little, I found myself buying recordings of Russian composers, Tchaikovsky, Rachmaninoff, Rimsky-Korsakov, then I moved on to German composers such as Beethoven and Brahms.

4. The next step was obvious, I began listening to opera and ballet music.
5. At first I thought I would have to give up all of my favorite rock singers and groups, therefore, I was about to offer all of my "golden oldies" to my younger brothers and sisters.
6. Fortunately, before I gave anything away, I realized something important, it is possible to like both kinds of music.
7. It did not have to be what my philosophy professor calls an "either/or" choice, it could be a "both/and" choice.
8. Now I feel comfortable owning symphonies by Bach, Beethoven, and Brahms, arias by Callas, Caballé, and Carreras, and rock songs by the Beatles, Billy Idol, and, of course, the Boss.
9. For me, the moral of the story is plain, the more kinds of music I like the richer my musical life is.
10. There is one problem, how do I keep track of my recordings?

21 ◆ DASHES

RULE 1 Use a **dash** instead of a comma to stress a sudden break in thought or an important introductory word or group of words:

They had won the big game—but the crowd was strangely silent.

Everest—it is the ultimate challenge for mountain climbers.

RULE 2 Use a **dash** instead of a comma or colon to emphasize a climactic word or group of words at the end of a sentence:

> Ahead of them stretched years of hard work before they could reach their goal—playing with the Philharmonic Orchestra.

RULE 3 Use a **dash** instead of a semicolon to emphasize a summarizing statement or comment at the end of the sentence:

> They faced long hours of practicing alone, of strenuous rehearsals with other members of the class, of criticism by their teachers, and of discouraging self-doubt—these were all part of the normal life of a serious ballet student.

RULE 4 Use a **pair of dashes** to set off an important insertion or side comment, including one that is a complete sentence in itself:

> The elderly couple reluctantly reached a decision—to sell their house and move to an apartment—after years of helplessly watching their property deteriorate.

CAUTION: Do **not** use two dashes acting separately in one sentence. Your readers may think that they form a pair and are enclosing the words between them, as in this confusing sentence:

> For fifty years they had lived in the same house—they had bought it before their marriage—an unusually happy one with many shared interests.

Do **not** use a single dash in a sentence in which you also use a pair of dashes. Your readers will not be able to see easily which dash is acting alone, as in this confusing sentence:

> The house had many old-fashioned features—a wide front porch, an attic for storage, and a real dining room—that no apartments would offer—even expensive ones.

RULE 5 **Use dashes sparingly.** They stand out more on the page than any other punctuation. If you sprinkle them around freely, they lose their effect, and readers will think that you did not take the trouble to punctuate carefully.

NOTE: When typing, indicate a dash by typing two hyphen marks, one after the other, with *no* spaces before, after, or between them.

22 ◆ PARENTHESES

The word *parenthesis* comes from Greek (*para* = beside + *entithenai* = to insert) and means an insertion of any kind or the curved marks used to enclose the insertion. Use parentheses to set off additional information— such as the source of an opinion or fact, a short side comment, an explanation, a date, or a statistic—and to enclose numerals or letters identifying subdivisions or information in a sentence.

> The earliest known example of insurance was a kind of accident insurance obtained in 3000 B.C. by shipown-

ers in ancient Babylon (Charles Panati, *A Browser's Book of Beginnings,* page 173).

While he was president, Andrew Jackson established a ten-hour working day in the national shipyards (until then, twelve to fourteen hours had been standard), and workers warmly applauded him.

Chief Justice Marshall's particularly notable decisions ranged from *Marbury* v. *Madison* (1803) to *Gibbons* v. *Ogden* (1824).

The report showed that the company must develop (1) better quality control, (2) more worker participation in decision making, and (3) increased productivity.

REMINDERS: (1) Parentheses themselves are punctuation marks; therefore, do *not* place any punctuation *before* them. After a parenthesis, use whatever punctuation would be appropriate if you omitted the parenthesized material. (2) Use a *pair of commas* to set off non-restrictive modifiers and most short insertions in sentences. (See **18**, rule 7.) (3) Use *dashes* to set off an insertion that you want your readers to be sure to notice.

23 ◆ QUOTATION MARKS

Quotation marks are used to indicate the nature or the source of the words they enclose. Unlike such marks of punctuation as the comma or semicolon, quotation marks do not indicate sentence structure. For most purposes, double quotation marks (". . .") enclose the words being marked off; but in special cases, single quotation marks ('. . .') are necessary.

Double quotation marks serve five purposes: they enclose direct dialogue, titles of short works, words used in a special sense, the meanings of words being defined, and short passages of prose or poetry quoted from another source. **Single quotation marks** serve only one purpose: they enclose dialogue, titles, and words that form part of material already enclosed in double quotation marks.

1. **Direct dialogue**   Use *double quotation marks* to enclose words being presented as conversation. Identify each speaker if the reader might have any doubts as to who is speaking. Set off each speaker's remarks as a separate paragraph.

> "It certainly is hot," Pat groaned as he caught up with Chris and Lee in front of Henderson's, the largest sporting goods store in town.
>
> "I heard on the radio that it's going to be one for the record books if the temperature goes up one more degree today," Lee answered.
>
> "Have you got any plans for this afternoon?" asked Pat.
>
> "Let's all go for a swim," Chris suggested, "to cool off before dinner."

NOTE: In the last remark, if the quoted words following "Chris suggested" had formed a complete sentence, a period would have been necessary after "suggested":

> "Let's go for a swim," Chris suggested. "I want to cool off before dinner."

Use *single quotation marks* to set off any words that a speaker quotes from another source:

"Let's all go for a swim," Chris suggested. "My doc-tor's orders are 'Exercise an hour a day.' I've found that 'An apple a day keeps the doctor away' doesn't work for me."

NOTE: Do not use quotation marks around indirect dialogue:

Pat groaned that it certainly was hot, and Chris suggested that they all go for a swim.

2. **Titles of short works** Use *double quotation marks* to enclose the titles of short written works, such as poems, essays, short stories, and magazine or newspa-per articles; short musical compositions; and the sub-divisions of longer works, such as book chapters and individual episodes or segments of television shows:

Frost's poem, "Mending Wall"; Orwell's essay, "A Hanging"; Poe's short story, "The Tell-Tale Heart"; Dave Anderson's newspaper article, "Another Knockout for Tyson"; Gershwin's com-position, "Summertime"; Douglas Grant's chap-ter in *Twain,* "The Gigantic Picnic"; *Nova's* epi-sode, "The Horsemen of China"

Use *single quotation marks* around the title of a short work mentioned in the title of another short work:

Carl Ketcham's essay, "Shelley's 'A Vision of the Sea' "

NOTE: British practice reverses our procedure: single quotation marks enclose dialogue and titles of short works, and double quotation marks enclose titles or material quoted in dialogue.

3. **Words used in a special sense**   Use *double quotation marks* to enclose slang or dialect words and words used humorously or ironically:

> It was his third stay in the "slammer" in less than five years.

> The infant "artist" gleefully splashed paint on the floor.

In serious writing, avoid the humorous or ironic use of quotation marks.

4. **Meaning of words being defined**   Use *double quotation marks* to enclose the definition of a word or expression:

> We usually think of *brave* as meaning "willing to face danger."

5. **Short passages of prose or poetry quoted from another source**   For a full discussion, see **52a–b**.

23a Combining quotation marks with other punctuation

When quoting, use the terminal punctuation that the grammar requires. Place a *comma* or a *period* **inside** the closing quotation mark, whether or not it is part of the original.

Original: Fourscore and seven years ago our fathers brought forth on this continent a new nation, conceived in liberty, and dedicated to the proposition that all men are created equal.

Quoted: In his Gettysburg Address, Lincoln gave this reminder to his listeners: "Our fathers brought forth on this continent a new nation, conceived in liberty."

Quoted: At Gettysburg Lincoln said that "our fathers brought forth on this continent a new nation," and he reminded the audience that this nation was "conceived in liberty."

Place an *exclamation mark,* a *dash,* or a *question mark* **inside** the closing quotation mark if it is part of the original and applies only to the quoted words. Place it **outside** the closing quotation mark if you have added it or if it applies to the whole combination of the quotation and your sentence.

Original: Shall I compare thee to a summer's day?

Quoted: Shakespeare begins a comparison between his lover and the weather with the words "Shall I compare thee to a summer's day?"

Quoted: Who wrote the poem that begins with the words "Shall I compare thee to a summer's day"?

Place a *colon* or *semicolon* following a quotation **outside** the closing quotation mark, even if it appeared in the original.

Original: The exact nature of Byzantine art can be properly appreciated only when the art itself has been fully examined; it can be more easily defined at the conclusion of a book on the subject than at the outset.

Quoted: The art historian David Talbot Rice points out that "the exact nature of Byzantine art can be properly appreciated only when the art itself has been fully examined"; he defines it at the end of his book, not at the beginning.

23b Sources of quotations

Identify the source even of well-known quotations to make sure that your readers will see their importance. Special methods for presenting sources are required in research papers and critical essays (see **52**). In less formal uses of quotations, these methods are appropriate:

1. *To identify a long quotation,* one presented in a block, use an introductory statement ending with a colon:

> In dedicating the National Cemetery at Gettysburg in 1863, Lincoln began his address with a sentence that has become famous:

>> Fourscore and seven years ago our fathers brought forth on this continent a new nation, conceived in liberty, and dedicated to the proposition that all men are created equal.

2. *To identify a short quotation,* several methods are appropriate.
    a. An introductory statement ending with a colon or, less formally, with a comma:

Lincoln began his Gettysburg Address: "Fourscore and seven years ago our fathers brought forth on this continent a new nation."

Lincoln began his Gettysburg Address, "Fourscore and seven years ago our fathers brought forth on this continent a new nation."

b. An introductory clause ending in *that* as a subordinating conjunction and therefore requiring no punctuation after it:

In his Gettysburg Address, Lincoln said that "fourscore and seven years ago our fathers brought forth on this continent a new nation."

c. An identifying clause or phrase after the quotation:

"Fourscore and seven years ago our fathers brought forth on this continent a new nation," Lincoln reminded his audience at the beginning of his Gettysburg Address.

d. An identifying clause or phrase inserted in the quotation:

"Fourscore and seven years ago," Lincoln began, "our fathers brought forth on this continent a new nation."

EXERCISE In the following sentences, add single and double quotation marks where they are needed:

179

1. The instructor asked the class what the word *haply* means.
2. A student in the back row said, The word *haply* means by chance or by fortune, doesn't it?
3. That is correct, said the instructor. We have the same root in words like *mishap* and *happen.* Do not confuse *haply* with *happily.* Originally they both meant the same thing, that is, by good fortune, but they came to mean different things. Now *haply* means by chance or by accident, whereas *happily* means either fortunately or in a happy way.
4. Can you give us an example in which it is used? asked another student. I'm not sure I understand.
5. Certainly, the instructor replied. In Shakespeare's Sonnet 20, there is a line that begins, Haply I think on thee. . . . In that poem the word's primary meaning is by chance; therefore, the expression means by chance you come into my mind.
6. Excuse me, said a student in the front of the class. I thought it meant I think about you in a happy way. Didn't you say that *haply* and *happily* used to mean the same thing?
7. The instructor grinned. You're right he said. In Shakespeare's time the two words were interchangeable, and both meanings were possible. He was probably playing with the two meanings.
8. The student in the front asked the instructor to give another example, so the instructor asked the class to read Keats's Ode to a Nightingale for homework.
9. What page? someone called out, but we knew the instructor's standard answer: Use the table of contents or the index.

10. The poem was in a chapter called The Romantic Poets.

24 ◆ ITALICS

Italics, like quotation marks, indicate the nature of the words they emphasize, not the structure of the sentence. Italics are letters slanted in a style first made popular in Italy in the fifteenth century and available in printing and on some typewriters and computer printers. When writing by hand or using a machine without italics, underline the words that should be printed in italic type.

Italics serve four purposes: they indicate the titles of long written works and works of art; words referred to as words; words in a foreign language; and words given special emphasis.

1. **Titles**   Use italics to indicate the titles of all long written works—books, magazines, newspapers, plays, movies, radio and television programs and their scripts, musical compositions, paintings, and sculptures:

> *Huckleberry Finn, Newsweek,* the *Boston Globe, Hamlet, The Color Purple, Miami Vice,* Beethoven's *Eroica*, Verdi's *Aida*, Picasso's *Guernica*, Rodin's *The Thinker*

EXCEPTIONS: There are some important exceptions to this rule. Do not italicize the Bible or the titles of any books in it; do not italicize titles of literary or musical works known by their form, such as Shakespeare's Sonnet 34 or Beethoven's Fifth Symphony; and do not italicize descriptive or unofficial titles of works of art, such as the Venus de Milo (a descriptive title meaning "the statue of Venus found at Milo") or the Mona Lisa (the unofficial name for *La Gioconda*).

CAUTION: Most newspapers do not set titles in italics. Do *not* follow their practice in your writing.

2. **Technical terms, key words, and words referred to as words** Use italics to call your reader's attention to technical terms and key words in your discussion the first time you use them and to words that you define or refer to as words:

> One basis for classifying flowers is by the edges of the petals, which may be *entire, lobed,* or *toothed.*

> In a description of the edge of a flower petal, *toothed* means "notched" or "indented," not that the petal has teeth. The petals of the starry campion are toothed.

3. **Words in a foreign language** Use italics to indicate that a word is not English:

> The *ejido,* or communal farmland, of Mexican villages is divided into small sections.

English is full of words once considered foreign but now completely adopted into the language:

ski (Norwegian)
trek (Afrikaans)
data (Latin)
thug (Hindi)
bamboo (Malay)
leprechaun (Irish)
pizza (Italian)
thesis (Greek)

tea (Chinese)
vodka (Russian)
restaurant (French)
karate (Japanese)
rodeo (Spanish)
kindergarten (German)
megillah (Hebrew)

Check your college dictionary before deciding whether to treat a word as foreign.

4. **Words given special emphasis**   Use italics to indicate that a speaker has given a word special emphasis or to call attention to an important word that your readers might overlook:

> Do *not* call before nine o'clock.

In formal writing, this use of italics is ordinarily out of place. Instead, make your sentence structure emphasize the important words, and choose words that are forceful in themselves.

EXERCISE   In the following sentences, add double quotation marks and italics where they are needed.

1. Our word freeway is Autobahn in German, autoroute in French, and autostrada in Italian.
2. The second book of the Old Testament is Exodus.
3. Although The Star-Spangled Banner is our national anthem, many people prefer America the Beautiful because it is easier to sing.

4. The opening words of Book I of Milton's Paradise Lost are Of man's first disobedience. . . .
5. James Dean is probably best known for his role in Rebel Without a Cause.
6. Beethoven's Seventh Symphony is popularly known as the Pastoral.
7. Araby is the third story in James Joyce's collection Dubliners.
8. Botticelli's famous painting The Birth of Venus has been jokingly referred to as Venus on the Half Shell.
9. The words cotton and coffee both originally come from Arabic.
10. We usually think of smart as meaning intelligent or clever, but as a verb it means to cause stinging pain.

25 ◆ APOSTROPHES

The mark for an apostrophe is the same as a single quotation mark, but the two have no connection with each other. We use apostrophes for four purposes:

1. In **possessive forms** of all nouns and of many pronouns:

> one student's books   two students' books
> children's toys   anyone's job
> another's work

CAUTION: Do *not* use an apostrophe in the possessive forms of the personal pronouns (hers, its, ours, yours, theirs) or of who (whose). For further discussion of possessive forms, see **4b** and **5b**.

2. In **contractions of verbs** with pronouns or with *not:*

    we're ready   we aren't ready
    it's cold   it isn't cold
    they'll leave   they won't leave

For further discussion of contractions, see **6h**.

3. In **contractions of the number for a year:**

    the class of '91   a bottle of '85 burgundy

4. In **plurals of words referred to as words**, lowercase letters, abbreviations that include periods, and years forming a decade:

    two *the*'s   four g's   two M.A.'s
    the 1980's (*also acceptable:* the 1980s; see **29**)

EXERCISE   In the following sentences, add apostrophes where they are needed.

1. They weren't invited to Franks party.
2. The Class of 80 will be having its tenth reunion soon.
3. There are two *a*s and two *e*s in the word *separate.*
4. The Smiths house is larger than the Joneses, but it doesn't have a garden.
5. Euripides tragedies are as moving as Shakespeares.
6. Whos going to believe your theory if youve given no evidence?
7. If theres no way to prove what youre saying, its better to call your ideas theories and not facts.
8. When were away on vacation, we board our dog at the vets.

9. Whats the name of the man who administered the oath of office at Washingtons first inauguration?
10. Marys fathers uncle is Marys great-uncle, isnt he?

26 ◆ HYPHENS

Hyphens have four uses:

1. To connect two or more words joined to form a compound word:

   sister-in-law   well-oiled engine
   ten-year drought   fifty-one

2. To connect certain prefixes and suffixes to words:

   ex-president   great-aunt
   senator-elect   self-conscious

3. To prevent ambiguity in pronunciation:

   anti-inflationary   re-present (in contrast to *represent*)

NOTE: For further discussion of these three uses, see **2d**.

4. To connect the syllables of a word split between two lines.

Always try to avoid splitting a word at the end of a line. A split word is always hard to read. Instead, leave the space at the end of the line blank and write the complete word on the next line. If you must divide a word between two lines, divide it between syllables. Your college dictionary shows the syllabication of every word.

Never divide a one-syllable word, no matter how long it is—*climbed,* never *clim-bed* or *climb-ed; straight,* never *stra-ight.* Never divide a syllable, no matter how many vowels it contains—*gor-geous,* not *gorge-ous; sensation,* not *sensati-on.* Similarly, do not split a word ending in *le,* even though pronounced as a partial syllable, so that only three letters are carried over to the next line—*credible,* not *credi-ble; prin-ciple,* not *princi-ple.* Such words as *people* and *title* should not be divided at all.

In applying these rules, use common sense. Do not divide a word so that only one or two letters are cut off by a hyphen. Despite the syllabic division, *unite* should not be split into *u-nite* or *acted* into *act-ed.* Do not divide a word that readers will be likely to misread—avoid splitting both *eve-ning* (time of day) and *even-ing* (making even).

CAUTION: Newspapers and magazines frequently violate these rules. Their narrow columns do not allow much adjustment, so they often use illogical hyphenation. Do *not* follow their practice.

27 ◆ ABBREVIATIONS

Use abbreviations in addressing envelopes or in heading a business letter (see **54**), in citing some sources in research papers (see **52a–d**), and in technical and scientific charts and formulas. In the rest of your writing, you should spell out words, with the few common exceptions that follow.

1. **Personal names**   Use initials only if the person named regularly used them:

> John F. Kennedy   George M. Cohan
> T. S. Eliot

When referring to a person only by initials, omit periods:

> JFK   FDR

Do not abbreviate given names:

> George Washington, *not* Geo. Washington

> Thomas Jefferson, *not* Thos. Jefferson

When *Saint* forms part of a person's name, follow that person's usage in choosing between *Saint* and *St.:*

> Ruth St. Denis   Augustus Saint-Gaudens

For Christian saints, use either *Saint* or *St.,* but be consistent. If you begin by using St. Francis, then use *St.* for all references to him and other saints you mention.

The designations *Junior* and *Senior* are considered part of the names they follow. They are regularly abbreviated *Jr.* and *Sr.* and are set off from the rest of the sentence by commas:

> Eugene O'Neill, Jr., was a classical scholar, not a playwright like his father.

Similarly, the numbers II, III, etc., or 2nd, 3rd, etc., are also considered part of the name, but they are not set off by commas:

> Cornelius Vanderbilt Whitney III was the great-grandson of Commodore Vanderbilt, who founded the family fortune.

Use *Jr., Sr.,* and numbers only after the full name. Do *not* write *Mr. O'Neill, Jr.,* or *Mr. Vanderbilt III.*

2. **Titles that precede names**
   a. **Social titles**   Always abbreviate these social titles:

> Mr.   Mrs.   Ms.

We use the French plurals for *Mr.* and *Mrs.: Messrs.* and *Mmes.; Ms.* is both singular and plural.
   b. **Civil and military titles**   Spell out most titles when giving only a person's surname:

> General Eisenhower   Professor Boas
> Senator Smith   Lieutenant Lopez

When giving full names, you may abbreviate these titles:

> Gen. Dwight Eisenhower   Prof. Franz Boas
> Sen. Margaret Chase Smith Lt. Ramon Lopez

   c. **Courtesy and religious titles**   Spell out *Reverend* and *Honorable* when you precede them with *the:*

> the Reverend Billy Graham

> the Honorable Mario Cuomo

> the Right Reverend Monsignor Paul Evans

When not preceded by *the*, these titles may be abbreviated:

> Present at the meeting were Rev. Graham, Hon. Cuomo, and Rt. Rev. Msgr. Evans.

3. **Degrees, titles, and honors that follow names**
   a. **Degrees** Abbreviate all professional and scholarly degrees. Most are based on Latin words. These are in general use:

B.A.	Bachelor of Arts (from Latin *artium baccalaureus;* some universities keep the Latin word order and abbreviate this degree as *A.B.*)
B.S.	Bachelor of Science
D.D.	Doctor of Divinity (from Latin *divinitatis doctor*)
D.D.S.	Doctor of Dental Surgery
D.V.M.	Doctor of Veterinary Medicine
J.D.	Doctor of Law (from Latin *juris doctor*)
J.P.	Justice of the Peace
Litt.D.	Doctor of Letters (from Latin *litterarum doctor;* note the use of lowercase letters in the abbreviation)
LL.B.	Bachelor of Law (from Latin *legum baccalaureus;* note the use of the double capital letter to abbreviate *legum*)
M.A.	Master of Arts (from Latin *artium magister;* some universities keep the Latin word order and abbreviate this degree as *A.M.*)

M.B.A.	Master of Business Administration
M.D.	Doctor of Medicine (from Latin *medicinae doctor*)
M.S.	Master of Science
Ph.D.	Doctor of Philosophy (from Latin *philosophiae doctor;* note the use of a lowercase *h* in the abbreviation)

Use commas to set off these degrees from the names to which they refer and omit *Mr., Mrs., Miss, Ms.,* or *Dr.:*

> Jane Smith, Ph.D., was one of the signers of the petition.

or

> Dr. Jane Smith was one of the signers of the petition.

b. **Titles** *Esquire* is sometimes used instead of *Mr.* as a mark of special respect. Use it if the person you are mentioning prefers it. Place it after the name and abbreviate it:

> James Robinson, Esq.

c. **Honors** Abbreviate military honors such as the Distinguished Service Order:

> Capt. James Robinson, D.S.O.

4. **Agencies and organizations** The names of government agencies, broadcasting companies, unions, some associations and businesses, and many other groups are known primarily by their initials. Give them in capital letters with no periods or spaces between them, for example:

UNESCO	NASA	UN	SALT
NBC	CBS	UAW	YMCA
NAACP	VFW	NFL	NBA
IBM	TWA	FBI	

5. **Geographical terms** In the text of your paper, spell out the names of the states, as in:

> The company has offices in Bangor, Maine, and Provo, Utah.

In business letters and lists, however, you may abbreviate the names of states when they follow the names of cities:

> The company has offices in New Haven, Conn., and Tampa, Fla.

Similarly, the District of Columbia is abbreviated *D.C.* when it follows *Washington.*

Spell out the prefixes of most geographic names, as in

Fort Wayne	South Bend
Mount Holly	Port Washington

Names of cities beginning with *Saint,* such as St. Paul and St. Louis, are the only exceptions.

Spell out the names of all countries except the Soviet Union, for which *USSR* is customary rather than *Union of Soviet Socialist Republics.* In referring to the United States, you may use *U.S.* as an adjective if it modifies the words immediately following it, as in "The U.S. Senate meets in Washington." Otherwise, spell out the name, as in "The Senate of the United States meets in Washington."

Spell out words in addresses that you use in a letter or essay, but use numerals for building numbers:

> They lived first at 527 Reed Avenue, then at 103 East Mautner Parkway, and finally at 6 Romm Square.

Before a ZIP code, always use the U.S. Postal Service's two-letter abbreviation for the state:

> Paterson, NJ 07513   Des Plaines, IL 60016

6. **References to time**
    a. **Years**   In traditional usage, the following abbreviations precede the number of the year:

    A.D.   (from Latin *anno Domini* = in the year of the Lord) used to distinguish dates in modern times from those in ancient times (Placing A.D. after the number of the year is becoming common practice.)

    A.H.   (from Latin *anno Hegirae* = in the year of the Hegira) used to distinguish dates in Mohammedan history

    A.H.   (from Latin *anno Hebraico* = in the Hebrew Year) used to distinguish dates in Jewish history

These abbreviations follow the number of the year:

    B.C.   (for *Before Christ*) used to distinguish dates in ancient times

    B.C.E. (for *Before the Common Era*), see C.E.

C.E.   (for *Common Era*), C.E. and B.C.E. replace A.D. and B.C. for those preferring to avoid a reference to religion

b. **Months**   Spell out the names of months except in the heading of business letters and in lists and charts; in those, the abbreviations *Jan., Feb.,* and so forth, are customary.

c. **Days of the week**   Spell out the days of the week except in lists and charts.

d. **Time of day**   When giving the hour in numerals, you may indicate whether it is before or after noon with abbreviations:

A.M. (from Latin *ante meridiem* = before midday) used to identify the hours between midnight and noon

P.M. (from Latin *post meridiem* = after midday) used to identify the hours from noon to midnight When giving the time in words, do not use *A.M.* or *P.M.* Instead, write "The meeting will be at ten-thirty on Tuesday morning" or "The client arrived at three forty-five in the afternoon."

NOTE: In print, the abbreviations A.M. and P.M. are usually set in small capital letters. In a typed or handwritten paper, use either ordinary capital letters or lowercase letters:

3:45 P.M.   *or*   3:45 p.m.

7. **Frequently used Latin expressions**   These Latin words and phrases are usually abbreviated:

c. *or* ca. ·   (for *circa*) meaning "around" or "approximately," as in "Caesar was born c. 100 B.C. and died in 44 B.C."

e.g.	(for *exempli gratia*) meaning "for example"
et al.	(for *et alii*) meaning "and others," and always written as two words; usually refers to people; see *etc.*
etc.	(for *et cetera*) meaning "and other things"
i.e.	(for *id est*) meaning "that is"; introduces an explanation
viz.	(for *videlicet*) meaning "namely"; introduces an example
vs. *or* v.	(for *versus*) meaning "against" or "opposed to"

Because these abbreviations are used often, they are not normally italicized, even though they stand for words in a foreign language.

Abbreviations with other punctuation If you use an abbreviation within a sentence, do not omit other punctuation that your sentence requires. However, if the abbreviation ends in a period and comes at the end of the sentence, do not add another period:

In 753 B.C., according to legend, Rome was founded.

According to legend, Rome was founded in 753 B.C.

28 ◆ CAPITALIZATION

Capitalizing a word for emphasis was common a hundred years ago. Now only six uses of capital letters are standard:

1. Capitalize the first letter of the first word of every sentence.
2. Capitalize the first letter of the first word of every quoted sentence that does not play a grammatical role in a sentence of your own. Compare these uses of the same quotation:

> Grant writes of *Huckleberry Finn,* "The book is a triumph of style."

> Grant writes of *Huckleberry Finn* that "the book is a triumph of style."

In the first, the quotation is treated as an independent sentence, despite the introductory clause, so it begins with a capital letter. In the second, the quotation is treated as a dependent clause introduced by "that," so it begins with a lowercase letter.
3. Capitalize the first letter of every line of poetry unless the poet has not capitalized it.
4. Capitalize the pronoun *I,* but not the other pronouns. Traditionally, pronouns referring to God have been capitalized, but many writers no longer follow this practice, and you are free to do as your beliefs dictate. Capitalize the exclamation *O* wherever it occurs, but capitalize *oh* only when it begins a sentence.
5. Capitalize the first letter of all proper names—the names of persons, places, languages, nations, organizations, religions, ethnic groups, historical events, days, months, holidays, academic degrees, titles that precede a name, and *Jr., Sr.,* and *Esq.* following a name.

NOTE: We usually capitalize modifiers derived from proper names:

Elizabethan era   Platonic philosphy
Freudian slip   Jeffersonian democracy

We also capitalize proper names and modifiers derived from them when they are part of a compound:

anti-Hitler   pro-American   mid-Victorian
ex-President Ferdinand Marcos

6. In the titles of all written and dramatic works, works of art, and musical compositions, capitalize the first and last words, any word following a colon or semicolon (whatever the word), and all words between the first and last except articles *(a, an, the)*, conjunctions *(and, but, or, nor, for, yet, so)*, and prepositions:

> *A Midsummer Night's Dream, Gone with the Wind, Romeo and Juliet,* "Ode on a Grecian Urn," *Shelley: A Life*

CAUTION: There are several exceptions to the preceding rules:

1. Do **not** capitalize the first letter of the first word of an independent clause that you insert as a parenthetic statement:

> The large painting—for once, the artist had worked on a grand scale—dominated the room.

2. Do **not** capitalize personal titles unless they precede a name:

28 Capitalization

They met with General Washington and two captains.

There are exceptions to this exception. When you refer only by title to a particular individual who is the political head of a country, the title is usually capitalized. Compare:

Several American presidents have visited Germany.

The President visited Germany in 1985.

Although current usage is moving away from capitalizing titles, some organizations and institutions capitalize when referring to their own officers, as in "Several students saw the Dean about their grades."

3. Do **not** capitalize verbs, participles, or gerunds formed from proper names; for example, *pasteurize, galvanized, mesmerizing*

4. Do **not** capitalize the name of a field of study, such as *physics, economics,* or *sociology,* unless it names a language; for example, "She majored in geology, but he majored in Italian."

5. Opinion is divided on capitalizing words naming family members when the words function as proper names. Both forms are correct:

"Is lunch ready, Mother?" the children asked.

"Is lunch ready, mother?" the children asked.

Do **not** capitalize these words in other uses:

The children asked their mother if lunch was ready.

Notice the differences in the use of capital and lower-case letters in the following cases:

Chemistry 101	the study of chemistry
the Ohio River	the rivers of Ohio
a city in the West	to the west of the city
Franklin High School	a high school building
Senator Byrd	several senators
Main Street, Iona	the main street of Iona
April, October	the spring, the fall
the Civil War	the civil wars of history
Aunt Jane	the children's aunt
the Democratic party	a democratic society
President Adams	Adams, our second president

EXERCISE In the following sentences, change lowercase letters to capital letters wherever necessary.

1. the reporter asked the press secretary, "does senator wilson want to comment on the president's speech?"
2. the romans persecuted both christians and jews.
3. do students read shakespeare's *much ado about nothing?*
4. in high school i read two plays, *julius caesar* and robert bolt's *a man for all seasons.*
5. who was president in 1923? was it harding or coolidge?
6. my american history course only goes up to the civil war.
7. ask me again in the spring, around the middle of march, when i'm taking american history 102.

8. robert frost's poem "mending wall" ends with these lines:

> he will not go behind his father's saying,
> and he likes having thought of it so well
> he says again, "good fences make good
> neighbors."

9. why did they major in latin instead of french?
10. my uncle is older than my father, but aunt edna is younger.

29 ◆ NUMBERS

With technical, statistical, and scientific material that involves many numbers, use figures throughout, including fractions and one-digit figures, but always spell out any number that begins a sentence (when typing on a typewriter that lacks a separate key for the number **1**, use the letter **l**, never the letter **I**).

With material that requires only an occasional number, spell out any that you can write in one or two words, such as fifteen, forty-two, three hundred, or nine million. Hyphenate compound numbers, such as forty-two; use figures for others such as 5¾, 102, and 2,450.

If you have several numbers fairly close together and could write some in one or two words but not the others, use one style for all:

> The farmer had forty cows and a hundred and ten chickens.

or

The farmer had 40 cows and 110 chickens.

CAUTION: Newspapers and magazines regularly use figures to save space, even for a single number. Do **not** follow this practice.

Use commas to divide figures of five or more digits into three-digit groups, counting from the right: 42,752; 2,873,649. In four-digit figures, the comma is optional: either $2500 or $2,500.

NOTES: (1) Do **not** leave a space between the comma and the number that follows it. (2) Do **not** use commas in four- or five-digit numbers in street addresses or book pages:

1573 Maple Drive   page 1287

If a hyphenated number is used to indicate a building spread over two or more lots, retain the hyphen in giving the address:

1815-17 Mountain Boulevard

With times and dates, you have a choice of styles, but use one consistently through any one piece of writing.

10:15 a.m. (*or* A.M. *or* A.M.) *or* ten fifteen in the morning *or* quarter past ten in the morning

May 3, 1988 *or* 3 May 1988

May third *or* the third of May *or* May 3 *or* May 3rd (Do not write *May 3rd, 1988,* which mixes styles.)

the twenties *or* the 1920's *or* the 1920s

the twentieth century or the 20th century

in 1983-84 *or* in 1983-1984 (a group of years as a unit)

CAUTION: Write "from 1983 to 1984," not "from 1983-1984"; a hyphen does not substitute for "to."

Never begin a sentence with a figure. Spell out the number or rewrite your sentence so that it begins with a word:

Two hundred and fifty guests attended the ceremony.

or

There were 250 guests attending the ceremony.

Use figures in addresses and in names that are usually printed with figures:

527 Fifth Avenue
Apartment 12-B
  or Apt. 12-B
Channel 13
Interstate 40

P.O. Box 1415
40 West 119 Street
  or 40 West 119th Street
Pope John XXIII
Route 18

Part Four
SENTENCE EFFECTIVENESS

30 ◆ EFFECTIVE STRUCTURE

How did the student who wrote this awkward, long-winded ending for an essay revise it to make the single, compact, and effective sentence of the final draft?

First draft

So it can easily be seen why Pete Rose deserves an award for being the most outstanding person in athletics in 1985. One reason he deserves it is because of his accomplishments on the baseball field. Another reason he deserves it is because of his positive attitude toward the game when he plays.

Final draft

We can easily see that, because of his accomplishments on the baseball field and because he never stops "hustling" when he plays, Pete Rose deserves an award for being the outstanding athlete of 1985.

Here is the student's first draft with all the revisions:

~~So it~~ _{we} can easily ~~be seen why~~ _{see that} Pete Rose deserves an award for being the ~~most~~ outstanding ~~person in athletics in~~ _{athlete of} 1985. ~~One reason he deserves it is~~ because of his accomplishments on the baseball field, _{and} ~~Another reason he deserves it is~~ because ~~of his positive attitude toward the game~~ _{he never stops "hustling"} when he plays,

Notice how the student eliminated the unnecessary words that weakened the first version, reducing its length by more than 35%. Notice, also, how the student combined the original two sentences into one and emphasized the most important words by moving them to the end to serve as the climax of the sentence and therefore also of the essay. Notice, finally, the change from the colorless wording of "his positive attitude toward the game" to the more precise and vigorous wording of "he never stops 'hustling,'" using the term often applied to Rose's energetic style.

This section discusses how to take advantage of sentence structure and word choice to make your meaning clear and forceful. The following techniques are particularly useful.

30a Coordination

Use compound sentences, compound subjects, and compound predicates to bring related points together and to show that they are of roughly equal importance. Readers notice the last compound element slightly more than the others simply because it is last. Take advantage of that fact in organizing your sentence.

> It was Sunday, the weather was warm and sunny, and many cars were on the road to the beach.

Compare that sentence with this version, which has no compounds:

> Because it was a warm, sunny Sunday, many cars were on the road to the beach.

Both versions are grammatically correct, but the effect and emphasis are different.

30b Subordination

Use prepositional, verbal, and appositive phrases and dependent clauses to create relationships among your thoughts. Emphasize more important points by subordinating others to them.

> A red BMW, which had been moving rapidly in the left lane, now cut sharply to the right in front of a blue Honda.

Compare that sentence with this version, which uses coordination:

> A red BMW had been moving rapidly in the left lane, and it now cut sharply to the right in front of a blue Honda.

30c Parallelism

Two or more groups of words are parallel when they have the same structure and function. For example, a series of three "if" clauses modifying the same verb will catch the attention of readers just as a set of triplets all dressed alike by their proud parents catches instant attention. Readers notice a series, and the last element somewhat more than the others. Arrange the parts of a series in climactic order, starting with the least important and ending with the most important.

> The driver of the BMW played games with the traffic—switching in and out of the right lane, slowing down suddenly for no apparent reason, then leaping ahead in a sudden burst of speed.

Compare that version with this one, which lacks parallelism:

> The driver of the BMW played games with the traffic as he switched in and out of the right lane, slowing down suddenly for no apparent reason before he leaped ahead in a sudden burst of speed.

30d Repetition

The repetition of key words and phrases helps readers to notice and remember them, especially when the repetition is reinforced by parallelism. Careless repetition wastes words and bores readers, but deliberate repetition can be effective.

The red car, red as a stoplight, red as a fire engine,
glittered like a danger signal.

Compare that version with this one, which lacks repetition:

The red car, the color of a stoplight or a fire engine,
glittered like a danger signal.

30e Anticipation

Introductory modifiers can stimulate curiosity by
making readers wait to find out what the sentence is
about. Structures such as *not only . . . but also . . .* and *if
it is not . . . it must be . . .* create suspense, making readers
expect to find important information at the end of the
sentence.

Swinging out suddenly from behind a big truck that had
blocked the view of the road ahead, the BMW skidded on an oil slick.

Compare that version with this one, which lacks anticipation:

The BMW skidded on an oil slick after swinging out
suddenly from behind a truck that had blocked the
view of the road ahead.

30f Contrast and variety

If several sentences in a row are the same length and
have the same construction but are not designed as a parallel series, they become monotonous:

> For a moment, the BMW went completely out of con-
> trol. It spun around wildly. It was in front of the
> oncoming truck. The truck tried to swerve out of the
> way. Then the two crashed.

The writer may also lose emphasis with one long sentence:

> For a moment, completely out of control, the BMW
> spun wildly in front of the oncoming truck, which
> tried to swerve out of the way, but the two crashed.

If the writer places a short, simple sentence after
longer and more complicated ones, it will stand out by
contrast, summing up material or pinpointing an important thought. Varied sentence structures and lengths keep
readers alert and interested:

> For a moment, completely out of control, the BMW
> spun around wildly in front of the oncoming truck,
> which tried to swerve out of the way. Then the two
> crashed.

30g Economy

Use relative pronouns, subordinate clauses, and verbal phrases to compress your ideas. One compact sentence
is more forceful than several sprawling ones that waste
words and make readers impatient.

> All the other cars and trucks on the highway came to a
> halt, with their tires screeching in the process. At the
> same time, the truck driver, who had not been in-
> jured in the crash, leaped out of the cab of his truck
> and ran over to the BMW.

Compare that version with this tightly constructed one, half as long but much more effective:

> As all the highway traffic came screeching to a halt, the truck driver, uninjured, leaped out of his cab and ran to the BMW.

Do professional writers consciously think of structure with each sentence they write? Of course not. But they look over what they write to see it with a reader's eye, watching for sentences that seem monotonous, awkward, unclear, or unemphatic. Then they revise what they have written to sharpen and strengthen it. Often, revising takes longer than composing a first draft.

Passages for analysis   The following paragraph is from the opening chapter of *Everything in Its Path* by Kai Erikson, a study of how the lives of people in a small coal-mining community in West Virginia were changed by a violent flood that swept through their narrow mountain valley (or "hollow") in 1972. A sentence-by-sentence analysis follows the paragraph.

Example 1

> So the residents of Buffalo Creek were fairly well off in the early days of 1972. Most of the men were employed and earning good wages, and if the hollow did not quite reach the national mean on the conventional indices of wealth, the people nonetheless owned their own homes, paid modest taxes, enjoyed a certain measure of security, and were generally satisfied with their lot. They had survived the crisis of automation and were even beginning to profit from it, and to that

extent, at least, they were one of the most affluent groups in an otherwise impoverished region. Most of them had worked their way out of the hardships their parents had known in the old coal camps and the poverty their grandparents had known in the remote mountains of Appalachia. Looking back, the men and women of Buffalo Creek remember it as a secure, honest, comfortable life.

The paragraph ends a description of what the community had been like before the flood, summarizing the important points for the reader. The writing is direct and simple, a style that is appropriate for exposition. Although the paragraph is informative rather than dramatic, Erikson makes his meaning clear and forceful by using compound structures, parallelism, varied sentence structures, and contrasts in length and complexity.

In the following analysis, each sentence is numbered for easy reference. The main sections of compound sentences are indicated by *a* and *b,* and dependent clauses are set off in parentheses.

1   So the residents of Buffalo Creek were fairly well off in the early days of 1972.

This simple sentence explicitly states the topic of the paragraph. It is also the shortest sentence in the paragraph. The beginning "So" links this paragraph to the preceding one.

2a   Most of the men were employed and earning good wages,

2b and (if the hollow did not quite reach the national mean on the conventional indices of wealth), the people nonetheless owned their own homes, paid modest taxes, enjoyed a certain measure of security, and were generally satisfied with their lot.

This compound-complex sentence supports the opinion expressed in sentence 1. Clause 2a gives the chief cause underlying the opinion in a compound predicate whose two verbs pinpoint the important elements of the underlying cause—employment and good wages. Clause 2b gives specific details to support the general facts given in 2a. The compound predicate with four verbs in parallel constructions emphasizes the elements supporting the claim made in sentence 1. It is four times as long as 2a, and its introductory modifier builds up to the main clause and emphasizes it.

3a They had survived the crisis of automation and were even beginning to profit from it,

3b and to that extent, at least, they were one of the most affluent groups in an otherwise impoverished region.

This compound sentence, whose parts are more equal than those of sentence 2, further supports the topic stated in sentence 1. Clause 3a has a compound predicate that gives two related general comments to summarize sentence 2. Clause 3b gives the results of sentence 2 and of the preceding clause.

4 Most of them had worked their way out of the hardships (their parents had known in the old coal camps)

and the poverty (their grandparents had known in the remote mountains of Appalachia).

This complex sentence gives the historical context for the general opinion stated in sentence 1. Two nouns are the parallel objects of "way out of"—"hardships" and "poverty"—and each noun is modified by an adjective clause with repeated key words to reinforce the parallelism.

5   Looking back, the men and women of Buffalo Creek
    remember it as a secure, honest, comfortable life.

This simple sentence sums up the paragraph. Its short introductory modifier prepares the reader for a summarizing statement, and its adjectives, "secure, honest, comfortable," reinforce the opinion in sentence 1.

Throughout the paragraph, Erikson writes with *economy.* For example, consider this long-winded version of sentence 5:

The men and women of Buffalo Creek look back over their life there, and then they remember their life as one that was secure, and honest, and comfortable.

This version takes 28 words to say what Erikson says in 17.

Also throughout the paragraph, Erikson *varies the structure and length of his sentences.* The first and last are simple, the second is compound-complex, the third compound, and the fourth complex; sentence 1 has 16 words, 2 has 49 words, 3 has 34 words, 4 has 33 words, and 5 has 17 words. Erikson also *varies the openings* of his sentences. In the first main clause of sentences 2 and 3 and in the main clause of sentence 4, the first words form the complete subject, but he begins the two simple sentences and the other main clauses differently: 1 begins with a conjunction, "So"; 2b with an adverb clause; 3b with two short prepositional phrases; and 5 with a verbal phrase.

In example 1, we see how Erikson uses *coordination*—compound sentences and compound predicates—to emphasize the peaceful elements in the lives of the people of Buffalo Creek. In example 2, notice how Erikson uses *subordination* to dramatize the violence of the first moments of the flood. Of eight sentences here, only one is compound, but altogether they contain *eight subordinate clauses* and *five verbal phrases.* The only compound predicate occurs in a subordinate clause. As in example 1, Erikson writes with *economy,* uses *introductory modifiers* to increase anticipation, uses *parallelism* to organize information and emphasize similarities, and *varies the length and structure of his sentences* to avoid monotony. *Short, simple sentences* emphasize the main point—the extraordinary suddenness and violence of the flood.

Example 2

At one minute before 8:00, the dam simply collapsed. There is little evidence that water came over the top of the dam, although that remains one of the obvious possibilities. It is a good deal more likely that the whole structure became saturated with moisture, dissolved into something resembling wet paste, and just slumped over on its foundation of silt and sludge. In any event, the entire lake of black water, all 132 million gallons of it, roared through the breach in a matter of seconds. It was already more than water, full of coal dust and other solids, and as it broke through the dam and landed on the banks of refuse below, it scraped up thousands of tons of other material, the whole being fused into a liquid substance that one engineer simply called a "mud wave" and one witness described as "rolling lava." The wave set off a series of explosions as it drove a channel through the smoldering trough of slag, raising mushroom-shaped clouds high into the air and throwing great spatters of mud three hundred feet up to the haul road where a few men were returning from the mines. The rock and debris dislodged by those explosions were absorbed into the mass too. By now, there was something like a million tons of solid waste caught up in the flow.

EXERCISE   How and where does Erikson make the sentence structure in this paragraph emphasize important words? Analyze the paragraph, using the methods applied to example 1. As before, each sentence is numbered for easy reference, the main sections of the compound sentence are indicated by *a* and *b,* and the dependent clauses are set off in parentheses.

1   At one minute before 8:00, the dam simply collapsed.

2   There is little evidence (that water came over the top of the dam), (although that remains one of the obvious possibilities).

3   It is a good deal more likely (that the whole structure became saturated with moisture, dissolved into something resembling wet paste, and just slumped over on its foundation of silt and sludge).

4   In any event, the entire lake of black water, all

132 million gallons of it, roared through the breach in a matter of seconds.

5a It was already more than water, full of coal dust and other solids,

5b and (as it broke through the dam and landed on the banks of refuse below), it scraped up thousands of tons of other material, the whole being fused into a liquid substance (that one engineer simply called a "mud wave") and (one witness described as "rolling lava").

6 The wave set off a series of explosions (as it drove a channel through the smoldering trough of slag), raising mushroom-shaped clouds high into the air and throwing great spatters of mud three hundred feet up to the haul road (where a few men were returning from the mines).

7 The rock and debris dislodged by those explosions were absorbed into the mass too.

8 By now, there was something like a million tons of solid waste caught up in the flow.

30h Varying structure for emphasis

We can also create more effective sentences by varying the position of the main subject and verb in relation to the rest of the sentence. A sentence may be *loose, balanced,* or *periodic.*

(1) Loose sentences In a loose sentence, the main subject and verb are at or near the beginning of the sentence and appear in natural order, subject first, verb second. Most of our sentences are loose.

So the residents of Buffalo Creek were fairly well off in the early days of 1972.

A particular type of loose sentence is called "cumulative." In it, several modifiers follow the subject and verb, piling one on top of the other. Some cumulative sentences are quite long. A typical one is sentence 6 in example 2 from Erikson. It contains 50 words. A fairly dramatic example is the following sentence, which contains 80 words:

The San Bernardino Valley lies only an hour east of Los Angeles by the Freeway but is in certain ways an alien place: not the coastal California of the subtropical twilights and the soft westerlies off the Pacific but a harsher California, haunted by the Mojave just beyond the mountains, devastated by the hot dry Santa Ana wind that comes down through the passes at 100 miles an hour and whines through the eucalyptus windbreaks and works on the nerves.

> —Joan Didion, "Some Dreamers of the Golden Dream," *Slouching Toward Bethlehem*

The effectiveness of a cumulative sentence depends on the piling up of facts or opinions and the connections that are thus suggested. Despite their length, cumulative sentences are easy to read because they begin with the main subject and verb.

(2) Balanced sentences A balanced sentence is a compound sentence with closely parallel clauses of approximately the same length and importance:

Not only do the tides advance and retreat in their eternal rhythms, but the level of the sea itself is never at rest.

> —Rachel Carson, *The Edge of the Sea*

A balanced sentence emphasizes the similarity or contrast between two or more points.

(3) Periodic sentences In a periodic sentence, an essential part of the main thought, usually the main subject and verb, is delayed until the last part of the sentence after a relatively long introduction. As a result, the ending forms a climax in which the writer's main point finally becomes clear:

> In the Soviet Union, for example, where world-class athletes are the diplomat-soldiers of ideology and where factory girls are forced to exercise to reduce fatigue and to increase production, the entire athletic apparatus is part of the government.
>
> — Robert Lipsyte,
> *Sportsworld*

A periodic sentence gives dramatic emphasis to the main subject and verb, but hasty readers have difficulty understanding it.

(4) Other variations in structure A **reversal** of normal subject-verb-object word order also catches readers' attention, making them notice an important point:

> High in the air soared the fighter pilots.
>
> — Winston Churchill, *Their Finest Hour*

> Nature I loved, and next to Nature, Art.
>
> — Walter Savage Landor,
> "On His Seventy-fifth Birthday"

In the first example, the verb *soared* catches our attention and becomes dramatic because we expect to find the subject in that spot. In the second, *Nature* is the more important of the two direct objects; it catches our attention by appearing before the subject and verb, where we do not expect to find it.

An **interruption** between subject and verb or between verb and direct object makes readers wait for the words that complete the meaning of the sentence and therefore emphasizes them:

> There was a quarter-page advertisement in the London *Observer* for a computer service that will enmesh your name in an electronic network of fifty thousand other names, sort out your tastes, preferences, habits, and deepest desires, match them up with opposite numbers, and retrieve for you, within a matter of seconds, and for a very small fee, friends.
>
> —Lewis Thomas, *The Lives of a Cell*

Here, the string of modifiers after the verb *retrieve* creates suspense by making us wait for the object, *friends,* which is essential to complete the meaning of *retrieve.* As a result, we notice *friends* much more, and it becomes a humorous climax for the sequence of four parallel clauses that begins with "that will enmesh your name."

Varying your sentence structure provides an effective way to make your readers notice important points. Of course, if you use special structures too often in a single piece of writing, they will seem like your normal style, and readers will stop noticing them.

EXERCISES

A. The selections that follow are by three writers with very different styles who are noted for their effective use of sentence structure to emphasize ideas. First, read each selection for the overall meaning. Then answer the following questions about it. The sentences are numbered for your convenience.

1. What is the writer's main point?
2. Give a specific example of each of the following methods that the writer uses to emphasize the main point:
   a. Coordinate structures to emphasize ideas of equal importance
   b. Subordinate structures to indicate contributing ideas
   c. Parallel structures to emphasize parallel ideas
   d. Repetition of words and word groups for emphasis
   e. Introductory modifiers to create anticipation
   f. Contrasting sentence lengths and structures to create variety and emphasize important ideas
   g. Economy—can you rewrite any sentences or parts of sentences in fewer words with no loss of meaning?
3. What examples, if any, do you find of the following, and what words or ideas do they emphasize?
   a. Cumulative sentence
   b. Balanced sentence
   c. Periodic sentence
   d. Reversal of normal subject-verb-object word order
   e. Interruption of normal subject-verb-object word order

Selection 1 These paragraphs begin a chapter called "The Birth of an Island" in *The Sea Around Us* by Rachel Carson.

[1]Millions of years ago, a volcano built a mountain on the floor of the Atlantic. [2]In eruption after eruption, it pushed up a great pile of volcanic rock, until it had accumulated a mass a hundred miles across at its base, reaching upward toward the surface of the sea. [3]Finally its cone emerged as an island with an area of about 200 square miles. [4]Thousands of years passed, and thousands of thousands. [5]Eventually the waves of the Atlantic cut down the cone and reduced it to a shoal—all of it, that is, but a small fragment which remained above water. [6]This fragment we know as Bermuda.

[7]With variations, the life story of Bermuda has been repeated by almost every one of the islands that interrupt the watery expanses of the oceans far from land. [8]For these isolated islands in the sea are fundamentally different from the continents. [9]The major land masses and the ocean basins are today much as they have been throughout the greater part of geologic time. [10]But islands are ephemeral, created today, destroyed tomorrow. [11]With few exceptions, they are the result of the violent, explosive, earth-shaking eruptions of submarine volcanoes, working perhaps for millions of years to achieve their end. [12]It is one of the paradoxes in the ways of earth and sea that a process seemingly so destructive, so catastrophic in nature, can result in an act of creation.

Selection 2 These paragraphs form the conclusion of a chapter in Richard Wright's autobiography, *Black Boy,* published in 1945.

[1]A quarter of a century was to elapse between the time when I saw my father sitting with the strange woman and the time when I was to see him again, standing alone upon the red clay of a Mississippi plantation, a sharecropper, clad in ragged overalls, holding a muddy hoe in his gnarled, veined hands—a quarter of a century during which my mind and consciousness had become so greatly and violently altered that when I tried to talk to him I realized that, though ties of blood made us kin, though I could see a shadow of my face in his face, though there was an echo of my voice in his voice, we were forever strangers, speaking a different language, living on vastly distant planes of reality. [2]That day a quarter of a century later when I visited him on the plantation—he was standing against the sky, smiling toothlessly, his hair whitened, his body bent, his eyes glazed with dim recollection, his fearsome aspect of twenty-five years ago gone forever from him—I was overwhelmed to realize that he could never understand me or the scalding experiences that had swept me beyond his life and into an area of living that he could never know. [3]I stood before him, poised, my mind aching as it embraced the simple nakedness of his life, feeling how completely his soul was imprisoned by the slow flow of the seasons, by wind and rain and sun, how fastened were his memories to a crude and raw past, how chained were his actions and emotions to the direct, animalistic impulses of his withering body. . . .

[4]From the white landowners above him there had not been handed to him a chance to learn the meaning of loyalty, of sentiment, of tradition. [5]Joy was as unknown to him as was despair. [6]As a creature of the earth, he endured, hearty, whole, seemingly indestructible, with no regrets and no hope. [7]He asked easy, drawling questions

about me, his other son, his wife, and he laughed, amused, when I informed him of their destinies. [8]I forgave him and pitied him as my eyes looked past him to the unpainted wooden shack. [9]From far beyond the horizons that bound this bleak plantation there had come to me through my living the knowledge that my father was a black peasant who had gone to the city seeking life, but who had failed in the city; a black peasant whose life had been hopelessly snarled in the city, and who had at last fled the city—that same city which had lifted me in its burning arms and borne me toward alien and undreamed-of shores of knowing.

Selection 3 This paragraph begins an essay called "James Weathercock," the name used professionally by Thomas Wainewright, a painter and essayist in the nineteenth century, who in less than two years poisoned three of his relatives for their money. The essay appears in *Singular Preference: Portraits and Essays,* by Peter Quennell.

[1]We have most of us contemplated committing a crime—and wished that that particular crime could be committed quietly, impersonally, without involving any danger of detection. [2]But the darkest intentions are not bad enough, for to commit a crime one must traverse, or allow oneself very gradually to drift across, a borderline that separates wishful thinking from desperate acting, his "fashionably dressed" audience from the man in the dock, ordinary human beings from legendary monsters. [3]The exact position of this frontier-zone is hard to decide. [4]Where does it begin? [5]Is there any point in his progress towards criminality at which the criminal recognizes that he has crossed the border and that wild imaginings have

assumed an uncomfortably concrete shape? [6]Or is the transition quite imperceptible? [7]Many celebrated felons have been habitual day-dreamers. [8]They are also—most of them—exceedingly conceited persons, either armored with an invincible self-righteousness or intoxicated with their own intelligence and virile bravado. [9]Hauptmann* (if we accept his guilt) was among the former. [10]"I feel I am innocent—I *am* innocent!" he is reported to have exclaimed during the course of the long, miserable, disgusting trial that sent him to the electric chair. [11]Landru† was a member of the latter class, a small-time swindler and petty amorist whose unconquerable egotism jutted like his famous beard. [12]What pigeon-hole can we find for Thomas Wainewright, amiable virtuoso and accomplished poisoner, who graduated as a criminal from the half-world on the fringes of art?

*Bruno Hauptmann was convicted in 1935 of the kidnapping and murder of the infant son of Charles and Anne Morrow Lindbergh.
†Henri Désiré Landru was executed in France in 1922 for the murders of ten women and a boy.

B. In constructing sentences, we can choose among many ways to organize information, eliminate useless repetition, and emphasize important words. For example, the information in these seven sentences with monotonously similar structures can be the basis for a variety of longer sentences, each with a different structure and each emphasizing a different part of the information:

Our house had an attic.
The attic was reached only through a trapdoor.
We climbed a stepladder to the trapdoor.
The attic was the darkest and strangest part of the
     house.
The attic was filled with unidentifiable articles.
The articles were no longer of any use.
The articles were too important to be thrown out.

To emphasize the problem of the articles in the attic, we can select information and reorganize it to form this *cumulative* sentence with parallel modifying phrases:

Our attic was the darkest and strangest part of the house, reached only by climbing a stepladder to the trapdoor and filled with unidentifiable articles too important to be thrown out but no longer of any use.

To emphasize that the attic was dark and strange, we can begin with modifiers and construct this *periodic* sentence, using a series of introductory modifiers to build up suspense:

Reached only by a stepladder to the trapdoor and filled with unidentifiable articles too important to be thrown out but no longer of any use, our attic was the darkest and strangest part of the house.

The final choice depends on what you wish to emphasize, and many other combinations are possible.

1. Using as much of the information as you need from the sentences in group 1, which follows, compose an example of each of the following constructions:

    a. A cumulative sentence containing at least three parallel coordinate structures

    b. A sentence containing at least three parallel subordinate structures

    c. A sentence in which you repeat a key word or short phrase for emphasis

    d. A sentence with an introductory modifier to create anticipation

    e. A balanced sentence

    f. A periodic sentence

    g. A sentence containing a reversal of subject and verb or of verb and direct object to emphasize the words that are reversed

    h. A sentence containing an interruption of a subject and verb or of a verb and a direct object to emphasize the words that are interrupted

    i. A short paragraph in which you vary the length and structure of your sentences to emphasize a relatively short sentence

REMINDER: Try to write with economy. Do not use more words than are necessary to present the information, but, of course, add any coordinating or subordinating conjunctions that you need to show the relationships among the parts of your sentences. Avoid the passive voice.

Group 1

a. The stock market crash of 1929 was the most dramatic economic disaster of modern times.

   b. Life savings were lost by millions of investors.

   c. Many businesses ended in failure.

   d. Many factories were closed.

   e. There were millions of unemployed.

   f. Many of the unemployed were walking the streets.

   g. Many of the unemployed were looking for work.

   h. There were no jobs to be found for most of the unemployed.

   i. Many of the unemployed were begging for food.

   j. Many cities and counties could not meet their payrolls.

   k. Thousands of families lost their homes when they could not pay the interest on their mortgages.

2. Follow the instructions for the previous exercise, using the sentences in group 2.

Group 2

   a. Many forces shaped American life in the nineteenth century.

   b. The most important force was the frontier.

   c. It shaped American life.

   d. It also shaped American character.

   e. The frontier was the border area.

   f. In the border area, population was scarce.

   g. In the border area, the people were chiefly engaged in clearing land and building homes.

   h. In the nineteenth century, the frontier moved across the continent.

   i. The frontier moved from the Atlantic seaboard to the Great Plains.

j. The frontier was a line on the maps.
k. The frontier was also a social process.
l. The frontier encouraged individual initiative.
m. The frontier broke down conservatism.
n. The frontier encouraged a spirit of independence in Americans.

31 ◆ THE ACTIVE VOICE

To make your sentences more direct and forceful, put verbs in the active voice as often as possible. In the active voice, the subject performs the action of the verb; in the passive voice, the subject receives the action of the verb. For discussion of active and passive verb forms, see **6d**. Compare these sentences:

The president vetoed the bill. (active)

The bill was vetoed by the president. (passive)

Although these two sentences convey the same information, they do not have the same emphasis. The active version emphasizes the **president** as the subject of the sentence, while the passive version emphasizes the **bill** with the noun *president* functioning merely as the object of a preposition in an adverbial phrase. Which one are you writing about? The active version would be more appropriate in a paragraph about the president, the passive version in a paragraph about the bill. Notice also that the active voice requires fewer words.

Professional writers consistently prefer the active

voice. For example, the two paragraphs by Erikson in **30** contain a total of 13 sentences with 34 verbs. Only two of those verbs are in the passive voice. The other five sentences given as examples, each by a different writer, contain a total of 18 verbs, 16 of them in the active voice. Notice how much less effective sentence 6 in Erikson's second paragraph would become, despite the dramatic material, if we put most of the verbs in the passive:

> A series of explosions was set off by the wave as a channel was driven by it through the smoldering trough of slag, mushroom-shaped clouds being raised high in the air and great spatters of mud being thrown three hundred feet up to the haul road where a few men were returning home from the mines.

In your own writing, choose the active voice for most of your verbs.

32 ◆ EFFECTIVE WORDS AND FIGURES OF SPEECH

Choose words that are appropriate to your subject, that give your meaning precisely, and that will make your material come alive for your readers. Choose words with *concrete, specific* meanings, and whenever possible, use *nouns* and *verbs* rather than adjectives and adverbs to describe something. Use comparisons to make your abstractions and generalizations concrete, specific, and easy to understand. For example, consider the differences between two versions of a single sentence—the meaning is essentially the same and only a few words are different, but the first is vivid and memorable while the second is colorless and unlikely to make much impression on readers. The author is describing a journey by camel across a part of the Arabian desert in which he thought that the land appeared not only empty but dead. Notice how he makes it seem repulsive without directly stating his opinion:

> Shallow depressions in the limestone floor held sloughs of glutinous black mud, crusted with scabs of salt and sand, like putrescent patches on a carcass rotting in the sun.
>
> — Wilfred Thesiger,
> *Arabian Sands*

> Shallow depressions in the limestone floor held large wet expanses of adhesive black moistened soil, covered with hardened areas of salt and sand, like sections of decay on something disintegrating in the sun.

Concrete, specific words will also help your readers to respond to what you are describing and therefore to share your ideas. However much we differ as individuals in our ideas and opinions, we have in common the experience of our five senses and the physical details of everyday life. Specific words that describe sensory details—colors, shapes, textures, flavors, sounds, smells—and references to specific physical experiences, such as eating ice cream or taking a hot shower, can make abstractions come to life.

32a Figures of speech

Comparisons help to make the unfamiliar more familiar and bring the abstract to life. There are several methods of comparison, and we have special terms to identify them. We can describe a tropical breeze with a direct, *factual statement,* such as "The wind speed was 5 miles an hour, the temperature 85° Fahrenheit, and the humidity 100%," or we can use a *simple comparison,* "The warm breeze was as sticky as syrup on our faces." This mentions two things and gives the element they have in common—both are sticky.

To emphasize the nature of the breeze still more, we can use any of the figures of speech:

simile (from Latin *similis* = similar):

The warm breeze was like syrup on our faces.

A simile says that *x* is like *y.* The breeze and syrup are compared, and the writer takes for granted that readers know that syrup is sticky.

metaphor (from Greek *meta* = over + *pherein* = to bear or carry, hence "a carrying over of meaning from one thing to another"):

The warm breeze was a syrup on our faces.

A metaphor says that *x* **is** *y.* The breeze and syrup are presented as one and the same, and the writer assumes that readers know they are really separate things.

implied metaphor:

The warm breeze oozed stickily over our faces.

An implied metaphor suggests, without stating it, that *x* is *y.* Syrup and other sticky liquids ooze, but no liquid is actually mentioned; the writer expects readers to realize that the breeze is being compared to a sticky liquid.

extended metaphor:

> The warm breeze was a thick, sweet syrup of tropical fruit that oozed over our faces and filled our nostrils with the essence of oranges and mangoes, a rich dessert after we had feasted our senses all day on the beauty of the island.

An extended metaphor develops in detail the idea that *x* is *y*. The sticky sweetness of syrup is developed through related ideas, in this case going from the physical to the psychological.

personification:

> The warm breeze stroked our faces with its sticky fingers.

A personification presents something inanimate as if it were a human being. The breeze is described as if it were a person whose fingers could stroke someone's face.

hyperbole (from Greek *hyperbole,* meaning "excess," which comes from *hyper* = beyond + *ballein* = to throw):

> The warm breeze was a dense syrup.

Hyperbole uses strong exaggeration for emphasis. This example exaggerates greatly because air can never be as dense as syrup.

understatement:

> With no breeze and the humidity and temperature nearing 100, our faces grew slightly warm.

An understatement is the reverse of a hyperbole; it deliberately reduces the extent or importance of something for effect.

litotes (from Greek *litos* = smooth):

> Our faces were not dry in the warm, sticky breeze.

Litotes is a form of understatement that asserts something by denying its opposite.

analogy (from Greek *ana* = according to + *logos* = reasoning, ratio):

> To picture the enormous distances in our universe, imagine the sun as the size of an orange; the earth will then be like a grain of sand 30 feet away from the sun and Jupiter like a cherry pit 200 feet away.

With an analogy, a writer explains the complicated or unfamiliar by comparing it to the simple or familiar. Unlike similes and metaphors, which appeal to our senses, analogies usually point out similarities to clarify our understanding.

Use figures of speech to enrich your words, but, by analogy, use them like salt, to heighten the flavor, not to overwhelm it.

Choose figurative language with appropriate associations. "The business was so successful that it spread like a brushfire" may be accurate—a brushfire does spread quickly—but it is inappropriate because readers will associate fire with danger and destruction, not with good business.

Make sure that your figures of speech are consistent and logical. A **mixed metaphor** is one that combines unrelated comparisons. The result may inspire a laugh the writer does not want, as in "The fire in his eyes froze their blood with terror." Fire does not freeze anything.

Avoid clichés, expressions that have grown tired through overuse, such as "good as gold," "green as grass," or "old as the hills," and adages, such as "Don't cry over spilled milk," unless you can breathe new life into them, as in "His face seemed as old as the hills, worn down to the granite of his strong character."

32b Improving word choice

Words with precise, concrete meanings are better for emphasis than tired hyperboles. Avoid modifiers like *awful* and *terribly* that have lost almost all meaning through overuse. For example, in writing "The show was terribly funny," would you really mean that terror was part of the humor? Write, instead, something like "The show made us laugh till our stomach muscles ached."

Simple, direct statements are better than flowery writing. Instead of "We embarked on our voyage of discovery to seek employment in the jungle of the great metropolis," write "We left to find a job in the city."

The following planning notes and rough draft were composed as an in-class exercise. This was the student's assignment:

> In one detailed paragraph, describe a visit to the campus cafeteria. Assume your readers are students at another college who have not seen the cafeteria. Hand in your planning notes with your paragraph.

NOTE: To make the student's notes and paragraph easier to read, they are presented here as if they had been typed, and errors in spelling and punctuation have been corrected.

The planning notes as they looked when they were first made:

chocolate cake   limp salads

greasy stew   burnt coffee

voices--general loud hum   string beans

noise--forks, knives,   struggle to dig

  plates   out money

ping of cash register   where is an empty

distinct words sometimes   seat?

spaghetti

After thinking over the notes, the student chose
which items to describe, decided on a sequence for presenting them, numbered them and added a note to the
instructor to explain the changes.
The notes then looked like this:

9 chocolate cake   7 limp salads

4 greasy stew   8 burnt coffee

2 voices--general loud hum   5 spaghetti

1 noise--forks, knives,   6 string beans

  plates   + spinach

3 distinct words sometimes

I decided to leave out the cash register,

digging out money, and finding a seat because

I figured the food was what people want to

know about--in a cafeteria that's what really

matters. I decided the chocolate cake would make the best ending. I saw that I forgot the spinach, so I added it with the string beans.

The paragraph written in class looked like this:

N. L. Baker

The Cafeteria

My first impression of the cafeteria as I pushed open the door was noise--clattering plates and silverware, and many voices, some loud, with an occasional laugh or a shout to a distant friend. I picked up a tray and went to the end of the line that was slowly moving toward the hot foods. When I reached the counter, I dropped my tray on the tray rail with a clank and stared at the offerings. A large pool of what the menu called beef stew looked disgusting and seemed to be still boiling. The spaghetti in the next pan was more attractive, with plenty of meat and tomato sauce. Next were rather unattractive piles of string beans and

spinach. They both looked old. In the
salads, the lettuce seemed old, too, and the
tomatoes were not red at all. An unpleasant
smell made it clear that the coffee had
boiled too long. Then I saw the chocolate
cake. The icing looked really good, just the
way I like it. Maybe lunch would not be so
bad after all.

At the next class meeting, the instructor returned the paragraphs and notes and asked the students to strengthen their descriptions by using more precise, concrete words, and by eliminating unnecessary words.

The copy with the student's revisions looked like this:

N. L. Baker

The Cafeteria

~~(My first impression of the cafeteria)~~ As I
pushed open the door, was noise--clattering
                the steady, loud hum of
plates and silverware, and ~~many~~ voices, ~~some~~
 punctuated by   *hoot of laughter*
~~loud, with~~ an occasional ~~laugh~~ or a shout to
        across the room.   *wet hot*
a ~~distant~~ friend, I picked up a tray and
joined
~~went to the end of~~ the line that was slowly

shuffling *steam table* *At*
~~moving~~ toward the ~~hot foods.~~ ~~When I reached~~

clanked *down*
the counter, I ~~dropped~~ my tray on the ~~tray~~

rail ~~with a clank~~ and stared at the

red-brown *wall*
offerings. A large pool of what the menu

was still boiling. Small bubbles broke through the
called beef stew ~~looked disgusting and seemed~~
grease, and gray lumps of meat floated among big, shiny
~~to be still boiling.~~ The spaghetti in the *chunks of potato.*

next pan was more attractive, with plenty of

ground *in the thick*
meat ~~and~~ tomato sauce. Next, ~~were rather~~
limp sagged in a pale green pile,
~~unattractive piles of~~ string beans and
lay collapsed in a dark tangle.
spinach. ~~They both looked old.~~ In the

tired drooped under slices of greenish white
salads, the lettuce ~~seemed old, too, and the~~
A stale bitter
tomatoes ~~were not red at all.~~ An unpleasant

announced that
smell ~~made it clear that the~~ coffee had

slices of
boiled too long. Then I saw ~~the~~ chocolate
—dark brown, almost black, with icing oozing onto the plate.
cake. ~~The icing looked really good, just the~~

~~way I like it.~~ Maybe lunch would not be so

bad after all.

The student's clean copy after revising looked like this:

N. L. Baker

The Cafeteria

As I pushed open the door, my first
impression of the cafeteria was

noise--clattering plates and silverware, and the steady, loud hum of voices punctuated by an occasional hoot of laughter or shout to a friend across the room. I picked up a wet, hot tray and joined the line that was slowly shuffling toward the brightly lit steam table. At the counter, I clanked my tray down on the rail and stared at the offerings. A large, red-brown pool of what the wall menu called beef stew was still boiling. Small bubbles broke through the grease, and gray lumps of meat floated among big, shiny chunks of potato. The spaghetti in the next pan was more attractive, with plenty of ground meat in the thick tomato sauce. Nearby, limp string beans sagged in a pale green pile, and spinach lay collapsed in a dark tangle. In the salads the tired lettuce drooped under slices of greenish white tomatoes. A stale, bitter smell announced coffee that had boiled too long. Then I saw slices of chocolate cake--dark brown, almost black, with icing oozing onto the plate. Maybe lunch would not

be so bad after all.

EXERCISE

1. Which of the five senses does the writer try to appeal to?
2. Explain where and how the writer makes each appeal.
3. Which revisions reduce the number of words needed to present the description?
4. Choose two specific changes in word choice that you think increase the appeal to one or more of the senses, and explain in detail why they seem more vivid than the first version.

33 ◆ LOGICAL EXPRESSION

The surest way to persuade readers that your ideas are worth considering is to support them with logical reasoning. We have two types of logical reasoning, **induction** and **deduction**, and we must avoid the mistakes in reasoning called **fallacies**.

33a Induction

Induction (from Latin *in* = into + *ducere* = to lead) is reasoning from the particular to the general. By examining specific cases, we arrive at a general conclusion about all similar cases. Induction is useful because it may not be possible to check every single case before reaching a conclusion. For example, if you have trouble falling asleep every time you drink coffee at night, you safely conclude that drinking coffee keeps you from sleeping at night. You will not keep trying coffee every night of your life to be sure. You have made a generalization about all cases after examining enough cases to convince you. Similarly, if you notice that your instructor has given an unannounced test every Monday since the semester began, you may reasonably conclude that your instructor will probably give an unannounced test next Monday too.

Induction is useful only when your conclusion is based on an adequate sampling of cases. How many cases you must examine will depend on the conclusion you are trying to reach. You do not need to stand in the rain ten times to conclude that you are likely to get wet; once or twice should be enough. If, however, you wish to conclude that students prefer afternoon classes to morning classes, you will need a much larger sampling of cases. Conclusions that are produced by induction should be qualified by such warning words as *probably, likely, usually, generally,* or *tend to* because there is always a chance, however remote, that later cases will contradict the conclusion.

33b Deduction

Deduction (from Latin *de* = away from + *ducere* = to lead) is reasoning from the general to the particular. A general conclusion that you or others have reached is applied to a specific case. Deduction allows you to interpret new cases by established conclusions. For example, you have concluded that coffee keeps you awake. When a friend suggests having a cup of coffee at a study break late at night, you may reply, "No thanks, I need a good night's sleep, or I'll do badly on the test tomorrow." You have applied your generalization that drinking coffee keeps you from sleeping to a specific case of needing sleep.

Your deduction, in its most basic form, can be expressed as a **syllogism** (from Greek *syn* = with + *logizes-thai* = to reason), or an argument made up of a *major premise,* a *minor premise,* and a *conclusion.*

Major premise: Drinking coffee at night keeps me from sleeping.

Minor premise: Lack of sleep causes me to do badly on tests.

Conclusion: Therefore, drinking coffee at night will cause me to do badly on the test.

In writing, we rarely use syllogisms in their basic form; instead, we omit the obvious steps. A syllogism with one of its parts missing is called an *enthymeme* (from Greek *en* = in + *thumos* = mind) because part of the syllogism is unstated. We use enthymemes frequently in writing and conversation:

The movie had no plot, so we hated it.

Unstated major premise: we hate movies without plots.

Minor premise: This movie has no plot.

Conclusion: Therefore, we hate this movie.

All dictators must be overthrown, so down with Caesar!

Major premise: All dictators must be overthrown.

Unstated minor premise: Caesar is a dictator.

Conclusion: Therefore, Caesar must be overthrown.

I am allergic to aspirin, and this is loaded with it.

Major premise: I am allergic to aspirin.

Minor premise: This contains aspirin.

Unstated conclusion: I am allergic to this.

Syllogisms are an important tool in logic because they allow us to test whether an argument is actually logical in all of its parts or whether it is built on hidden assumptions that are not logical. Your readers will not accept a syllogism unless both the major and minor premises are convincing. For example, a syllogism that starts with the major premise "All humans believe in ghosts" is not likely to yield a believable conclusion.

Even when the premises of a syllogism are true, the conclusion may not be valid if it is not properly deduced from the premises. Consider this syllogism:

Major premise: Children like candy.

Minor premise: You like candy.

Conclusion: You are a child.

The premises seem reasonable, but the conclusion is not valid. What went wrong? The major premise is deceptive; it speaks about what children like, not about all people who like candy. If we change the major premise so that the syllogism is logical, then we have a major premise that few readers would accept:

Major premise: All people who like candy are children.

Minor premise: You like candy.

Conclusion: You are a child.

Now the conclusion is properly deduced from the premises, and we can see that the major premise is not believable.

Although induction and deduction are separate processes, they regularly work together. You are unlikely to gather evidence without having some idea of the conclusion that you wish to prove, nor do you want to start a syllogism with premises for which there is no evidence. Your readers will expect you to provide facts, reasons, examples, and the statements of recognized experts to support your conclusions.

33c Fallacies

Fallacies (from Latin *fallax* = false, deceiving) are errors in reasoning or in the use of evidence. Because evidence is vital to induction and deduction, you should be aware of the basic fallacies that interfere with logical thinking and distort your evidence.

Hasty generalization is the fallacy of basing a conclusion on too little evidence. If your flight to Chicago on Supersky Airlines is delayed, that does not entitle you to claim that Supersky Airlines is always late. You need more than a single case to support such a conclusion.

Overgeneralization is the fallacy of assuming that all members of a group do what most members of the group do. Many Japanese eat raw fish regularly, but you overgeneralize if you claim that all Japanese eat raw fish. Similarly, not all Italians like spaghetti, and not all Republicans voted for Ronald Reagan. Be cautious in using such words as *all, no, always,* and *never.* Instead, qualify broad generalizations with words like *many, most,* and *few,* or *frequently, often, rarely,* and *seldom.*

Non sequitur (Latin = it does not follow) is the fallacy of claiming a conclusion that does not follow logically from the premises; for example, "The chorus wore such ugly costumes that I was surprised they sang so well." What does clothing have to do with how well people sing? You must establish a clear connection between premise and conclusion before readers will accept such a cause-and-effect relationship.

Post hoc, ergo propter hoc (Latin = after this, therefore, because of this) is the fallacy of claiming that one event is the cause of another from the mere fact that the first occurs earlier than the second; for example, "I found a four-leaf clover so I got an A on my Spanish test." This is a *post hoc* fallacy because a causal relationship is claimed where none exists. Most superstitions are the result of this kind of fallacy.

Begging the question is the fallacy of offering a conclusion that simply rewords the premise. If you claim that parallel lines never meet because they are parallel, you are restating the premise instead of providing evidence for it. To avoid begging the question, be sure that you support your ideas with evidence instead of merely restating them.

Argumentum ad hominem (Latin = arguing against the man) is the fallacy of attacking an opponent personally rather than disproving an opponent's ideas. "The candidate comes from a wealthy family, so he can never understand the problems of poor farmers." Such a claim appeals to your readers' prejudices against wealth, but it does not address the candidate's proposals for helping poor farmers. This fallacy is often the basis for attacking critics rather than responding to their criticism. A music critic who had condemned a singer's performance was asked if he could sing any better himself. "No," he wisely replied. "And I cannot lay an egg either, but I know a rotten one when I smell it." To avoid the *ad hominem* fallacy, aim your arguments at the issues and not at personalities or personal circumstances.

False analogy is the fallacy of comparing two things that are not sufficiently alike to be fairly compared. If you claim that the United States is becoming as sexually permissive as ancient Rome and, therefore, will fall just as Rome did, you are offering a false analogy. The comparison concentrates on a single similarity but ignores all differences. A good analogy clarifies an unfamiliar or difficult concept by comparing it with something more familiar or more easily understood.

"Stacking the deck" is the fallacy of presenting only the evidence that supports a premise while ignoring or withholding contrary evidence. If you claim that we should not re-elect Governor Green because he has raised taxes and not built new prisons, you may be stacking the deck. Have you fairly described the governor's accomplishments? Or did he also reform the legal code, balance the budget, and improve schools? To avoid stacking the deck, be sure that you examine serious evidence on both sides of an issue.

Using **loaded words** is the technique of slanting an argument with words that prejudice readers about the evidence. If you claim that a book is "long-winded" and "boring," you encourage disapproval. Could someone else describe it as "richly specific" and "probing"? Would it be more unbiased to describe the book as "six hundred pages of detailed prose"? Choosing more neutral words may allow readers to draw their own conclusion.

Either/or is the fallacy of offering only two choices when more possibilities exist. If you adopt the political slogan "America, love it or leave it," you are guilty of this fallacy. It is possible to love a country *and* leave it or live in a country without loving it. The either/or fallacy most often occurs when we attempt to reduce a complex issue to its bare essentials. To be sure, if there are only two possibilities—for example, either you are pregnant or you are not—there is no fallacy.

The **complex question** is the fallacy of asking a simple question that contains a hidden second question. In the classic example, a prosecutor asks a defendant, "When did you stop beating your wife?" Of course, the unasked question that should come first is "Did you beat your wife?" Similarly, a politician may ask, "How long are we going to allow other countries to control our foreign policy?" If we are alert to the fallacy, we may ask, "What evidence do you have that other countries control our foreign policy?" To avoid this fallacy, point out the complexity of the question, analyzing its parts one by one.

The **bandwagon appeal** is the fallacy of claiming that "everyone" is doing something and that readers should therefore "jump on the bandwagon" and do the same thing. This fallacy is particularly common in advertising, which often includes an appeal to the reader's vanity: "Smart shoppers all choose Sudso. Don't you?" In most cases we are asked to join a group, not to weigh the evidence about a product or candidate.

EXERCISES

A. We often encounter fallacies in casual conversation as well as in careless writing. Which kinds of fallacies can you detect in the following statements? Some have more than one fallacy.

1. There must be more Republicans than Democrats, or Ronald Reagan would not have won the election in 1984.
2. The desk clerk at the hotel didn't even say "Thank you," but, of course, the French are always rude to American tourists.
3. I canceled my appointment at the doctor's yesterday, and I'm sure that is why I came down with a sore throat today.
4. Jane has a new boyfriend every month, so I am certainly not going to vote for her for class president.
5. I have to buy a class ring because everybody is getting one. Do you want me to be the only one without a ring?
6. Choosing among all the candidates is just like buying new shoes. Look them all over, pick the ones that fit your ideas best, pay your money, wrap them up, and take them home.
7. Tom did not like *Ghostbusters* at all; he said it was a silly, empty, juvenile movie.
8. I think English should be the only language in this country. After all, you are either a real American or you are not. It's as simple as that.
9. I would not take a class with Professor Clark if I were you. She gives surprise tests, does not grade on a curve, and assigns a lot of reading every week.

10. I like adventure stories because I like stories with plenty of action and excitement.

B. The following items are enthymemes. Can you supply the missing premises or conclusions to make them into full syllogisms?

1. The Fosters bought a new car last week. They must be rich.
2. Jones is an American citizen. He was born in Idaho.
3. People who tell lies cannot be trusted. I don't trust Bill.
4. We hate soap operas, so we do not watch *Dallas* or *Dynasty.*
5. Every one of the fifty states has two senators, and, of course, Hawaii is a state like all the others.

Part Five
PARAGRAPHS

34 ◆ ORGANIZING THE PARAGRAPH

A **paragraph** contains one or more sentences and presents one main thought. The paragraph as a unit helps readers to see each important subdivision of thought within a larger work. To emphasize the subdivisions visually, we surround each paragraph with blank space, indenting the first line and leaving the last line blank after the last word. The word *paragraph* (from Greek *para* = beside + *graphein* = to write) originally named the symbol (¶) that medieval manuscript writers placed in the margin to mark the main divisions of their thought. Because the vellum on which they wrote was costly, they could not afford to leave blank spaces.

A paragraph may be of any length, from one sentence to hundreds, just as a sentence may have from one word to hundreds or a book from a few pages to thousands. The average paragraph is from three to eight sentences long and occupies roughly one-third to two-thirds of a typed page. Too many short paragraphs will make writing seem choppy, but a series of paragraphs each a page long may discourage readers from even starting. Newspapers use very short paragraphs, often only one sentence, because their narrow columns cause most sentences to occupy several lines and therefore to appear longer than they are. In most forms of writing, paragraphs are longer, and one-sentence paragraphs are rare except as emphasis for a very significant point.

Whatever its length, each paragraph should be **unified** and **coherent.** It should present only **one main topic** or controlling idea. The other information in a paragraph should be there to make the main idea clear and should be organized so that readers will see the logical connections. In most paragraphs, the basic organization is *beginning, main body,* and *ending.*

34a The beginning

The **beginning of a paragraph** in the most common pattern presents the topic or controlling idea of that paragraph in a single sentence, which we call a *topic sentence.* A clear, straightforward statement of the topic is best if your material is complicated or unfamiliar to your readers. With familiar material, however, you can interest your readers and rouse their curiosity with a direct question that the paragraph answers, a challenging remark, or a provocative detail that the paragraph then relates to the topic. Whatever form you choose, keep the opening brief. Remember that its chief function is to lead readers to the real substance in the main body of the paragraph.

34b The main body

The **main body** of a paragraph provides support for the topic statement by developing the idea with specific, detailed information and logical reasoning. To develop the main body, take advantage of the different methods discussed in **35**—description, narration, exemplification, process, comparison and contrast, classification, analysis, cause-and-effect relationships, and definition. Use them singly or in combination, as they seem suited to your purpose and likely to interest your readers.

Organize the main body in a pattern that will make your material clear and interesting for your readers. Ask yourself what is most likely to catch their attention and what they will need to know first to understand your main point, what they will need next, and so on. The six patterns most likely to be useful are *chronological, spatial, general to particular, particular to general, climactic,* and *supporting.*

(1) Chronological Present events or opinions in the order in which they occurred, were observed, or developed, starting with the earliest and ending with the most recent; *or,* as in many investigations, starting with the most recent material and moving back in time to the earliest; *or* starting with a striking event or opinion and moving backward and forward in time to establish both its roots and development. This example gives a short biography in simple chronological order:

Example 1

The facts of Aristotle's life are easy to summarize, and his importance to Western culture has been great. Aristotle was born in 384 B.C. in Macedonia. Starting at the age of seventeen, he studied under Plato, who was his mentor for twenty years at the Academy at Athens. After the death of Plato, Aristotle left Athens, going first to teach at Assos, next on the island of Lesbos, and later still in Macedonia at the royal court, where he was tutor to a young prince, soon to be known as Alexander the Great. In 335 B.C., when Alexander became king and began his conquest of the ancient world, Aristotle went back to Athens, where he founded a school of his own.

It was called the Peripatetic school because Aristotle taught his pupils while strolling in the school gardens along the shady paths, called *peripatoi* in ancient Greek. Later, when political opponents accused him of breaking the laws, he went into exile in Chalkis, where he died in 322 B.C. Aristotle was one of the most influential philosophers of ancient times, and his theories form the basis for much modern thought, especially in philosophy, logic, and literary criticism.

(2) Spatial Arrange your material according to the physical relationships in space of the people or objects concerned, so that readers can imagine them easily. Start with the nearest and move by degrees to the farthest, *or* from the farthest to the nearest, *or* from right to left, east to west, or in some other physical sequence. This example uses a near-to-far arrangement, beginning with a clear physical position in relation to the scene:

Example 2

If we could stand on top of the Great Pyramid at Giza in Egypt, we would have a surprising perspective. To the south, but almost at our feet, would be the Sphinx and the other two famous pyramids. These monuments are familiar to most of us from movies and travel posters. If we looked further south, however, past Giza, we could easily see the low mounds of two unfinished pyramids about three miles away at Zawyet el-Aryan. Still further to the south, almost as far as the eye can see, we could distinguish four more pyramids at Abusir. Beyond the range of vision, another five or six miles to the south of Abusir, a dozen or more pyramids cluster at Saqqâra, and the tourist who travels to them can, by gazing south, discern four more pyramids still farther south at Dahshur, eight miles away. The grouping at Dahshur is the continuation of a long line of pyramids, dotting the west bank of the Nile, from Abu Rawash, just north of the Great Pyramid at Giza, all the way to el-Kula, some four hundred miles to the south. There are more than ninety pyramids in the chain, and archaeologists are certain that others still lie buried under the desert sands.

(3) General to particular Present the general information first to give your readers an overall view, and follow it with particular details to support, explain, or exemplify it. This pattern is especially useful for material that your readers are likely to find difficult or unfamiliar:

Example 3

No one knows when humans first made wine out of grapes, but most wine lovers agree that the greatest wines in the world are made in several different regions of France. The most famous areas of wine production are Bordeaux, Burgundy, and Champagne, but less than one third of France's wines come from these areas. Burgundy is the smallest of the three famous areas, and its greatest wines all come from a narrow strip of hills in eastern France that is only a mile or two wide and about twenty-five miles long. Probably the single most prized wine of Burgundy is made from grapes grown on a small part of one slope at a little 4½-acre vineyard called La Romanée-Conti. A bottle of this precious liquid costs more than $300, or roughly $50 a glass. To wine lovers, however, the price is not important; for them, a glass of Romanée-Conti may be the wine-drinking experience of a lifetime.

(4) Particular to general Present the particular details first, then give generalizations to interpret the importance of the details and show relationships among them:

Example 4

Robert Price, head of Price Company in San Diego, is offering a special bargain. For just a $25 fee, shoppers can become one-year members of Price's enormous chain of cash-and-carry wholesale outlets. Members pay nearly wholesale prices for everything from televisions to T-shirts. Price himself secures interest-free capital, in effect, from the membership fees, and he also generates the steady repeat business that he requires to make his paper-thin markups profitable. His warehouse shopping-club approach is the most recent innovation in the deep-discounting movement that has been invading retail selling in the past decade, but fresh concepts like Price's are as unusual as they are profitable. Price Company's five-year profitability outdoes that of any of the thousand largest public companies in America. Clearly, many Americans are changing their buying habits radically; they are now willing to shop in windowless, unadorned warehouses with bare concrete floors in order to get a better price.

(5) Climactic Build up to the most important point, which you save until the end of the paragraph:

Example 5

They were brothers, one thirty-six years old, the other thirty-two. They had been building and repairing bicycles for eight or nine years. Now they designed and constructed their own wind tunnel to learn the facts about air and air currents, about "lift" and "drag." They shaped their own wings; they built their own engine. With twelve horsepower and four cylinders, they made their first four attempts on December 17, 1903, at Kitty Hawk, North Carolina. Their best effort lasted only fifty-nine seconds, their highest speed was a mere thirty miles an hour, and their greatest distance less than three hundred yards. On that day, Wilbur and Orville Wright made their first successful flight in a heavier-than-air machine, and modern aviation was born.

(6) Supporting Present the most important point first, and give the rest of your material as an explanation or answer. This method is used most often in expository writing because it guides readers through material that they might otherwise find difficult:

Example 6

In many ways, 1813 marked the beginning of the end of Spain's control of South America. It was then that Simón Bolívar began his career as liberator by arguing persuasively that the primary task was to break Spain's grip on Venezuela. In what is modern Colombia, Bolívar convinced the revolutionary government to give him 800 fighting men to oppose the 15,000 royalist troops of Spain, and he started his military campaign.

By August 6, when Bolívar entered Caracas in triumph, he had fought six major battles and crossed 700 miles of mountain and jungle in only ninety days. Although Spain recaptured the city within a year and Bolívar suffered years of defeat and exile, he returned in 1821 to liberate the city again. The second battle for the city lasted only an hour, but it was decisive: Venezuela was free. In the next four years, Bolívar drove the armies of Spain out of Colombia, Ecuador, Peru, and Bolivia, and the long struggle that had begun with the capture of Caracas was complete.

EXERCISE   Compose six versions of the same descriptive paragraph using a different method of organization for each version. To gather material, stand for about five minutes in one spot on the campus or in a neighborhood you know well. Choose a busy time of the day or night and observe what happens. With each paragraph after the first, add a short statement in which you explain why you added to the material that you used for the first version or why you omitted any part of it.

> *First version:* Compose a paragraph describing the appearances, actions, and events in chronological order as you observed them, starting with the earliest. Begin your paragraph with a general statement identifying the time and place, and end with another general statement summing up your impressions.
>
> *Second version:* Drawing on the observations you used in version one, compose a paragraph in which you arrange the material in *one* of these

spatial sequences: what you observed from one spot by looking from one side to the other, *or* what you observed as you looked from what was nearest to what was farthest away or from what was farthest to what was nearest.

Third version: Drawing on the observations you used in versions one and two, compose a paragraph in which you begin with a general description of the scene and then narrow your attention to smaller and smaller elements, ending with a particular detail that is representative of the whole scene.

Fourth version: Drawing on the observations you used in versions one, two, and three, compose a paragraph in which you begin with a particular detail and gradually fill in the background against which you observed it, ending with a general statement summing up your overall impression and reminding readers how the detail with which you began fits into the whole picture.

Fifth version: Drawing on the observations you used in versions one through four, compose a paragraph in which you begin with the material you find least interesting or important, and then work up to the material you find most interesting or important, presenting it as a climax for the paragraph.

Sixth version: Drawing on the observations you used for versions one through five, compose a paragraph in which you begin with a statement indicating what you found most interesting or important, and then present the rest of your material, organizing it to support and explain your opening statement.

34c The ending

The **ending** of a paragraph suggests or directly states the main point that the writer wants readers to accept and remember. The more compact you can make the ending, preferably a single sentence, the more easily your readers will remember it. It may be a *forceful restatement* of your topic or controlling idea presented in the light of what you have said in the main body, as in example 5 in **34b.** It may be the *answer* to the question or problem raised in the beginning, as in example 6 in **34b.** It may even pose a *new question* based on the main body to make readers rethink what they have just read. It may be an especially *convincing example* to illustrate the main point of the paragraph and clinch the argument, as in example 3 in **34b.**

Your ending may also act as a *transition* from one paragraph to the next. For example, the ending of example 1 in **34b** could lead to a more detailed discussion of Aristotle's life or his influence. The ending of example 2 could lead to a more detailed examination of one of the pyramids, to a discussion of their historical or architectural significance, or to advice on planning a visit to them. The ending in example 3 could lead to a detailed discussion of Romanée-Conti wines. The ending in example 4 could lead to a discussion of changing American buying habits or a more detailed analysis of the success of Price Company and of Robert Price. The ending in example 5 could lead to a more detailed description or analysis of the work of the Wright brothers or of the latest developments in aviation. The ending of example 6 could lead to a detailed discussion of Bolívar's career or of Spanish domination in South America.

34d Variations

If you are sure that your subject matter will seem familiar and uncomplicated to your readers, you may vary the pattern described earlier. For example, you may save your topic sentence until the end of the paragraph so that it will come as a climax, like the solution of a mystery story, as in examples 3 and 5 in **34b.** This method can be effective with a narrative or a study of cause and effect when you wish to surprise your readers with an unexpected outcome. You may omit any direct statement of the topic or controlling idea and only *imply* it, trusting your readers to react in the way you wish. This method can be especially effective in a description, a narrative, or a comparison, when the details by themselves will create the impression you intend.

34e Connections

Make the connections clear among the thoughts and pieces of information in each paragraph. Transitional expressions, such as *also, similarly, moreover, for example,* and *in another example,* tell readers that you are adding material to expand or reinforce what you have already written. Such expressions as *nevertheless, however, in contrast,* or simply *but* indicate that what follows contradicts or contrasts with what has preceded it. To point out a cause-and-effect relationship, use *as a result, for this reason,* or *therefore.* Some transitional expressions always act in pairs or series, for example, *first, second, third; in the first place, in the second place; on one hand, on the other hand.*

NOTE: Remember that we have only two hands. Do not go on to introduce a third item with "on the other hand." If you introduce something with "first," readers will expect a "second" and may be confused if you omit it or, worse, forget to include a second item.

You may also connect your thoughts by using *this, these, that,* and *those* as demonstrative adjectives or pronouns to remind readers of what you have mentioned earlier. Similarly, the *repetition* of a key word or phrase can help to remind your readers of an important point. Beware, however, of repetitions that are not important. Another very effective and rather subtle way to indicate connections is to use *parallel sentence structures* (see **30c**).

35 ◆ DEVELOPING THE PARAGRAPH

Each paragraph presents a topic or idea, and it **develops** that topic by providing specific details, examples, or logical reasoning to expand and clarify the idea. Nine basic methods help in developing paragraphs—description, narration, exemplification, process, comparison and contrast, classification, analysis, cause and effect, and definition—and these methods are often combined even in a single paragraph.

35a Description

You will use description in almost everything you write. Readers need to see in their imaginations—and sometimes to hear, smell, touch, even taste—what you are writing about. You may organize descriptive details in several ways: chronologically, in the order in which you observed them; spatially, according to where they are in relation to each other and the observer; by relative importance, giving a quick view of less important details and working up to the most important; or the reverse, starting with close attention to important details and giving less attention to others that fill in the picture.

Two examples of description follow, one of a relatively static scene and the other of violent action. In the first example, James Herriot arranges details in a *spatial pattern,* moving from near to far. He begins with a general overview of the room; then mentions its most noticeable feature, the fireplace; looks farther away to a window at the end of the room; and then, still farther, through the window; and on to the farthest sight of all, the distant hills.

It had been built in the grand manner, high-ceilinged and airy with a massive fireplace flanked by arched alcoves. One end was taken up by a French window which gave on a long, high-walled garden. I could see unkempt lawns, a rockery, and many fruit trees. A great bank of peonies blazed in the hot sunshine, and at the far end, rooks cawed in the branches of a group of tall elms. Above and beyond were the green hills with their climbing walls.

—James Herriot, *All
Creatures Great and Small*

In the first sentence, "It" refers to "a sunlit room," mentioned at the end of the preceding paragraph, and therefore helps to connect the two paragraphs. Notice Herriot's use of specific detail to make readers see the scene. There is no topic sentence; the simplicity of the description makes one unnecessary.

The "I" in the following paragraph is a black high school student in a small southern town at a time when racial discrimination was strong. For the amusement of the town's leading white male citizens, the students were blindfolded and forced to take part in a free-for-all boxing match. The narrator, able to see a little despite his blindfold, describes the scene and his own reactions. In the opening sentence, *everyone* refers to the narrator's classmates, mentioned at the end of the preceding paragraph, and therefore helps to connect the two paragraphs.

Everyone fought hysterically. It was complete anarchy. Everybody fought everybody else. No group fought together for long. Two, three, four, fought one, then turned to fight each other, were themselves attacked. Blows landed below the belt and in the kidney, with the gloves open as well as closed, and with my eye partly opened now there was not so much terror. I moved carefully, avoiding blows, although not too many to attract attention, fighting from group to group. The boys groped about like blind, cautious crabs crouching to protect their mid-sections, their heads pulled in short against their shoulders, their arms stretched nervously before them, with their fists testing the smoke-filled air like the knobbed feelers of hypersensitive snails. In one corner I glimpsed a boy violently punching the air and heard him scream in pain as he smashed his hand against a ring post. For a second I saw him bent over holding his hand, then going down as a blow caught his unprotected head. I played one group against the other, slipping in and throwing a punch, then stepping out of range while pushing the others into the melee to take the blows blindly aimed at me. The smoke was agonizing and there were no rounds, no bells at three-minute intervals to relieve our exhaustion. The room spun round me, a swirl of lights, smoke, sweating bodies surrounded by tense white faces. I bled from both nose and mouth, the blood spattering upon my chest.

— Ralph Ellison, *The Invisible Man*

The two short sentences at the beginning present the topic and set the scene in general terms. Longer sentences *develop the topic* by illustrating the opening generalizations with *specific supporting details* arranged both *spatially* and *chronologically*. Throughout, Ellison implies the psychological effect on the student and ends the paragraph with two sentences stating specific physical effects. Notice the vivid comparison of the boys to "blind, cautious crabs" and of their hands in boxing gloves to "the knobbed feelers of hypersensitive snails."

35b Narration

A narrative is the retelling of one or more related events and usually presents them in chronological order. Everyone enjoys a story, and a short narrative can give a memorable illustration of a point you wish to explain to your readers or an opinion you wish them to accept.

In the following paragraphs, Edith Hamilton uses short narratives to support her interpretation of the personality of Alexander the Great. In the first sentence, "he" refers to Alexander and "In those early days" to the time established in the preceding paragraph, helping to connect these paragraphs with the one before them.

In those early days, he showed himself again and again to be the perfect knight-errant. During a journey through a burning desert when the water supply failed and the army was almost dying of thirst, a man offered him a skin full of water. Alexander took it; then looking at the thirsty soldiers around him, he gave it back saying, "There is not enough for all." Of course his men adored him.

No one, not Arthur or Galahad, could have improved upon his behavior to the wife of Darius, whom he captured. He restored all her treasures of gold and jewels and sent her word that he would not come into her presence unless she summoned him. A king whom he took captive when he was advancing into India showed a haughty defiance in his presence, and Alexander, interested, asked him, "How shall I treat you?" "As a king," answered the other, with the result that Alexander restored to him the kingdom he had just taken from him. Once when he was ill and his physician was mixing a draught for him, a letter was brought to him from his most trusted general telling him that the physician had been bribed by the Persian king to poison him. Alexander raised the draught to his lips with one hand and with the other gave the letter to the physician. By the time the letter had been read the medicine had been drunk. No harm was done; the physician was trustworthy, but Alexander appears here in his true colors. He was the adventurer complete. He loved to stake his all upon a chance. He was a gay gambler with life, almost to the end.

—Edith Hamilton, *The Echo of Greece*

Hamilton begins the first paragraph with a *topic sentence,* narrates an incident to illustrate that topic, and ends with a very short sentence summing up the effect of Alexander's personality on others. She *connects* the second paragraph to the first by beginning it with a stronger version of the same topic sentence—according to legend, Galahad was an ideal knight in the court of King Arthur, who was himself a model of chivalry. She then narrates three more episodes to illustrate Alexander's personality, developing the third at more length because it provides a dramatic climax, and ends the paragraph with three short sentences that *sum up her interpretation.*

35c Exemplification

Examples help writers to make their ideas and opinions clear and convincing to their readers. How many examples to use and how much detail to include with each will depend on the importance of the point that you wish to illustrate and on how difficult or unfamiliar it is likely to seem to your readers. Notice how many examples the writer uses in the following paragraph:

> What has made humanity the most dreadfully successful species of animals on earth? Simply that human beings learned how to carry their environment with them. When the climate was no longer warm, clothing kept out the cold. In the absence of natural caves for shelter, artificial ones were contrived of walls and roofs, or of stretched skins. When game was hard to find, animals were bred domestically. When legs did not serve to pass over a sea, floating craft supported them. To keep *his* environment hospitable to him, man has made the environment his own, modifying it to the point that a city-bred child rarely sees anything that has not been arranged at least partly by human hands.
>
> —Dwight Bolinger,
> *Language: The Loaded*
> *Weapon*

Bolinger begins with a challenging question to catch the reader's attention. He answers it briefly, then devotes the main body to *four short, familiar examples* that illustrate his answer. The *parallel structure* of the three sentences that begin with *When* helps to emphasize that they present parallel information. Bolinger ends the paragraph with a *simple, specific example* to emphasize his main point—how much human beings have modified the environment.

35d Process

To make your subject matter clear to readers and to convince them that you have not jumped to hasty conclusions, you may sometimes need to explain a process—how to do something or how something occurs. In the following paragraph, the author describes the process of a scientific experiment. His main point is that laboratory experiments on animals have shown that genetic factors may contribute to alcoholism.

Another kind of abnormal behavior in humans which can be conveniently studied in animals is addiction. It has long been known that some animals, again especially monkeys and rats, can become addicted to certain drugs such as morphine and alcohol. The advantage of working with laboratory animals in this type of problem does not need stressing. New techniques and new cures can be tried out with greater rapidity and certainty than with a group of human patients suffering from addiction. Here again there seem to be the predisposing genetic factors involved to some extent, and these can be studied only in the laboratory. Thus, while most rats and mice prefer plain water to water containing a proportion of alcohol, there are some which prefer the cocktail consistently. This is shown by arranging in each cage two sources of water supply instead of the usual single one, so that each animal can choose to drink from the bottle on the left or the one on the right. These bottles are carefully graduated so that each day it is easy to read how much has been drunk from each. In this way it is possible to determine the preference for whatever is in the bottles, merely by seeing which one has most consumed from it. It is necessary to switch the bottles around from time to time for it has been found that even if both contain exactly the same liquid, pure water, for example, rats and mice will develop a preference for a certain position, one side or the other. There is then the danger, without precaution of changing the bottles around, that what may seem to be a genuine preference for one or other substance may merely be a preference for one side over the other. Now, when such a preference has been established, it is of great interest to discover what is determining it. One cause so far discovered is the hereditary one—some strains of mice will prefer alcohol whereas others dislike it, and this innately determined preference may be related to the addiction to the drug. Much work remains to be done in this connection, . . . but the advances made are encouraging and speak well for progress in surmounting some of the difficult problems in the understanding and care of mental illness.

—P. L. Broadhurst, *The Science of Animal Behavior*

The author begins with a *broad generalization* on his topic, then quickly narrows it to the *specific topic* of alcoholism in rats and mice. To convince his readers that some animals chose the alcoholic drink because they liked it, not because of some other factor, he gives the main steps of the process followed in the experiment and the reasons for each step. He ends by *restating his thesis* in the next-to-last sentence and, in the last sentence, *looking toward future developments.*

35e Comparison and contrast

Comparison and contrast are useful, often essential, in evaluating and explaining everything from abstract ideas to people and objects. Generally, we use both processes together because they complement each other. A comparison points out similarities; a contrast points out differences. There are two basic patterns for organizing a comparison. With the *block pattern,* the writer gives all the significant characteristics of one thing in a block, then all the matching characteristics of another in a matching block, and makes a comparison and contrast at the end of the paragraph. With the *alternating pattern,* the writer moves back and forth between two things, comparing and contrasting them on each characteristic discussed. Many writers combine the two patterns because, with the block pattern, readers may forget one part of the comparison while reading about the other; with the alternating pattern, they may feel like observers at a tennis match, constantly glancing back and forth between the subjects of the comparison. How would you describe the pattern that the author uses in the following paragraph? Her topic is the plight of the many black women in South Africa who are required by the government to live in segregated areas far from the work centers where their husbands are.

At the close of day they light their fires to prepare the evening meal. The fortunate ones milk and shut in the stock, but for most there is no stock to shut in, and their children do not know the milk from the family cow. For some there is a letter of good news from the father and husband far away in the work center— the long awaited letter with money has come—part of the debt at the trader's will be paid off. There will be bread, sugar, tea and a few extras to eat for at least a few weeks. For others it is bad news. The loved one far away is ill, has met with an accident, has been thrown in jail because he failed to produce his papers when demanded by some government official. Not that he did not have them, but just that by mistake he forgot them in the pocket of his other jacket. A black man in South Africa cannot forget! It is a sad day for this one. Her children look up anxiously in her face. They fear to ask her any questions, and she does not know how much to tell them. "Tata sends his greetings," she manages to say at last, "but says we will have to be patient about the money we asked for; he has had some trouble and has used up all the money." The rest of the evening is spent in silence. And when they kneel down to pray, this lonely woman sends to heaven a prayer with an "Amen." Small wonder most such women are old at the age of thirty, emaciated, tired and worn out.

> — Phyllis Ntantala, "The Widows of the Reserves"— from *An African Treasury*, edited by Langston Hughes

In the first sentence, *they* refers to all the women. The author then uses details to contrast the lives of the more prosperous wives with those of the majority. Next, after more details in two sentences on the fortunate few, she uses a very short sentence, "For others it is bad news," to signal her shift to the sufferings of the majority of the women. To emphasize these sufferings, she devotes the rest of the paragraph to the example of one typical woman.

35f Classification

Classification uses comparison and contrast to help to identify one or more things by showing how they resemble or differ from other related things. For example, librarians arrange books by classifying them according to subject matter and author, and supermarkets group foods according to ingredients, purpose, and method of packaging. As the following paragraph shows, classification is particularly important in the sciences and social sciences. The author, an anthropologist, distinguishes among three major groups involved in the religious ceremonies of the Zuñi Indians of the American Southwest.

This ceremonial life that preoccupies Zuñi attention is organized like a series of interlocking wheels. The priesthoods have their sacred objects, their retreats, their dances, their prayers; and their year-long program is annually initiated by the great winter solstice ceremony that makes use of all the different groups and sacred things and focuses all their functions. The tribal masked-god society has similar possessions and calendric observances, and these culminate in the great winter tribal masked god ceremony, the Shalako. In like fashion the medicine societies, with their special relation to curing, function throughout the year and have their annual culminating ceremony for tribal health. These three major cults of Zuñi ceremonial life are not mutually exclusive. A man may be, and often is, for the greater part of his life, a member of all three. They each give him sacred possessions "to live by" and demand of him exacting ceremonial knowledge.

—Ruth Benedict, *Patterns of Culture*

In subsequent paragraphs Benedict describes the functions and duties of each group in detail. In this paragraph, after an *introductory generalization,* she gives a one-sentence description of each subdivision and includes the chief ways in which these resemble and differ from each other. She *concludes the paragraph by explaining in general terms* what roles an individual Indian may have in the three ceremonial groups.

35g Analysis

Another method by which you can help your readers to understand complicated or unfamiliar subject matter is analysis—the breaking down of the material into its component parts so that the underlying causes can be examined. In the following paragraph, the author, a scientist, answers a question he has raised earlier about the need for more supersonic travel: "The question, I think, is not: Can we go faster? but Do we have to?"

Most of the demand for high-speed long-distance travel comes from businessmen and government officials who need to have conferences with their opposite numbers in other states or countries. But what is really involved here is not the transportation of material but the transportation of information. I think much of the necessity for high-speed transport could be avoided if the existing communications technology were better used. I have many times participated in government or private meetings in which there were, say, twenty participants, each of whom was paid $500 for transportation and living expenses merely to attend the meeting—the cost of which was therefore $10,000 just to get the participants together. But all the participants ever exchange is information. Video phones, leased telephone lines, and facsimile reproducers to transmit paper copies of notes and diagrams would, I believe, serve as well or even better. There is no significant function of such a meeting—including private discussions among the participants "in the corridor"—that cannot be performed less expensively and at least equally conveniently with communications rather than transportation technology.

—Carl Sagan, *Broca's Brain*

Sagan begins his analysis with a *generalized statement* of a fact and then points out the *underlying cause.* This leads him to his *main point,* given in the third sentence: modern communication methods can replace high-speed travel at much lower cost. He *supports his claim* with *specific details* of a *typical example* from his own experience and with a specific suggestion for achieving the same results without high-speed aircraft. He ends by *restating his claim* in the light of what he has just said.

35h Cause and effect

An analysis of the causes of a condition or problem and of the effects it produces can help your readers to accept your opinions as valid. The following paragraph comes from a book in which the author, a social psychologist, examines the hidden causes and the widespread effects of the universal need for self-esteem.

In childhood we see the struggle for self-esteem at its least disguised. The child is unashamed about what he needs and wants most. His whole organism shouts the claims of his natural narcissism. And this claim can make childhood hellish for the adults concerned, especially when there are several children competing at once for the prerogatives of limitless self-extension, what we might call "cosmic significance." The term is not meant to be taken lightly, because this is where our discussion is leading. We like to speak casually about "sibling rivalry," as though it were some kind of by-product of growing up, a bit of competitiveness and selfishness of children who have been spoiled, who haven't yet grown into a generous social nature. But it is too all-absorbing and relentless to be an aberration, it expresses the heart of the creature: the desire to stand out, to be *the* one in creation. When you combine natural narcissism with the basic need for self-esteem, you create a creature who has to feel himself an object of primary value: first in the universe, representing in himself all of life. This is the reason for the daily and usually excruciating struggle with siblings: the child cannot allow himself to be second-best or devalued, much less left out. "You gave him the biggest piece of candy!" "You gave him more juice!" "Here's a little more, then." "Now *she's* got more juice than me!" "You let her light the fire in the fireplace and not me." "Okay, you light a piece of paper." "But this piece of paper is *smaller* than the one she lit." And so on and on. An animal who gets his feeling of worth symbolically must minutely compare himself to those around him to make sure he doesn't come off second-best. Sibling rivalry is a critical problem that reflects the basic human condition: it is not that children are vicious, selfish, or domineering. It is that they so openly express man's tragic destiny: he must desperately justify himself as an object of primary value in the universe; he must stand out, be a hero, make the biggest possible contribution to world life, show that he *counts* more than anything or anyone else.

—Ernest Becker, *The Denial of Death*

Becker *begins with a general statement of the topic* and then *restates* it more specifically in the next two sentences. In the main body of the paragraph, he *shows the effects* of a child's need for esteem, *analyzes the causes,* and gives *general descriptions* and *specific examples* of the effects. In the last two sentences, he *reinterprets his opening claim,* stating it more fully and more precisely in light of what he has said in the main body.

35i Definition

A **definition** (from Latin *de* = from + *finire* = to limit) establishes the limits of something. The methods of development described so far, especially description, exemplification, and analysis, help you *define your subject matter* so that your readers will understand it fully and accept your interpretation. These methods will also help you clarify whatever special terms you use. *Define any key words* that may be unfamiliar to your readers, such as scientific terms or words that you are using in a special way. The following definition comes from a handbook on North American shells that includes scientific information but presents it in a form the general reader can understand.

The family Veneridae is the largest pelecypod family, and it has the greatest distribution, both in depth and in range. Named for the goddess Venus, the shells of this group are noted for their graceful lines and beauty of color and sculpture. The shells are equivalve, commonly oblong-oval in outline, and porcellaneous in texture. The mollusks are burrowers just beneath the surface of sand or mud, and are never fixed in one place. They are native to all seas, and since ancient times many of them have been used by man for both food and adornment.

— Percy Morris, *A Field Guide to the Shells*

The author follows a *conventional sequence for presenting scientific identifications.* He begins by placing the smaller group (the family) in the larger group (the class) of which it is a part and then gives the distinguishing characteristics of the smaller group: first the physical construction; then color, behavior, habitat; and finally the uses.

The second definition comes from a book on changing fashions in American clothing and is less formal. In her previous paragraph the author defined *camp* as a term that in the sixties came to mean "a kind of exaggerated style that was anti-fashionable, anti-tasteful, and anti-aesthetic." In this paragraph, she defines two related terms, *funky* and *kitsch.*

Funky was a kind of updated version of camp, except that it applied specifically to outmoded styles. Anything that was definitely *out* of fashion could not be considered *in* fashion. In this same category, the term **kitsch** has been used by the avant-garde to designate anything considered to be in bad taste. Kitsch was defined as anything copied from a work of art but done in another medium, form, or setting. The Parthenon copied in plastic and a replica of the Venus de Milo made into a cigarette lighter are examples of kitsch. The Mona Lisa's face printed on a sweatshirt is a pure example, but the term *kitsch* would probably also cover a $6000 mink coat design made in authentic Orlon, or vinyl alligator shoes.

—Marilyn Horn,
The Second Skin

Horn first **distinguishes** *funky* from *camp,* then **relates** *kitsch* to *funky,* and finally **illustrates** *kitsch* with four specific examples. Notice her use of repetition for emphasis in the second sentence.

EXERCISES

A. Compose a paragraph of roughly 150 to 200 words in which you use concrete details to describe one of the following:

   your favorite dinner

   getting up early on a cold morning

   the physical appearance of a movie or TV star you admire

B. Compose a paragraph of roughly 150 to 200 words in which you narrate in detail one of the following experiences:

   the actions and conversation in a classroom from the moment you enter until the moment the class begins

the most exciting moments in a sports event that you
watched recently

the actions and conversation during a meal in a coffee shop or fast-food restaurant

C. Compose a paragraph of roughly 150 to 200 words in
which you use at least three specific examples to support your opinion on a sports event, a movie, a TV
show, or a political speech that you watched or heard
recently.

D. Compose a paragraph of roughly 150 to 200 words in
which you give detailed directions on one of the following to a visitor from another country who is unfamiliar with the style of equipment here:

how to use a coin-operated telephone

how to find a book in the college library without
asking anyone for help

how to make a photocopy in a coin-operated machine

E. Compose a paragraph of roughly 150 to 200 words in
which you compare and contrast one of the following:

two teachers you had in high school

two makes of cars or other machinery that you know
well

two political leaders

F. Compose a paragraph of roughly 150 to 200 words in
which you describe a different way of classifying the
items for sale in the college store or in a local variety

store or food store. First, describe the principles of classification used in the store, and then present a contrasting way. For example, foods can be classified by the types and sizes of the containers, by color, or by origin instead of by purpose.

G. In a paragraph of roughly 150 to 200 words, analyze your reasons for deciding to go to college. Go deeper than such obvious reasons as "to get an education," "to prepare for a career," or "to make new friends," and find the reasons behind the reasons.

H. Trace the links of cause and effect in some action, large or small, that you took recently. For example, if you visited friends at their home, what were your reasons for going, and what were the effects of your visit on you and them? Go beyond such vague reasons as "I went because I like them" or such vague results as "We had a good time."

Part Six
ESSAYS

36 ◆ ESSAYS: AN OVERVIEW

The word *essay* comes from the French verb *essayer,* meaning "to try" or "to try out," which in turn comes from the Latin *exagium,* meaning "a weighing." As a verb in English, *essay* means "to attempt" or "to try out," and as a noun it means "a testing," "an attempt," "a trying out" of something. In writing an essay, you *try out* your ideas on your readers—you attempt to persuade them that your material is interesting and that your opinions are valid or at least deserve serious consideration.

Essays are commonly classified as descriptive, narrative, expository, or argumentative, depending on the chief methods the writers use for making their points clear to their readers. A descriptive essay, like a descriptive paragraph (see **35a**), gives details about one or more persons, places, objects, or events so that readers can imagine them vividly. A narrative essay, like a narrative paragraph (see **35b**), tells the story of an event or sequence of events, real or imagined, to illustrate a point or provide a record of what happened. An expository essay (from Latin *ex* = out + *ponere* = to put or place) places an idea, a procedure, or an object fully before the readers by describing, analyzing, and explaining its nature and significance. An argumentative essay uses logical reasoning, an emotional appeal, or both to persuade readers to agree with a particular opinion.

Most college and business writing is expository, argumentative, or a combination of the two. For example, a paper for a natural science course giving the latest information on acid rain will be expository, but if the writer uses the information to persuade readers that government should more strictly regulate factory emissions, the paper will be argumentative. Similarly, a report to a company manager describing methods for promoting a new product will be expository, but a detailed recommendation for a particular sales campaign will be argumentative. Newspaper editorials are usually short argumentative essays; feature articles that include the writers' opinions are usually longer essays that combine exposition and argument.

NOTE: A distinction is sometimes drawn between argumentative and persuasive writing. The two types use the same general methods, and they have the same purpose: to influence readers so that they will agree with the writer's opinions. The persuasive essay relies particularly on an appeal to the emotions of readers to make them change their opinions. The argumentative essay relies particularly on logical reasoning to prove that an opinion is right or wrong.

In each type of essay, the writer may take advantage of the methods of the other types to make the main point clear and vivid for readers. An argumentative essay, for example, may present parts of the material through description and narration and will almost certainly include some exposition.

An essay may be of any length, from one paragraph to hundreds, just as a book may be of any length; but very short essays and very long essays are both rare. Most are from five or six to fifteen or twenty paragraphs long. Whatever its length, a good essay, like a good paragraph, is unified and coherent. It presents only one main topic or controlling idea, although it may include many related ideas and pieces of information to make the main idea clear. It presents the material in a sequence that will help readers to see relationships among the writer's thoughts and to follow them easily. The basic pattern for the overall organization of an essay, like that of a paragraph, has three elements: a beginning, a main body, and an ending.

The beginning of an essay acts as an introduction (from Latin *intro* = into + *ducere* = to lead). It leads readers into the main body of the essay, first by catching their attention and then by giving them whatever information and directions they need to begin following the writer's line of thought in the main body. The main body contains the real substance of what the writer has to say. It develops, explains, and supports the writer's thesis (Greek *thesis* = a placing, position, or proposition), which is so named because it places the writer's main point before the readers. The ending acts as a conclusion (from Latin *com* = together + *clausus* = closed up) by impressing the writer's thesis on the minds of the readers.

In composing an essay, it is usually wise to make a rough draft of your thesis statement and at least a plan for organizing material in the main body before you compose a beginning for the essay. You will then be better able to choose a beginning that will catch the attention of your readers and lead them into the main body of the essay.

If you have had frequent experience in writing essays and, on the whole, have been satisfied with what you wrote, you may not need the suggestions that follow. If, however, you are like most people and wonder each time where to begin and how to proceed, these suggestions may help you.

There are as many ways to go about writing an essay as there are essay writers. At one extreme are a few writers who make such detailed plans and follow them so carefully that they write only one rough draft and make only minor changes in it for the final copy. At the other extreme are writers who find their ideas and a way of organizing them only in the process of free writing. They jot down whatever occurs to them as they let their minds wander freely over, around, and sometimes off the general topic, and they discover their ideas when they see their words and sentences. They may write many rough drafts, throwing out big chunks, adding and rearranging others, and sometimes completely changing the thesis or even the topic before they at last produce an essay that satisfies them. Most writers are somewhere between these two extremes. By frequent practice and experimentation and by close attention to your instructor's comments, you will find the process that helps you most.

Although writing procedures may differ dramatically, they all include the following, though not necessarily in this order: **choosing or being assigned a general topic; gathering, sorting, and reviewing material** on the general topic; **narrowing attention to a specific topic; formulating a thesis; choosing material** and **organizing it** in the order most likely to be clear and convincing to readers; **composing a stimulating beginning** that will introduce the topic and thesis to the readers and catch their attention; and **composing an effective ending** to make readers remember the main point—the thesis—of the essay.

Many rough drafts and revisions may be necessary to produce an essay that presents your thoughts effectively. *Revision,* as the word itself shows, means "seeing again," a new vision of your material—seeing it with fresh eyes, from a new angle, or in relation to new things. Revision is a continuing activity. By keeping your mind open to new impressions during the whole writing process, you will be able to *re-see* your material, your approach, and your readers' possible reactions. You will reject many of the new ideas that occur to you, but some will prove valuable, and one or two may become the most effective parts of your essay.

37 ◆ HOW ONE ESSAY DEVELOPED— A CASE HISTORY

The development of the following student essay, from the assignment through the final draft, provides an example of the composing process in action and shows how much rethinking and re-rethinking the process may require. This is the assignment that one student in a college composition course received:

> In an essay of about 500 words, describe your bedroom at home or your dormitory room. Assume that your readers will be students at another college who have never seen your room. As you proceed, make notes describing how you composed the paper and hand them in on Monday with your rough draft (or drafts) and your final copy.

The student's notes and rough drafts were handwritten but, to make them easy to read, they are presented here as if they had been typed; also, errors in spelling, punctuation, and grammar have been corrected so that you can concentrate more easily on the essential elements in the composing process.

<u>Day 1</u>--Came back to the dorm, sat on my bed, and took a good look around the room. Made a list of what to describe:

desk	dresser
desk chair	posters and calendar
bookcase	armchair
closet	night table with clock and stereo

Almost forgot the bed because I was sitting on it. Added colors of the walls, floor tiles, woodwork, bedspread. It's so easy to forget obvious things because you don't notice them anymore.

Made another list--what someone can see from the doorway, starting from that end of the room and moving to the other:

bookcase

desk, desk chair, wall calendar

bed, posters

night table with tape deck, armchair

Left out the dresser because it's a built-in, part of the same wall as the door; you see it only if you're already in the room.

How do I organize these things into a
paper? By what interests me? By what I
think is most important? Is this about <u>me</u> or
about the <u>room</u>? What would anyone notice
about this room? An outsider would need some
background to picture this room and how it's
arranged. Made another list:

    dorm rooms in this building
        basic shape like a shoe box
        furniture always the same--plain style,
            wooden bed, desk, two chairs,
            bookcase, built-in dresser
        colors always the same too--walls/
            cream, woodwork/dark brown,
            furniture/dark brown, floor/medium
            brown
    my room, seen from the doorway (visitor's
        view)
        bed--against the left wall with head in
            far corner by the window--biggest
            thing, so obvious place to start
        night table and stereo next to head of
            bed

armchair in right far corner by window

desk, with desk chair--in middle of
>   right hand wall

bookcase--four shelves high, against
>   right wall between desk and door--
>   shells and rocks

closet door and built-in dresser in
>   wall to left of door

Lots of details. How can readers keep
them all straight? And what's the point?
Got to have a <u>thesis</u> of some kind.

The assignment was what <u>someone else</u>
would see if they looked into my room. But
it's really what <u>I</u> want them to notice
because <u>I'm</u> the one who's doing the
describing. There's a big difference. What
do I want someone to notice? Dorm rooms are
pretty much the same, at least the ones here
are. I don't want to be boring, but if I try
to make it too special, it'll sound phony.
Looked over my lists again.

I've got to use more <u>details</u> to try to

make this paper interesting. Maybe the
details should be my main point. That can be
my <u>thesis</u>--the dorm rooms all start out the
same, so only the little details make them
individual. Or put that in the <u>conclusion</u>--
it will give me something to lead up to, and
then the ending won't be just a boring
repetition of the topic.

<u>Day 2</u>--Wrote the first draft as fast as I
could, without stopping to check spelling or
find the "right" word. When I get the whole
thing down, I can see it as one piece. Then
it's easier to tell if it makes any sense--I
can always play around with it later and
change the parts that don't sound right.

First draft

One Room in Whittier Hall

All the rooms in Whittier Hall have the
same basic furniture. There is a cot bed, a
night table, a plain wooden desk, a
four-shelf bookcase, a straight chair, a
plain wooden armchair, and a built-in

dresser. Also, all the rooms have the same basic shape. They are like shoe boxes, long and narrow. Another thing makes them all look alike. The walls in all of them are painted in the same cream color, and the woodwork is all stained brown to look like oak. The floors are all covered with the same dark-brown linoleum tiles.

Standing in the doorway of my room, a visitor would probably first notice the bed because it is the largest thing in the room and the cover is bright red. It is against the left wall, with the head of the bed in the corner next to the window, and beside the head of the bed is a small night table. My alarm clock is on top, and my stereo is on the shelf below. The armchair, which my father says is in a kind of Windsor chair style, is in the corner on the other side of the window. The desk is in the middle of the right-hand wall, and the bookcase is against the same wall between the desk and the door. My collection of shells and rocks is on the

two top shelves. There are two travel
posters on the left wall over the bed, and
there is a wall calendar over the desk. The
chest of drawers is built into the wall with
the door, in the corner beyond the closet.

No two rooms that I've seen in Whittier
Hall look exactly alike, in spite of having
the same furniture, and the same layout, and
the same colors for the walls and floors.
Some rooms are neat, and some are messy, like
mine. Everybody has different posters and
pictures and banners on the walls, and their
bedspreads are different colors. Also, what
they have in their bookcases and on their
desks are different. Even in small rooms
like these with the same basic equipment,
there is still room to show a little
individuality.

Day 2 continued--Sat around in my room
with RH and CJ and talked about the
assignment. Read them my rough draft. They
said I needed more about my travel posters

because that's what anyone would notice first. And they joked about the mess on my desk--it's really special, the messiest they've ever seen. I need to <u>support</u> that with <u>evidence</u> so readers can picture it.

Then we talked about my rocks and seashells. They'd never even noticed them, although they've been in my room dozens of times. What's so special about the rocks and shells? When I explained, they said to put that in the paper. Besides, the rocks and shells connect up with the posters because one poster shows mountains and the other shows a beach. That would help readers imagine the room and make it a little different.

After dinner, wrote a description of the posters and an explanation about the rocks and shells. And about the mess on my desk. Not too much though--I'm not going to brag about being messy! I'll add this stuff to the paper tomorrow.

Day 3--Took the descriptions I wrote last night and taped them into the paper so that I could get a better picture of the whole paper. This would sure be a lot easier with a word processor.

Reread the whole paper. It sounds awkward and repetitious. The main point about the rooms being different isn't clear. The ending is pretty weak. Need to give the main point at the end of the first paragraph--otherwise it doesn't come until the very end, and readers won't know why all the details are in the main body.

Revised the beginning. Added a little to help readers get into the picture and emphasized how the rooms are really all the same, kind of like jail cells almost. Can they sue me for libel? Cut out part of the ending to make it more forceful. Added some description of the calendar. Put in a bit about the closet and the dresser but then cut it out. Cut down the ending some more to try to make it more forceful.

Talking last night with RH and CJ made me realize what a difference the details can make. It's so hard to figure out how other people will see things, and in this paper it's the details that really matter. What about "Important Details" for the title? It gets the main idea across right from the beginning.

First draft with additions and revisions The numbers in the left margin indicate the sequence in which the additions and major revisions were made.

~~Important Details~~ A Matter of Detail

A ~~One Room in Whittier Hall~~ ∧

4

The rooms in a college dormitory at the end of summer, before the students move in, look almost like jail cells because they have no individuality.⌐

⌐where I live, are no exception. They all⌐
— The rooms in Whittier Hall have the same

¶ Also, they all have the same basic
∧ basic furniture / — ~~There is~~ a cot bed, a night table, a plain wooden desk, a four-shelf bookcase, a straight chair, a plain wooden
   a closet and   to the left of the door.
armchair, and a∧built-in dresser∧ ~~Also, all~~

~~the rooms have the same basic~~ shape, ~~They~~

(--with the door at one end and the window at the oth
~~are~~ like shoe boxes, long and narrow⟩ ~~Another~~

~~thing makes them all look alike.~~ The walls ~~in~~
        all
~~all of them~~ are∧ painted in the same cream
        all
color, ~~and~~∧ the woodwork is ~~all~~ stained brown
       and⟩
to look like oak, ∧~~The floors are all covered~~
⟨cover all the floors.⟩ ⟨But the similarities end ther
~~with~~ the same dark brown linoleum tiles⟩
   → New ¶ ← put at end of new ¶
       Standing in the doorway of my room, a
          ~~the~~ bright red cover on my
visitor would probably first notice the∧ bed,

~~because it is the largest thing in the room~~
         which
~~and the cover is bright red.~~ ~~It~~∧ is against
        its
the left wall, with ~~the~~∧ head ~~of the bed~~ in

the corner next to the window,

       Over my bed hang two travel posters. In
        dashing   steep
one, a skier is ~~going~~∧ down a∧ slope, ~~with his~~

knees bent,~~down and his~~ poles tucked under

his arms, ~~There is an~~ orange scarf ~~that is~~

flying over his shoulder, and ~~there is~~

powdered snow ~~that is~~ swirling around behind

him. In the other poster, ~~there are~~ palm

trees ~~that are~~ lean~~ing~~ over the white sand of

a beach that curves around the blue-green
         A couple
water of a small bay. ~~A man and a woman~~ in

1

1 | bathing suits are stretched out on their
backs. Their eyes are closed and their skins
glistening with suntan oil.

By
~~and beside~~ the head
of the bed is a small night table. My alarm
clock is on top, and my stereo is on the
shelf below. The armchair, which my father
calls
~~says is in~~ a kind of Windsor chair, ~~style,~~ is in

My
¶ the corner on the other side of the window. ¶ ~~The~~
~~which~~   in the middle of the right hand wall,
desk, ~~is~~ would never win a prize for neatness.

3 | ~~The top is always cluttered with~~ Books,
notebooks, stray papers, pens, pencils, paper
clips, my old portable typewriter, and a
(are always cluttering the surface.)
gooseneck study lamp. A large college
hangs
calendar ~~is~~ over the desk, ~~decorated~~ with a
of
photograph ~~showing~~ the campus in spring.

A sharp-eyed visitor might guess that the
most personal detail in the room is
~~and the bookcase is~~
~~against the same wall between the desk and~~
the small   rocks and seashells
~~the door.~~ ~~My~~ collection of ~~shells and rocks~~
of the bookcase,
~~is~~ on the two top shelves, which is between

2 | the desk and the door, where most visitors

don't notice them. I picked up the rocks

last year on a camping trip to Colorado, and

I found the shells on the beach ~~when~~ ^while^ I was

visiting my grandparents ~~who have moved to~~ ^on^

the Gulf Coast of Florida. ^The rocks remind me of^ ~~Every time I look~~

~~at the rocks, I imagine that I am~~ breathing

that clean mountain air, and ~~every time I~~

~~look at~~ ^bring back^ the shells ^dazzling white^, ~~I see~~ that ^beach and^ ^its clear, blue-green^

^the^ water. ~~again.~~ ~~There are two travel~~

~~posters on the left wall over the bed, and~~

~~there is a wall calendar over the desk. The~~

~~chest of drawers is built into the wall with~~

~~the door, in the corner beyond the closet.~~

^When the rooms in Whittier Hall are inhabited^
^No~~No~~ two rooms~~ ~~that I've seen in Whittier~~

~~Hall~~ look exactly alike. ~~in spite of having~~
~~all the sameness~~
~~the same furniture, and the same layout, and~~

~~the same colors for the walls and~~

~~floors. Some rooms are neat, and some are~~

~~messy, like mine. Everybody has different~~

~~posters and pictures and banners on the~~

~~walls, and their bedspreads are different~~

~~colors. Also, what they have in their~~

5 | ~~bookcases and on their desks are different~~.
~~Even in small rooms like these with the same~~
~~basic equipment, there is still room to show~~
~~a little individuality~~. What makes each one

different ~~from all the others~~ is ~~just like~~
each person and each experience different
~~what makes even the most average people~~
              ~~particular~~ unique
~~different from each other~~--a combination of

small details. ~~Taken separately, none of the~~
~~details may seem important, but the~~
~~combination is always unique~~.

Final copy

                                    M. B. Wilson

                  A Matter of Detail

    The rooms in a college dormitory at the
end of summer, before the students move in,
look almost like jail cells because they have
no individuality. The rooms in Whittier
Hall, where I live, are no exception. They
all have the same basic shape, like shoe
boxes--long and narrow, with the door at one
end and the window at the other. The walls

are all painted the same cream color, all the woodwork is stained brown to look like oak, and the same dark brown linoleum tiles cover all the floors.

Also, all the rooms have the same basic furniture--a cot bed, a night table, a plain wooden desk, a four-shelf bookcase, a straight chair, a plain wooden armchair, and a built-in closet and dresser in the wall to the left of the door. But the similarities end there.

Standing in the doorway of my room, a visitor would probably first notice the bright red cover on my bed, which is against the left wall, with the head in the corner next to the window.

Over my bed hang two travel posters. In one, a skier is dashing down a steep slope, knees bent, poles tucked under his arms, orange scarf flying over his shoulder, and powdered snow swirling behind him. In the other poster, palm trees lean over the white sand of a beach that curves around the

blue-green water of a small bay. A couple in
bathing suits are stretched on their backs.
Their eyes are closed and their skins
glistening with suntan oil.

By the head of the bed is a little night
table. My alarm clock is on top, and my
stereo is on the shelf below. The armchair,
which my father calls a Windsor chair, is in
the corner on the other side of the window.

My desk, in the middle of the right-hand
wall, would never win a prize for neatness.
Books, notebooks, stray papers, pens,
pencils, paper clips, my old portable
typewriter, and a gooseneck lamp are always
cluttering the surface. A large college
calendar hangs over the desk, with a
photograph of the campus in spring.

A sharp-eyed visitor might guess that the
most personal detail in the room is the
collection of rocks and seashells on the two
top shelves of the bookcase, which is between
the desk and the door, where most visitors
don't notice them. I picked up the rocks

last year on a camping trip to Colorado, and
I found the shells on the beach while
visiting my grandparents on the Gulf Coast of
Florida. The rocks remind me of breathing
that clean mountain air, and the shells bring
back that dazzling white beach and its clear,
blue-green water.

When the rooms in Whittier Hall are
inhabited, no two look exactly alike. What
makes each one different is what makes each
person and each experience different--a
unique combination of details.

38 ◆ GATHERING MATERIAL AND DEFINING YOUR AUDIENCE

When you receive a specific topic as a writing assignment, your first steps are to gather material for your essay
and to define your audience. To make these activities
clear, let us assume that you receive the following assignment and have a weekend in which to complete it (if you
are free to choose your own topic, see **42** for suggestions
on how to make the choice):

A prize committee wishes to award a prize to the
outstanding person, team, or group, either professional

or amateur, in each of the following fields: popular music, classical music, sports, acting (television, film, or stage), local politics, and national politics. In the field that interests you most, which person, team, or group would you nominate and why? Write a 500-word essay in which you try to persuade the judges that your nominee deserves the prize in that field.

First, choose whichever field you know best—the more knowledge you have, the more information you will be able to draw on and the better your selection is likely to be. With only a weekend for the assignment, you will not have time for extensive research. For our example, assume your interest is sports, particularly basketball, and that you consider one team outstanding. That opinion will be your **general thesis.** For a more specific thesis, ask yourself what information is likely to convince your readers that the team is outstanding. The reporter's standard questions are helpful: *Who? What? Where? When? Why?* Consider the team's record, and **analyze** and **define** the strengths and weaknesses of the team and the individual players. Consider any problems the team has had to overcome—such as illness, injury, or a change of coach—and what other activities the team may have been involved in, such as working with the disabled or with disadvantaged teenagers. **Compare and contrast** the team with its competition.

Ask friends and acquaintances who are interested in basketball for their opinions—they may offer material you have overlooked or help you to see flaws in your logic. If you have time, consult recent sports sections of newspapers and magazines. The **opinions of others,** particularly people with special knowledge of the subject, will give you a sense of how readers will react. The more clearly you can imagine your **audience**—in this case, the hypothetical committee on awards—the better you will be able to direct your argument to them and make it convincing. To help yourself in imagining your readers clearly, ask yourself:

What do they probably already know about the subject?

What background information are they likely to need?

What opinions are they already likely to have on the topic?

What facts and what kind of presentation are most likely to convince them?

As you gather material, separate fact from hearsay by reading background material and checking sources to make sure that your information is unbiased and accurate. Also, try to make it as up-to-date and thorough as time allows.

Take notes on everything that occurs to you and everything that others suggest, even on what seems likely to be of little use. Something you thought unimportant at first may later be a source of inspiration.

When you have gathered as much material as time allows, review it and formulate a **working thesis**—a rough draft of your main point, based on your material. Your working thesis should go beyond merely making a claim that X deserves the prize. It should **summarize the reasoning** behind your claim: "X deserves the prize as outstanding basketball team **because.** . . ." Your working thesis will guide you in the next stage: selecting material that will make your thesis not only clear to your readers but also convincing.

As you sort out your notes and thoughts so that you can see them and select the best material, you will find two methods useful: (1) arranging your material in **satellite patterns** around your central point, and (2) choosing appropriate **categories** and listing all the material that can go in each. The two methods overlap and complement each other; you may wish to use both so that you can view your material in as many ways as possible.

A **satellite pattern** for this topic might look like this, with the thesis stated briefly in the center and the main points grouped around it, some of them with satellites of their own:

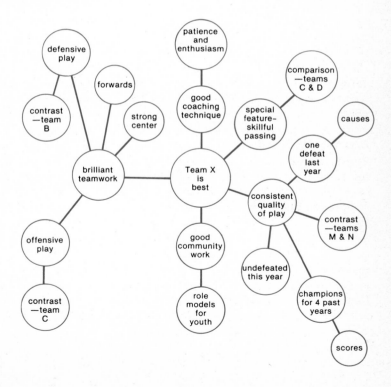

With the satellite method, you can see at a glance which parts are related to which other parts and how closely each is connected to the thesis. It leaves you free to choose the order in which you will take up the main points—according to chronology, relative importance, complexity, and so on.

A list of **categories** for this topic might look like this: chief technical strengths of individual players, chief technical weaknesses of individual players, colorful personalities, most important victories, surprising victories, significant features of typical games, significant features of recent games, training methods, personality of coach, early record, chief rivals and their strengths and weaknesses, probable future of the team.

Obviously, some material will fit in more than one category—for example, the players' strengths and weaknesses are probably related to their training and to their personalities and may have a decisive influence on teamwork. **Lists** emphasize the natural subdivisions of your material. With fresh lists, you can easily arrange new categories and combinations, exploring many different arrangements to find the most effective one. Lists can also reveal how your readers will follow your reasoning, since readers will take up your points in the order of your final listing.

Lists and patterns will help you in two essential steps: **recognizing relationships** among the parts of your material so that you can see what is connected to which and which is more important than what, and **organizing** them in the order that will be easiest for your readers to follow and most likely to convince them to accept your thesis.

While you arrange and rearrange your material in different patterns, keep your mind open for other interpretations, other ideas, other conclusions, and make notes of whatever occurs to you. At any point, even when writing the final draft, you may find something to add or change that will strengthen your thesis.

39 ◆ ORGANIZING AN ESSAY

To organize your opinions and material for the main body of an essay, you have the same choices as you have for organizing a paragraph: **chronological, spatial, general to particular, particular to general, climactic,** and **supporting.** Any of these could be appropriate for the hypothetical essay on team X or for an essay on almost any topic. Your choice will depend on what you wish to emphasize, how complicated or difficult your supporting material is likely to seem to your readers, and whether or not your readers are likely to agree with your opinions.

In choosing the best way to organize a particular essay, try all the ways that seem promising. First, jot down all your main points with a few notes on each giving the chief material you plan to use in developing it. Next, for each method of organization, list your main points and notes according to the order necessary for that method. You will then be able to compare and contrast them at a glance and see how each would appear to your readers— what they would read first, what second, and so on.

Chronological Using a chronological order, you could give highlights of the team's most notable games, starting with the earliest and ending with the most recent, *or* you could describe a single especially important or representative game from start to finish, making brief references to other games played before it and then to games after it, and ending with the most recent game to prove that the one you have chosen is truly important or representative. Yet another possibility would be to start with the most recent game and then go backward in time to show how the team's methods have evolved. With most material, a chronological order is easy for readers to follow, and in this case it would help you to emphasize that the team has always been very good or that it has improved with experience.

Spatial Using a spatial order, you could emphasize how the teamwork of the players is affected by whether they are defending their own basket or are in the other half of the court trying to score. A spatial order would also help you to emphasize the precise technical nature of the teamwork and would appeal to readers who know a lot about basketball.

General to particular Using a general-to-particular order, you could begin with a broad claim about the team's general ability to work together and then move from one or more general examples to a claim about the specific nature of their teamwork, giving examples pinpointing the qualities or techniques of the teamwork that you find most impressive. You could emphasize the most impressive example by saving it for last. Going from general to particular is effective when you have complicated or technical material about which your readers are likely to know little. The general beginning gives them an overall picture into which they can fit the details.

Particular to general Using a particular-to-general order, you could reverse the order just described, beginning with a specific example of teamwork and then widening your examination, first to the type illustrated by the example, then to other similar types, and finally to teamwork in general. Going from particular to general is effective when you can begin with an especially clear and impressive example or with an easily understood and important detail that will stimulate the curiosity of your readers and make them want to read further.

Climactic Using a climactic order, you could begin with examples of ordinary, routine teamwork shown by X and then go by degrees to the most impressive and unusual example, making it the climax of your account. A climactic order is effective if you can save your strongest and most essential material until the end without confusing your readers. The result will be similar to the final moments of a well-constructed drama, and your readers will remember it vividly.

Supporting Using a supporting order, you could begin with a full presentation of your thesis, giving your definition of X's teamwork and perhaps including a list of X's most important victories, *or* you could begin with a detailed description of the most impressive example of X's teamwork and follow it with your definition of teamwork and your thesis. In either case, you could continue by giving several further examples with plenty of details to explain and illustrate your thesis or to show that the impressive example, while exceptional, is still characteristic of the special qualities of the team. A supporting sequence is effective for presenting evidence when your material is complicated or when your readers are likely to be unfamiliar with it or when you think that they may be difficult to convince. It is the most widely used method for organizing factual material because it makes the main point clear from the beginning and emphasizes the abundance and quality of evidence supporting the thesis.

In organizing the main body of an essay, you should also consider the principal methods you will be using to develop it to make it convincing to your readers. You will need some or all of the methods for developing paragraphs: *description, narration, exemplification, process, comparison and contrast, classification, analysis, cause and effect,* and *definition* (see **35**). In an essay on team *X*, for example, you will certainly need to present examples of teamwork, and you will need narration and description to make the examples vivid. Be sure to include **negative examples,** if any exist—times when the players failed to show good teamwork—so that your readers will not accuse you of being one-sided. Analyze your negative examples to explain why, in spite of them, you think that the team is outstanding.

You may also need to explain the *process* of playing basketball, giving the kinds of planning and actions required in the game. To convince your readers that *X* is the most outstanding team, you will need to compare and contrast individual players with each other and the team with other teams, and you will need to classify and analyze the kinds of teamwork to show which are the most important and impressive. In showing how the players' personalities and styles and the team's training and background make the team outstanding, you will need to analyze cause and effect, and throughout your essay you will need to define any special basketball terms that your readers may not know.

To make a final choice for the organization of the main body, look over the lists that you made for organizing your material in different ways. As you do so, consider how complicated or difficult the material is likely to seem to your readers, how much they are likely to know about it already, and what their opinions of your thesis are likely to be. Then ask yourself these questions:

Which organization will make the thesis and material clearest to readers?

Which organization will emphasize the most important points most strongly?

Which organization will show the connections among the parts most clearly?

Your answers to these questions will guide you in choosing the best organization for the main body of your essay.

When you have chosen the organization, you are ready to **begin writing a rough draft**—perhaps the first of several—of your whole essay. At this stage, do not take time to compose the beginning unless a striking one has already occurred to you. The essential part of any beginning is the thesis statement, and that alone can temporarily serve to introduce the rough draft. Start, instead, with the main body.

40 ◆ COMPOSING AND REVISING
A ROUGH DRAFT

With your notes on your working thesis and your rough plan for the main body spread in view to help focus your thoughts, compose a *rough draft of the main body.* Try to work quickly. Do *not* edit your writing now. Remember that this is a *rough* draft and that you will polish it later, when it is complete, not while your ideas are still taking shape.

As you work, keep your thesis and your readers in mind. What you write must be relevant to your main point, and it must be clear and coherent to your readers. Do not let your special knowledge of your topic or your interest in it tempt you to write too much and lose valuable time. If you know a great deal about basketball in general and team X in particular, you could probably write 10,000 words, but if the assignment calls for a 500-word essay, you must adjust your plan to fit the requirement.

Set your rough draft aside for a while after you have finished it—if possible, for several hours. When you return to it, you will be able to bring a fresh perspective. Then read it rapidly to form an overall impression of the logic and forcefulness of what you have written. Ask yourself:

Does each part of the main body help in some way to develop the thesis?

Will the order in which these parts are arranged be easy for readers to understand?

Are the connections between the parts clear?

Is the reasoning logical throughout?

Revise any parts that seem weak, awkward, or unclear until you are satisfied that the main body will say to readers what you want it to say. This is an excellent time to compose the beginning and ending of your essay—immediately *after* you have reread the main body and made any major revisions you think necessary.

The **beginning** of your essay should catch the attention of your readers and lead them into the main body. If your readers are likely to be unfamiliar with your subject, then a brief, clear description of the subject will be best, with a statement of your position. For example, in recommending team X for the prize, you might start with a simple paragraph giving your opinion that the team is the most outstanding one in its league and that its success is largely due to remarkable teamwork. If readers are likely to be familiar with your subject or to disagree with your opinion, a more striking beginning would be advisable. The following suggestions can be adapted to most subjects:

1. A *direct statement* of your thesis, with a brief indication of how you plan to support it, is the simplest and easiest way to begin an essay. It is especially appropriate if your material is complicated or likely to be unfamiliar to your readers.

2. A *question,* such as "What has made team X successful and brought it to the top of the league?" followed by a brief identification of the team, may make your readers start to think. You could then withhold your thesis—that the key to their success is their teamwork—

until the end of the first paragraph or the beginning of the second to give it special emphasis. This kind of beginning is effective when your readers know at least something about your specific subject.

3. A *short narrative,* such as a colorful, brief anecdote about *X,* will appeal to almost all readers. At the end of the narrative or at the beginning of the next paragraph, you can explain that the narrative is an example of the teamwork that you think is *X*'s special strength and then present your thesis. Everyone enjoys a story, and a narrative makes an effective beginning when readers know enough about the general subject to be able to follow the story easily.

4. The *quotation of an expert's praise* of *X*'s good teamwork, with a brief identification of the expert and an indication that you agree with the praise, will support your thesis and suggest to readers that your opinion has a solid foundation. This is effective when you think your readers are knowledgeable but likely to be difficult to convince.

5. Conversely, the *quotation of a well-known expert's criticism* of *X*'s teamwork, with a brief identification of the expert and an indication that you disagree with the criticism, will show your independence of mind and challenge readers to make up their minds. This makes an effective beginning when you are very sure of your ground and when your readers are likely to be familiar with your subject.

For the **ending** of your essay, consider the overall effect you wish to have on your readers, what their opinion of your thesis is likely to be, and what you most want them to remember. Any of the methods suggested for an opening can be adapted to make an effective ending.

1. A forceful, brief *restatement of your claim* that X deserves the prize, perhaps including a very condensed *summary* of the main points of your argument, is the clearest and simplest type of conclusion and the one used most often.

2. A *rhetorical question,* implying the answer you expect, such as "What other team can claim to have the fine teamwork that X has shown?" makes readers think and also makes you seem less dogmatic than does a plain statement of opinion.

3. The *quotation of a well-known expert's comment,* such as a mention of X's teamwork, will support your thesis and suggest that you are knowledgeable.

4. An especially vivid and clear *example of your thesis* presented in a brief narrative or description will stimulate your readers' imagination and be easy for them to remember.

5. A *connection between your thesis and your readers*—such as a mention of the value of teamwork in almost every phase of life and the importance of our honoring a conspicuous example of it—will encourage your readers to relate your essay to their own experience and help them remember it.

Whatever forms you choose for the beginning and ending of your essay, both should be brief, especially the ending, so that they will be memorable. Remember that the main body contains the real substance of your essay.

When you have composed a suitable beginning and ending, you will have a rough draft of the entire essay. Read it straight through again, preferably out loud. If possible, read it aloud to a cooperative friend. You will not only benefit from any comments or questions but will also *hear* your own sentences, an excellent way to catch needless repetitions and awkward constructions that you should revise.

Choose a title that is appropriate to your subject, to your readers, and for the occasion. A short, informative title is best for most college writing, for example, "The Importance of Teamwork," "The Outstanding Basketball Team," or "*X*'s Outstanding Teamwork." A subtitle can stimulate reader interest, with a colon or dash to emphasize it: "*X:* Team of the Year" or "*X*—Candidate for an Award." A question may catch the attention of readers, for example, "What Makes *X* Outstanding?" or "Is *X* the Most Outstanding Team?"

Polishing the rough draft

Read the rough draft again, this time **very slowly,** checking it sentence by sentence, word by word, to make sure that you have taken advantage of paragraph and sentence structure to emphasize important words and phrases. Use the following checklist as a guide in revising and correcting your essay:

1. **Paragraphs**

   Each paragraph should have only one main topic.

   The topic should be clearly stated or strongly implied.

   Paragraph development should be adequate and appropriate for the topic.

Transitions and connections between sentences and between paragraphs should be clearly indicated by transitional words or phrases, by parallel structures, or by repetition of key words or phrases.

2. **Sentence structure**

Every sentence should be complete, with its own subject and predicate.

Information and opinions of equal importance should be in compound, coordinate, or parallel structures.

Information and opinions that are less important than other parts of a sentence should be in subordinate structures.

Modifiers should be close enough to the words they modify for readers to see the connection with no chance of confusion.

3. **Sentence consistency**

Verb tenses should be consistent and logical; change tenses only to indicate a change of time.

Regular verbs should have a *d* or *ed* ending in the past tense (see **6j** for the principal parts of common irregular verbs, or check a dictionary).

Verbs should agree with their subjects in number; a singular subject takes a singular verb form, and a plural or compound subject takes a plural verb form.

Third-person singular verbs in the present tense should have an *s* ending.

Pronouns should be consistent; change from *it* to *they* to show a change from singular to plural or from *you* to *they* to show a change in reference.

Pronouns should agree in number with the nouns they replace; the cases of personal pronouns and of *who, whom,* and *whose* should fit their role in the sentence.

Sentences should be logically consistent: every *either* should be followed by *or,* every *first* by a *second,* and so on.

4. **Punctuation**

Each sentence should begin with a capital letter and should end with a period; questions should end with a question mark.

Independent clauses joined by a coordinating conjunction should be separated by a comma.

Independent clauses not joined by a coordinating conjunction but meant to form a sentence should be divided by a semicolon or colon.

Introductory modifiers should be followed by a comma.

Non-restrictive modifiers should be set off from the rest of the sentence by punctuation.

Items in a series should be divided by commas or semicolons.

Two or more words used as a single word should be hyphenated.

5. **Words**

Words should present your meaning precisely and accurately; avoid clichés and colorless expressions, but use figurative language for special emphasis.

Idiomatic usage should follow standard conventions; remember that small words, especially prepositions and prepositional adverbs, can make a big difference in meaning.

Word choice should be compact and economical; avoid redundancies—they waste your readers' time and weaken the effect of your writing.

6. **Spelling**

Use standard American spelling.

Watch out for words that sound like other words but that are spelled differently; see the lists in **2b–c.**

Consult a dictionary whenever you are in doubt.

41 ◆ PREPARING THE FINAL COPY

For the final copy of your essay, use the following standard format and ask your instructor for any additional specifications.

Use white, standard-size paper (8½ by 11 inches). Do **not** use pages torn from a spiral binder or very thin paper, such as onionskin or airmail paper.

For handwritten work, use wide-lined paper (about ⅜ inch between lines) and black or dark-blue ink.

For typewritten work, double space and use a black ribbon.

Type or write on only **one** side of each page.

Give your name in the upper right corner of the first page and, below it, the name or number of the course, the name of your instructor, and the date on which you will submit the paper.

Center the title of your essay on the top line of a lined page or about 2 inches from the top of an unlined page; do **not** set the title off in quotation marks unless it is entirely composed of a quotation of another person's words; if you include a quotation in your title, set off only the quoted words. Capitalize the first and last words, whatever they are, and all other words except articles, coordinating conjunctions, and prepositions of less than five letters. (For longer papers—roughly five pages or more—your instructor may require a separate title page. For a sample title page, see **53b**).

Leave blank at least one line, or the equivalent space, between the title and the first line of your essay.

Write or type the number of each page after the first in the upper right corner, using Arabic numerals. (If you have a title page, do not include it in the numbering.)

Leave margins about 1½ inches wide at the left side and at the top and bottom of each page; in a typewritten paper, leave a right-hand margin of about 1 inch.

Indent the beginning of each paragraph the equivalent of a five-letter word.

Spell out all numbers below ten unless you are using several close together (many authorities recommend spelling out all numbers below 100). Spell out any number, no matter how large, that begins a sentence. If the result seems awkward, as it will in a sentence with other numbers that are not spelled out, revise your sentence to begin with a word instead.

Avoid splitting words at the ends of lines; split words are difficult to read. Instead, leave the space at the end blank. If splitting a word is a necessity, check your dictionary for the correct syllable divisions, and use a hyphen to mark the split.

CAUTION: Newspapers often violate the rules for splitting words because their columns leave no space for adjustments. Do *not* follow their practice.

In a typewritten paper, observe these typing conventions: skip two spaces after all terminal punctuation and one space after all internal punctuation except dashes. Indicate a dash by typing two hyphens with *no* space before, after, or in between. Add in ink any symbols that your typewriter does not have.

In a handwritten paper, make your writing as legible as you can. Avoid special flourishes such as a circle instead of a dot over an *i* or *j.* With each *t,* make the horizontal line really cross the vertical line, and make capital letters distinctly larger than lowercase letters.

Proofread your final copy with the greatest possible care. In the details of writing, accuracy will not guarantee you a good grade, but it is essential. The best subjects and plans will not impress readers who are constantly distracted or confused by errors in spelling, punctuation, or grammar. Correct slips of your pen or typewriter by firmly crossing out the error and neatly writing the correction above it. Avoid erasures; they are usually messy. If you find several errors on a page or if an error involves several words, recopy the page.

Fasten the pages of your paper together with a clip, staple, or binder. Ask your instructors which they prefer.

42 ◆ CHOOSING YOUR OWN TOPIC

Most of what we write in our lives is required or at least suggested by circumstances. For some of your college essays, however, you may be expected to select your own topic. If you are puzzled about how to do so, think over the material of the course, your reading assignments, the lectures and class discussions; check your textbook to see if the author offers suggestions; and think back over any relevant newspaper and magazine articles you may have read recently.

Look for an event, fact, problem, comment, or personality that catches your interest and that you would like to explore. For a course in American government, you might compare a historical figure or event with one currently in the news; for example, you might choose John Jay and William Rehnquist, both chief justices of the Supreme Court, and describe and analyze the personalities and policies of both in order to evaluate Rehnquist or to re-evaluate Jay. If a current government policy is causing discussion, you might make an informal survey of student opinion on your campus, weigh the pros and cons, arrive at a conclusion, and try to persuade your readers to agree.

For a course in expository writing, your choice of topics may be as wide as your interests—anything from the laboratory sciences, the social sciences, or the arts to sports, business, or your own experiences as an individual. Describing and analyzing the causes and effects of a childhood problem and how you overcame it could be humorous or dramatic. Comparing and contrasting two or three neighborhoods where you have lived can interest readers unfamiliar with your material and will amuse readers familiar enough to compare their knowledge with yours.

Think over what you yourself enjoy reading—faced with a long wait in a doctor's office and only a pile of magazines to help pass the time, what kinds of articles do you turn to first, and why? What kinds hold your attention best? Whatever interests you as a reader can be of interest to other readers, and we all write best about the subjects we know best. In writing on those subjects, we can supply the specific details that are essential in making material come alive for our readers.

To arrive at a specific topic and formulate a thesis, follow the process that was suggested for the essay on the basketball team. Think over the general areas of your knowledge and experience, choose the one that interests you most, and, on the basis of your knowledge, narrow this to a specific area. Reviewing what you know about it, decide what you want your readers to notice most in it, what opinions of it you want them to develop, and how you can stimulate their interest. Formulate a general thesis on the basis of what you want your readers' reactions to be. For example, any of the following might provide the basis for an effective essay: "My neighborhood has undergone many changes since I was a child, some good and some bad"; "In the first grade, I learned a painful lesson about how to get along with members of the opposite sex"; or "My grandfather was the family tyrant, but maybe his demands were good for us." Remember that you are most likely to interest readers in a topic or material that you yourself find interesting.

When you have chosen a topic and formulated a general thesis the process of writing the essay will be the same as that described in **38–41**.

43 ◆ WRITING UNDER PRESSURE

The same basic principles apply whether you are writing in a classroom with a strict time limit or at home with a distant deadline. Remember: because of the time limit for most in-class writing, your first draft must also be your final draft. Careful planning is essential.

Begin by **not** beginning to write the essay. Instead, read the question very carefully at least twice to make sure that you understand exactly what you are asked to do. If you are at all uncertain of the meaning of the question, how much material you should cover, or how you should present it, ask your instructor for clarification before you begin.

Some questions for in-class essays and examinations ask primarily for facts rather than for your opinions. For example, you might be asked, "Trace the growth of federalism in the American colonies from 1643 to 1765." With such a question, run rapidly through what you know of the subject, jotting down brief notes on scratch paper if your instructor allows you to use it or on the last page of the test booklet. When you think that you have remembered all the important points, look over your notes with the examination question in mind as your thesis and decide which points to emphasize, which to subordinate to others, and how to arrange them to make a clear, logical essay that will answer the question. Cross out any notes that you think you may not need, but leave them legible—they may be a source of inspiration later. Choose the sequence that will present your material most clearly, and number your notes accordingly. Then start writing the essay. Be sure to skip a line after each line of writing and to leave a wide margin on the left so that you will have space for later changes. Use the restatement of the test question itself or a brief answer to it as the chief element in the beginning of your essay unless something more striking has already occurred to you. Then write the main body, following the sequence you have indicated in your notes. The best ending for an examination essay is usually a firm restatement of a brief answer to the original question. You can strengthen it by an especially forceful supporting detail or brief example or by a statement summarizing the main body of the essay in two or three sentences.

Some questions ask you not only to present facts but also to develop an opinion and defend it. For example, you might be asked, "Which of the ten amendments to the Constitution in the Bill of Rights do you consider the most important to American society today?" or "In 'The Killers,' how and to what extent does Hemingway develop the characters?" Begin as before by jotting down notes on the topic; then review them to decide which are more important and how they relate to one another and to the question. On first reading a question, you may think you already have a firm opinion on the topic, but in looking at your notes closely, you may gain new insight and find your opinion changing. When you feel confident that you can support a firm opinion with facts and logic, first define your claim in a brief statement to serve as a beginning, and then follow the usual procedures for composing an essay— choosing the material necessary to support and explain your opinion and organizing the material to make it clear to your readers.

No matter how much you have to say on the assigned topic, always save time to *review your essay at least once*— if possible, twice. First, glance over it for a general impression to make sure that you have included all the material you meant to include and have arranged it in an order that will be easy for a reader to follow. If you discover an important omission, mark the spot on the line with a caret (⌃) and write the additional words on the line above. If the addition is too long to fit there, use the margin at the top of the page or a page at the end of the test booklet, taking care to include a note in the left margin directing your reader where to find the addition.

Now, read your essay again carefully to check your grammar, spelling, and punctuation. This is an essential step. Many students skip it because they have not used their time wisely or because they mistakenly think that quantity is more important than quality in an examination and that the reader will "understand" what they mean, even if it is not entirely clear. Be especially alert to catch the kind of small error or omission that can change the meaning of a sentence. Make sure that the reference of each pronoun is clear and that what each phrase or clause modifies is also clear. Check the spelling of any words that have given you difficulty before, and be alert for slips of the pen, such as writing *were* for *where,* that will confuse your reader or even change the meaning of an entire sentence. Cross out errors neatly and write corrections in the space directly above.

The most important element in writing an effective examination or in-class essay is having plenty of information in a well-organized form so that you can draw on it easily and quickly. From the start of each course, make informal outlines for your own use of the lectures and of your reading. Then, in studying for a test, make a fresh outline of the main points in the earlier outlines. This will let you see the material for the course as a whole. With that overall structure firmly in mind, you will handle any part of the material more intelligently because you will be able to show its significance in relation to the whole. Also, by establishing in your own mind how the parts of your material are related, you will be much better able to remember them in the pressure of the test situation. Memory is largely a matter of making associations, and outlining is an organized way of associating the parts of any subject. For unannounced tests, your memory of your outlines can be even more helpful, giving you the security of an organized body of information on which to draw.

If in the past you have had difficulty in writing fast enough to put all that you know about a particular topic on paper, practice writing under pressure at home. Choose a likely topic—many textbooks include questions on the material, and most chapter and section headings can easily be converted into questions. Place an alarm clock or kitchen timer in front of you, set it to ring in 45 minutes (or whatever time you are usually given for an examination essay), and go to work. A loudly ticking clock or timer may also help to re-create the tension of test-taking, giving you a valuable practice session in learning to withstand the strain. Keep checking the time to see how much you spend on the various stages of composing the essay, such as gathering your thoughts, selecting the material, deciding on a sequence for presenting it, and so on. Remember to allow several minutes for revision and correction—5 to 10 minutes is average for a 45-minute test, proportionately more for a longer one.

The more you practice in this way, the better you will be able to cope with the strains of a real test, because you will learn your own individual capacities—how much you can write in a given length of time, how much time you should allow for revising and correcting, which stages in planning you are likely to need most time for, and so on.

44 ◆ WRITING ABOUT LITERATURE

We read fiction, poetry, and drama for our own enjoyment, but we may also read them in order to study the literary methods of the author or in order to participate in an exchange of ideas. When we write about literature, we usually write *analytically* if we are examining the author's literary methods, or *argumentatively* if we are taking sides in a debate about ideas.

Read critically and take notes When you are reading a work for pleasure, you are likely to read it only once, probably fairly rapidly; but when you want to study an author's methods or ideas, you must become more intimate and familiar with the text. You will need to **read the whole work more than once,** rereading important passages or chapters several times to observe and appreciate less obvious details.

Read slowly and carefully, asking yourself questions and taking notes along the way. Each time that you reread the work, take fresh notes, because your attitudes and ideas will change as you grow familiar with the work and you do not want to lose your first insights when you begin to focus on details.

If you are preparing to write about a novel or short story, keep asking yourself about the five basic elements of fiction—plot, setting, characterization, point of view, and theme.

1. **Plot** What events make up the action or story line of the work? What is the significance of the way they have been arranged? The events of a novel or short story are usually presented in chronological order, starting with the earliest and moving forward in sequence to the latest. Other arrangements are possible, of course, such as "flashbacks" or events in the order that they become known to an individual character. In some fiction, instead of using conventional events to make up the plot, the author may present intellectual and emotional experiences as events in the development of a character.

2. **Setting** Where and when do the events take place? What is the significance of the location and time? In

some fiction, the setting is of minor importance, but more often it contributes significantly to the author's ideas.

3. **Characterization** How is each character created? Are the characters static, or do they develop and change? How do they create and solve problems? How do they react to each other and to their environment? In many works of fiction, particularly short stories, character is more important than plot.

4. **Point of view** Who is telling the story? Through whose eyes do we see the events and characters? In third-person narration, the narrator is completely outside the story and is never actually identified. The author is implied as the narrator (often called the "omniscient author"), but such a narrator usually goes inside the minds of only one or two of the characters. Which characters does the narrator choose? Why? In first-person narration, a fictional character narrates the events. Remember that such a narrator is not the author, even though the narrator's use of *I* may suggest that the author is speaking. It may even be the author's primary intention to show us that the narrator is misinformed or dishonest about the event.

5. **Theme** What is the subject of the work as a whole? What is the general thesis or controlling idea that the whole work is illustrating? The theme of a novel or short story is generally a fairly broad comment on our experience of being human rather than a specific remark about one character or one character's experience. In questioning theme, do not try to find a single word to sum up everything; use a complete sentence to formulate your claim about the theme.

As you read and reread, ask yourself about other important aspects of the work and how they relate to these basic elements. What is the significance of the *title?* What can you observe about the author's use of *language, symbols,* and *irony?* What is the general *tone* of the work—that is, what is the author's attitude toward the theme or subject of the work?

To write about a play or poem, adapt the list of basic elements. In considering a work of drama, you will probably not be concerned with point of view because there is not likely to be a narrator. Setting may be defined in much less detail than in fiction; in fact, it is often only briefly described in stage directions. Naturally, then, your attention in reading will be directed more toward plot, characterization, and theme; also, the author's special use of language to create and reveal characters may be an important feature to observe.

By contrast, in reading poetry, you will often find that there are no events that form a plot and no characters in the usual sense. Instead, you may need to analyze a sequence of ideas or images and their arrangement, and your attention may be focused more strongly on point of view.

Poetry usually demands a greater attention to language and form than do drama and fiction. In analyzing the language of a poem, ask several questions. Are the author's words abstract or concrete? Are words used literally or figuratively? What sounds are repeated or stressed? What figures of speech does the author use? What kinds of imagery has the author chosen? How does the author's choice of words affect the tone of the poem? How does the author's word choice help to express the theme? The form of the poem may also be significant. Do the lines vary in length, or does each contain the same number of syllables as the others? Is the poem subdivided into groupings of lines or into stanzas? How does the author use rhyme and meter? If you need help with the specialized vocabulary of poetic language and form, consult a handbook of literary terms; your library will have many to choose from, and your instructor can advise you in choosing.

Review your notes and choose a topic As you become familiar with the work by repeated reading, you will accumulate enough notes to help you decide on a topic. Review your notes carefully, arranging and organizing them so that you have a clear overall impression of your materials (see chapter **38** for specific advice on arranging and organizing your notes). If you have taken good notes, they should direct you to the richest areas for your topic. Be sure to choose an appropriate topic, one that is suitable to your own interests and to the nature of the work; a short story focusing on the psychological development of one character, for example, may not contain enough material for an essay analyzing the author's use of setting.

You may have to adjust your topic to fit the length of your assignment. If your topic is too broad, you will not have space in your paper to support your generalizations with adequate evidence; if it is too small, you will be tempted to repeat your ideas unnecessarily or to weaken your insights by padding them. If your assignment calls for approximately 500 words, you will not be able to examine the development of all of the characters in a novel. In such a case, you should narrow your topic; for example, examine the development of a minor character, or choose a major character and examine the development of that character in a single scene or chapter of the novel.

If you find it difficult to choose a topic, consider some of the traditional approaches. For instance, examine the significance of one of the basic elements, presenting and analyzing evidence that will support your view. Or examine a particular part of the work in relation to the whole. If you have knowledge of another field such as psychology, philosophy, art, or one of the sciences, consider the work in the light of that field. Examine the work in its biographical, social, or historical context. Or, if you have done other reading for the course, compare the work with another in terms of theme, tone, language, or literary method.

Formulate a thesis statement and plan its development Once you have selected a topic, develop a specific statement of your thesis that will allow you to analyze or argue about a single significant aspect of your topic. A clear, limited thesis statement will enable you to organize the useful material in your notes and to prepare a plan for your evidence just as you would for any other essay. For patterns of organization, see chapter **39**.

Special problems of the literary paper

Assume that your reader has read the work. You do not need very long quotations, paraphrases, or summaries. Imagine that your reader has read the work once, and you are providing additional insights based on closer examination.

Write about the work, not about yourself. Avoid using the first person pronouns *I* or *we.* When you offer ideas and evidence, such expressions as *I think* or *I feel* put the spotlight on you rather than on the work.

Use the present tense. Write about works of literature and authors in the present tense in literary discussions except when you are citing historical fact. For example, write "Shakespeare creates a public setting for Juliet's first meeting with Romeo" but "Shakespeare wrote *Romeo and Juliet* in 1595."

Identify quotations and references. After a quotation or reference, place the page number or numbers of the work in parentheses. For poetry, give line numbers; for drama, give act, scene, and line or page numbers.

Credit your sources. If you include the ideas of other critics as part of your evidence, identify the critics and the source of their words.

45 ◆ OUTLINES

If you were reviewing the first chapter of this book for a test, which of these versions of notes based on the first five paragraphs of section 1a would be more helpful?

Summary of 1a   English has many sources, but the basic framework of the language is Old English, also called Anglo-Saxon, from which come many of the words we use most often—all of our prepositions, conjunctions, and pronouns and many familiar nouns, verbs, adjectives, and adverbs. The Norman Conquest (1066) brought many French words into the language, particularly legal and military terms and words associated with a more cultured, leisurely life. We call this transitional stage in the development of the language Middle English. The revival of classical learning in the Renaissance brought in many Greek and Latin words. Of all the languages in the world, English has the most words, making many shades of meaning possible.

Informal outline of 1a

English has many sources:
  Old English—basically Anglo-Saxon
    all our prepositions, conjunctions, pronouns
    many familiar nouns, verbs, adjectives, and adverbs
  Middle English—many French words incorporated
    legal and military terms
    cultural terms
  Renaissance—beginning of modern English
    revival of classical learning
    many Latin and Greek words
Results:
  more words in English than in any other language
  more precision possible in shades of meaning

Summaries can be very useful because they give the content of what we read in short understandable form, but outlines are best for an overview. They let us see a whole essay, a lecture, or even a book at a glance. With an outline we can not only record the main ideas—any notes can do that—but also show their relationships and degrees of importance. An outline can therefore give essential help in studying and writing. Some of your instructors will ask you to submit an outline with each paper, and later, if you write reports in connection with your work, you will often be expected to include an outline.

A **formal outline** is merely a conventional, labeled arrangement of logical indentations. For a short paper, an informal outline will usually prove adequate, but the more complex your material is, the more detailed and careful your planning should be. Also, after you have written what you hope will be your final rough draft, making a formal outline will help you to see your essay in perspective and check it for the coherence and development of your ideas.

Two systems are widely used for labeling the parts of an outline to indicate their connections and their relative importance. In the humanities, the outline system combines Roman and Arabic numerals with upper- and lower-case letters. The standard system for the sciences and social sciences, business, and engineering uses only Arabic numerals. The method of indentation is the same in both systems.

45a Outline style for the humanities

An outline for use in the humanities follows this plan:

Thesis statement: Brief statement of topic and of conclusions drawn from it

I. First major point
    A. First point to illustrate or explain I
    B. Second point to illustrate or explain I
        1. First subpoint for B
            a. First sub-subpoint for 1
            b. Second sub-subpoint for 1
        2. Second subpoint for B

II. Second major point
    A. First point to illustrate or explain II
    B. Second point to illustrate or explain II
    C. Third point to illustrate or explain II

You will rarely need further subdivisions beyond the level of *a.*, but if you do, then label the next level below *a.* with (1), (2), and so on, and label subdivisions of those with (a), (b), and so on.

Notice how the indentations help to emphasize relationships among thoughts by grouping points visibly according to their relative importance. The more important a point is, the closer it should be to the left margin. In the following diagram, notice how the labels are aligned in relation to each other and to the words they introduce. The Roman numerals are aligned by the periods that follow them; each fresh level of indentation is aligned under the first letter of the words in the preceding level:

```
  I.  - - - - - - - - - - - - - - - - - - - - - - - - - - - - - - -
      A.  - - - - - - - - - - - - - - - - - - - - - - - - - - -
      B.  - - - - - - - - - - - - - - - - - - - - - - - - - - -
          1.  - - - - - - - - - - - - - - - - - - - - - - - - -
              a.  - - - - - - - - - - - - - - - - - -
              b.  - - - - - - - - - - - - - - - - - -
          2.  - - - - - - - - - - - - - - - - - - - - - - - - -
 II.  - - - - - - - - - - - - - - - - - - - - - - - - - - - - - - -
      A.  - - - - - - - - - - - - - - - - - - - - - - - - - - -
      B.  - - - - - - - - - - - - - - - - - - - - - - - - - - -
      C.  - - - - - - - - - - - - - - - - - - - - - - - - - - -
          1.  - - - - - - - - - - - - - - - - - - - - - - - - -
          2.  - - - - - - - - - - - - - - - - - - - - - - - - -
              a.  - - - - - - - - - - - - - - - - - -
                  (1).  - - - - - - - - - - - - - -
                  (2).  - - - - - - - - - - - - - -
                        (a).  - - - - - - - -
                        (b).  - - - - - - - -
              b.  - - - - - - - - - - - - - - - - - -
III.  - - - - - - - - - - - - - - - - - - - - - - - - - - - - - - -
```

45b Outline style for the sciences

The same outline labeled with Arabic numerals for use in the sciences, business, and engineering follows this plan:

1. First major point
   1.1 First point to illustrate or explain 1
   1.2 Second point to illustrate or explain 1
      1.2.1 First subpoint for 1.2
         1.2.1.1 First sub-subpoint for 1.2.1
         1.2.1.2 Second sub-subpoint for 1.2.1
      1.2.2 Second subpoint for 1.2
2. Second major point
   2.1 First point to illustrate or explain 2
   2.2 Second point to illustrate or explain 2
   2.3 Third point to illustrate or explain 2

The two labeling systems work equally well for both topic and sentence outlines.

45c Topic and sentence outlines

A topic outline presents each point in a phrase or a single word. A sentence outline presents each point in a complete sentence. For your own use and for readers likely to be familiar with your material, a topic outline is preferable because it can be seen at a glance, but for readers likely to find your material unfamiliar or complex, a sentence outline will be more helpful. When an instructor asks you to submit an outline of your work, be sure to ask which type you should prepare.

The following example of a topic outline was composed to accompany the first sample research paper in **53a**, which was written early in 1986.

Thesis: An examination of the three major news magazines and of three major daily newspapers suggests that many problems of 1985 will continue in 1986.

I. Overview of 1985
  A. Negatives
    1. Disasters
      a. Natural
        (1) Earthquakes
        (2) Famines
        (3) Incurable disease
      b. Man-made
        (1) Air crashes
        (2) Terrorism
        (3) Racial oppression in South Africa
    2. Financial problems
      a. National deficit
      b. Bank failures
  B. Positives
    1. Dow-Jones at record high
    2. Large donations to Live Aid
    3. Individual successes
      a. Bruce Springsteen
      b. Pete Rose

II. Opinions presented in weekly magazines
    A. *Time:* mixture of good and bad in news and forecasts
        1. Deng Xiaoping as "Man of the Year"
        2. Life in China today
    B. *Newsweek:* mixture of good and bad in news and forecasts
        1. "Abandoned": the plight of homeless mentally ill
        2. Increased minority representation in Congress
        3. "Portrait 85": some admirable and some destructive people
    C. *U.S. News & World Report:* great optimism for 1986 based on very positive interpretation of 1985
        1. Signs of re-awakened American spirit
        2. Continuing economic growth
        3. Interviews with happy immigrants and satisfied families

III. Featured news in three major newspapers
    A. *San Francisco Chronicle*
        1. Ricky Nelson's death
        2. Dangerous error by "Dr. Ruth"
        3. Killer squads in Lebanon
    B. *Chicago Tribune*
        1. McCormick Place trade center
        2. Bombing in Beirut
        3. Italy's reduced tolerance for PLO
        4. Budget delay by Regional Transportation Authority
        5. New racial bans in South Africa

   C. *New York Times*
      1. Front-page news
         a. Bombing in Beirut
         b. Winnie Mandela's supporters dispersed by police
         c. Libya linked to terrorist attacks
         d. Foreclosures threatened on farmers' debts
      2. Other news
         a. California farmers facing foreign competition
         b. Kidnapping-rape of 12-year-old girls in Georgia
         c. Threats by PLO
         d. Signs of failure for Deng Xiaoping's farm policies

IV. Concluding evaluation: 1985's problems will continue into 1986.

Sentence outlines differ from topic outlines only in the structure of each point. For example, in sentence outline form, section I.B of the outline just given would become this:

   B. Several positive events occurred.
      1. The Dow-Jones average reached a record high.
      2. Live Aid Concerts received large donations.
      3. Two people achieved big individual successes.
         a. Bruce Springsteen's album sold 15 million copies.
         b. Pete Rose made his 4,204th hit.

45c Outlines

REMINDER: Every *A.* should be followed by a *B.*, every *1.* by a *2.*, and so on. If at first you think you have only one point to present at a particular level, analyze your material again. The single point is probably too much a part of the point on the level above it to be separated; you should reword the point above to make it more inclusive. For example, the student writer of the research paper topic outline first wrote:

> I.B.2.   Large charitable donations
>   a.   Live aid concerts

Then, realizing that no other big charity drive had made headlines, the student revised I.B.2. as "Large donations to Live Aid."

Whether you choose to make a sentence outline or a topic outline, be sure to be consistent throughout. In a topic outline, present each point at every level in a single word or short phrase, and use parallel structures for phrases in the same group (see **30c** for details on parallelism). In a sentence outline, be sure that each point at every level is a complete sentence.

Part Seven

RESEARCH PAPERS

345

46 ◆ RESEARCH PAPERS: AN OVERVIEW

The term *research paper* covers a wide range of writing and often serves as a synonym for *report;* but in serious scholarly work, you will find important differences between the two terms. Both require information that a writer gathers from various sources, and for both this process of gathering facts and opinions is "research." There the similarity ends.

Report writers work with available facts and interpretations, and when they offer opinions, they do not claim that their opinions are new. Many journalists perform this kind of research. Their information may be new to their readers, but it was not first discovered by the writers. Writing reports can be a rewarding activity; you encounter new material, and you inform others about it. You do not, however, add anything new to the existing body of facts and opinions. The first sample research paper in **53a**, "As 1986 Begins," is an example of this kind of paper.

The writer of the true research paper, on the other hand, shines new light on a subject either by uncovering new facts and forming new opinions, by re-evaluating known facts and opinions, or both. The writer of a true research paper reports clearly on information gathered from various sources and uses that information to say something original. As you go on in scholarly work, you will increasingly perform research of this kind.

As an undergraduate, you are unlikely to discover something that is both new and important, such as a cure for AIDS or clear proof that the ancient Greeks visited Brazil 2,500 years ago. But you can do original research that will be interesting and valuable. Two general approaches are open to you:

1. You can gather information on a relatively small subject that no one has examined before or that no one has examined thoroughly. For example, you can collect all the available facts on a local political situation or environmental problem, use newspaper files to put together the story of an unsolved crime and work out your own suggestions for the solution, or interview an elderly person and—with the help of background reading in appropriate historical material—write a chapter in a projected biography of that person. There are thousands of such subjects, full of facts that have not yet been sorted out and interpreted. The second sample research paper in **53b**, "Shelley's 'Ozymandias,'" examines a poem that, although well-known, has received little attention from critics.

2. You can examine a well-known subject in a new light. For example, new theories are appearing on the sudden extinction of the dinosaurs, and a good researcher will examine each new theory, comparing and contrasting it with earlier ones. Each new theory forces researchers to re-assess all previous theories, even if only to conclude, with supporting evidence, that the new theory changes nothing.

Whichever general approach you take, you will be gathering information from printed sources of all kinds, laboratory experiments, opinion surveys, or a combination of these. The more you can learn about your subject, the more authoritative you will be and the more likely to say something significant.

Writing a research paper is hard and exacting work, most of which takes place before any actual writing begins. You will spend hours finding and selecting source materials, perhaps reaching dead ends, or having to reconcile contradictory opinions or evidence. The process is often like detective work. Even if the answer you are seeking escapes you, the search itself can still be exciting, and discovering new evidence can make you feel triumphant.

To write a research paper you must follow five major steps: (1) choose a subject, (2) build a bibliography, (3) gather information from reading and other appropriate sources, (4) sort and organize the information to define your specific topic and determine your main point, and (5) write and document the paper.

47 ◆ CHOOSING A GENERAL SUBJECT

Choosing a general subject, then narrowing it to a specific topic that you can handle in a paper of the assigned length, and finally forming an opinion—a thesis—on that topic will be a long procedure. The more you learn about your subject in general and your topic in particular, the more precisely you will be able to define what you wish to cover and the main point that you wish your readers to see. Also, you will probably find, as you gather material, that at least some of the opinions you held at first have changed. Be sure to keep your mind open for such changes. They are at the heart of the research process.

The more interesting your subject is to you, the better your research paper is likely to be. Compared with other writing assignments, a research paper is a long, demanding task, and you will have to live with your subject for several weeks. What interests you? What would you like to know more about? As a business major, you might examine the economic forecasts published in newspapers and business magazines in a particular month and then determine their accuracy by examining the present state of the economy. As a science major, you might examine the published evaluations of a new drug or a new health threat, research its history, ask several doctors for their opinions, and arrive at your own conclusions. As a sports fan, you might analyze your favorite team's performance in the last year, the opinions of sportswriters, and the views of the coach and the players themselves. If your interest is history, you have an irreplaceable resource in any elderly person you know, for you can write a biographical study, placing the facts on part of your subject's life in an appropriate historical context. If you are curious about human behavior, you can devise a questionnaire on a controversial topic, make a survey of student opinion on your campus, and use the results—along with your reading on the subject—as a basis for an analysis of the psychological, political, or social significance of the students' answers. The opportunities are as wide as your interests.

Whatever subject you choose, plan to *limit* it so that you can cover it thoroughly. For example, if you decide to write a biography of your grandmother, concentrate on a few years or even a few months or weeks and give those in full detail, with only a brief summary of the rest of her life as a frame for the part you have chosen.

48 ◆ USING THE REFERENCE COLLECTIONS

The reference collections in your college and local libraries will be essential to your research. They are your chief means of locating information. Familiarize yourself with what they contain. Walk beside the shelves, reading titles and leafing through any work that seems promising. Knowing how to take full advantage of a reference collection is as necessary for a researcher as knowing how to use the telephone is for most Americans.

Begin by obtaining a bird's-eye view of what is known on your subject. Look it up in several sources of general information. Encyclopedias are most likely to be helpful. These include not only the *Britannica, Americana,* and *New International,* but also those specializing in a single field, such as religion, sociology, or art; collections of brief biographies, such as the international *Who's Who,* the *Dictionary of National Biography* for the British, and *Who's Who in America* for Americans; and collections of facts and statistics, such as the *World Almanac* and other yearbooks. *Winchell's Guide to Reference Books,* kept up-to-date by occasional supplements, classifies by type and subject matter all kinds of reference works besides the famous ones just mentioned.

Browse through the whole reference collection to form an overall picture of what is available. As you do, make notes on index cards (the most convenient sizes are (3 by 5 inches and 4 by 6 inches). Record the names and facts they emphasize. Write only one note on each card, so that you can arrange and rearrange them later as you explore relationships in the material you have gathered. On each card, write the title, page number, and library call number of the work from which you made the note. These notes will help you keep your subject in focus so that you can see the significance and relationships of the parts. If an encyclopedia article mentions important books on your subject, make notes of these by author and title on separate cards so that you can later check on their availability in your library.

The **library catalog** and **periodical indexes** are your two best sources of information about material printed on your subject.

The **catalog,** whether on cards, in book form, or computerized, lists every book in the library alphabetically by both author and title and usually under several headings for the subjects with which the book deals. For example, you will probably find *The Uses of Enchantment* by Bruno Bettelheim listed not only under *B* (by the author's name) and under *U* (by the title) but also in several subject categories, such as "Fairy Tales—History and Criticism," "Psychoanalysis," "Folklore and Children," and "Child Psychology."

The **periodical indexes,** probably shelved in the reference room of the library, will help you find articles in periodicals—newspapers, magazines, and journals of all kinds.

The *Reader's Guide to Periodical Literature* is issued monthly in magazine form and at intervals cumulated into volumes covering several years. It indexes, under both author and subject headings, the contents of the better-known American (and a few British) periodicals on general subjects since 1900.

Poole's Index covers British and American periodicals from 1802 to 1906.

The International Index covers a selected list of American and European periodicals in the humanities, social sciences, and science, from 1916 to 1965. The *Social Science and Humanities Index* covers about 175 American and British periodicals from 1965 to 1974. Two separate indexes continue the listings: the *Social Sciences Index* and the *Humanities Index.*

There are many specialized indexes for particular fields, such as agriculture, engineering, psychology, industrial art, literature, dentistry, medicine, and law. Some of these list books and bulletins as well as periodical articles.

The *New York Times Index,* published annually, covers all that newspaper's stories and articles. Since most major news is handled on the same or the following day by all the major newspapers, this index can help guide you to material in other papers as well.

Check the catalog to determine which periodicals your library carries; ask a reference librarian what others are available at nearby libraries and how to arrange for photocopies of periodical articles available in libraries you cannot visit.

Reference librarians can be the most valuable source for information in the library: they specialize in information retrieval. Turn to them whenever you find yourself in a blind alley, but always first try to solve problems your-self—the more practice you have, the more efficient you will become as a researcher.

IMPORTANT: In your preliminary survey of resources, do not try to make a thorough search, or you will be over-whelmed by what is available. Instead, make sure that material on your general subject is plentiful and up-to-date—check publication dates. While you are looking over the catalog and the indexes, watch for clues that will help you narrow your subject to a manageable topic. The titles of books and articles will give you an overall impression of what others have written and may suggest a topic that will be appropriate for you. Keep your mind open for such possibilities, and be sure to jot them down as they occur to you.

49 ◆ NARROWING THE SUBJECT TO A SPECIFIC TOPIC

When you have a clear idea of what resources are available to you—books and periodicals, laboratory facili-ties, knowledgeable people—you are ready to decide on a specific topic. First, make a quick review of the available material. Then, think over what you now know of your subject. Keep in mind the constraints of the project: the **length** of the paper, the **deadline,** and the importance of giving your readers **something fresh** on the subject—facts, or opinions, or both—that they will not find elsewhere. Choose a specific topic that will suit your needs and theirs, but remember that you will revise it more than once as you continue your research and think over what you find.

50 ◆ BUILDING A WORKING BIBLIOGRAPHY

Keep a list of every printed item you find mentioned that seems worth examining. Later, this will be the basis for the list of your sources that must appear at the end of your paper.

With a good supply of index cards, go back to the catalog and the periodical indexes. The overview acquired by surveying encyclopedias and library resources will help you recognize what may prove useful, as may the titles of the works. For every entry that looks promising, **take down *all* the information you need to find it in the library,** using one card for each item. If you are unsure about the value of an item, make a card for it anyway. It is better to discard items later than to miss a good one.

The information that you need about **each book** includes the library call number for locating it later in the stacks, the full name of the author (last name first, for easy alphabetizing), and the title (underlined because it is a book). Also record the publisher, date and place of publication, and any other information that the catalog gives, such as an editor, translator, or edition other than the first. You will need all this for your final bibliography. A typical card will look like this:

```
                                    PR
                                   13. B8
  Crutwell, Patrick                no.191

  The English Sonnet

  London: Longman, 1966
```

The information you need about periodical articles is slightly different. For **each article,** give the author, with last name first, as before (if the article is anonymous, leave blank the line where the author's name would regularly go and alphabetize the card by the article title instead), the article title (in quotation marks), the title of the periodical (underlined), the volume and issue numbers (if it is not a weekly or monthly periodical), the full date of the issue that contains the article, and the first and last page numbers of the entire article.

There are two kinds of source material: **primary** and **secondary**. If your topic is a particular company's chance for future success, then any information issued by the company and any statements made by its officials, either oral or written, are primary sources. Information and opinions of writers discussing the company in books and periodical articles are secondary. But if your topic is an evaluation of the accuracy of the forecasts about the company made by financial analysts, then their opinions become primary sources; secondary sources for such a study would be other analysts' opinions of their opinions.

Use primary sources wherever possible—information "straight from the horse's mouth." Use secondary sources for general background and to show how much you agree or disagree with others who have written on the subject. If your topic is a biographical study of your grandmother and her struggles as a housewife in the Depression of the 1930s, your chief source of information will be what she and any of her contemporaries can tell you (primary evidence) and economic reports published at that time (primary). For background material you should rely on facts and opinions about the period given in books and articles by respected authorities (secondary), especially the more recent ones, since those writers will have the benefit of greater perspective.

Examine all of your sources with a sharply critical eye. When you begin your project, you may not know which writers are respected, well-known authorities; which are respectable though little known; and which are questionable. Your ability to judge will grow as your familiarity with the subject grows. Watch for any signs of biased opinions, illogical deductions, unsupported claims, or sweeping generalizations in your secondary sources. What sources do the writers use? What other writers on the subject do they refer to as authoritative? If you doubt the value of a book, check what reviewers have written in *Book Review Digest* and in scholarly journals, and ask your instructor.

NOTE: Remember that articles in newspapers and popular magazines usually serve as introductions to a subject, providing up-to-the-minute information. For more thorough analysis, you must go to specialized magazines, scholarly journals, and books. Always check the most recent publications as well as the famous and basic ones.

51 ◆ RESEARCHING THE TOPIC

Begin serious reading and note-taking when you have listed on your index cards all the promising materials on your subject that are available in the library.

1. Skim through all the available material to select what you will look at carefully later. Remember that the preface to a book often indicates if it is likely to include anything you need. The table of contents is even more useful; its chapter headings may direct you quickly to the sections that you need. Learn to *skim*—to glance rapidly through material in search of the significant. Eliminating items that now seem unsuitable, you can settle down to a thorough reading of what seems really worthwhile.

2. Take accurate notes, while reading, of any facts and opinions that you may wish to quote or refer to in your paper. Good notes will form the basis of your paper and help you to organize it. As you form a general picture of your subject, decide on your main headings and subheadings and use these on your note cards. Remember that you can add fresh subheadings or change a note from one heading to another at any time. For example, for a biographical study of your grandmother, you might subdivide a preliminary heading "education" into "education—elementary school" and "education—high school" or into "education—formal" and "education—practical."

3. Write your reading notes on cards. Limit each card to a single note on a single topic taken from a single source and give each a classifying heading. Then, instead of a hodgepodge, you will eventually have a mass of material that you can arrange easily under common headings and will be able to rearrange and discard items without disturbing the rest. The flexibility of such notes makes selecting and organizing the material relatively simple.

NOTE: Write on only one side of each card so that you can see the whole note at a glance. If a note is too long for one card, continue it on a second card, marking it with the source and "card 2" so that you will know instantly where it belongs.

4. Record the exact source of the borrowed material on each note card. Your finished work must show the book or article from which the words or idea came *and* the page number. For each note, jot down all page numbers on which you found the information. Use the author's last name or a short form of the title to identify the source as briefly as possible, but be specific enough to avoid any confusion with another author or work with a similar name.

5. Copy accurately any material you wish to quote. Most of your notes will be summaries; they will give in your own words the gist of what you have read. But in your paper you may wish to support important points with the exact words of your source. Copy them *precisely* as they appear in the original—even if they contain errors in fact or writing. Enclose each one in clear quotation marks so that later you will recognize at a glance that they are quotations. Photocopy any material of more than four or five lines to ensure accuracy. Although you may use only a few of these quotations, remember that you can summarize a quotation later, but you cannot turn a summary back into a quotation unless you have the exact words in front of you.

6. Learn to combine reading and note-taking. If you read a long article without taking notes as you read, you will almost certainly have to reread parts of the article, but if you pause too often to make notes, many of your notes will repeat each other. How much to read before taking notes depends on the nature of the material and the strength of your memory.

IMPORTANT: Be prepared to add to your bibliography as you go along. You may discover some of your best material through references and bibliographies that appear in your reading.

When you have gathered most of what you think will be your important material—by reading, interviewing, conducting a survey, performing an experiment, and doing whatever else is necessary for your project—begin composing your paper. For detailed advice on composing, review **39** and **40,** and read the logs kept by the student writers while they worked on the research papers given as samples in **53a** and **b.**

52 ◆ DOCUMENTING SOURCES: GENERAL ADVICE

You must document all your sources for your research paper. The chief support for your opinions will, of course, be the facts you have gathered and the opinions of others that you quote, paraphrase, or summarize. Whenever you use facts or opinions that can in any way be considered the property of someone else and whenever you quote the words written or spoken by someone else, you must give full credit to your sources by documenting them. Failure to do so is *plagiarism*—a form of theft that is legally punishable as a crime.

You need not give sources for well-known facts mentioned by many writers, such as the date of the signing of the Declaration of Independence, or for widely held opinions, such as that Michelangelo was a great painter. If, however, you use another writer's exact words to present such facts or opinions, you must acknowledge that writer as your source, no matter how familiar the facts or opinions are. Conversely, if you present a little-known fact or opinion, even in wording that is entirely your own, you should give your source. Notice how the writers of the sample research papers in **53a** and **b** support their opinions by drawing on other writers and how they document their sources. Any reader who wishes to check their accuracy or read more on their topics can quickly learn from their documentation exactly which books and essays they consulted *and* the precise pages on which they found material.

Two systems for documenting the printed sources of scholarly writing are widely used: that of the Modern Language Association, or MLA, and that of the American Psychological Association, or APA. The MLA style was created for research in the humanities, but it is also used to document works, regardless of subject matter, directed to the general reader. In its latest version, the MLA style is similar to the APA style, which is used, with minor variations, for research in the social and laboratory sciences. Ask your instructor which style you should use.

Whatever the style, you must make an alphabetized

list of all the sources you mention in your paper, whether they are quotations, paraphrases, summaries, or direct references. This list is often simply called a bibliography, a term which originally meant "a description of books" but now usually covers any printed materials, such as articles in magazines and newspapers. The MLA recommends *Works Cited* as the heading for this list, even if it includes materials that have contributed ideas but are not specifically cited in your paper. The APA recommends *Reference List* as the heading. **Reminder: Alphabetize all entries in the *Works Cited* or *Reference List* sections according to the first word of each entry.**

52a Documenting in the MLA style

If your instructor asks you to use the MLA style, follow the forms given in this section. Pay close attention to the kinds of information given in each example and the arrangement, punctuation, and use of abbreviations. The MLA style is described in complete detail in the *MLA Handbook* (1984) and the *MLA Style Manual* (1985).

52a(1) Source list: MLA style

In the MLA style, the alphabetized list of sources is called the **Works Cited**, but it should include all the sources used by the writer. Because your entries will be arranged in alphabetical order, the author's last name appears first in each entry in the list, followed by a comma and whatever form of first name or initials the author uses.

Alphabetize unsigned works by title, always ignoring *A*, *An*, and *The*. Use a period after each of the three main divisions of each entry: (1) the author's name, (2) the title of the work, and (3) the publication data, which for books includes the place of publication, the name of the publisher, and the date of publication. Use periods also after any additional information, such as the edition or number of volumes, that comes between the title and the publication data. Use parentheses only around a year that is preceded by a volume number in a periodical entry.

Underline (italicize) the title of each book and periodical. Enclose the title of each shorter work in quotation marks, and end the entry for it with inclusive page numbers to show all the pages it occupies in the larger work. If the book title you are citing contains a title normally enclosed in quotation marks, such as that of a poem or essay, keep the quotation marks and underline the entire title. If a book title contains a title normally underlined, such as the title of another book or periodical, do not underline the shorter title or set it off in quotation marks.

Use reverse paragraph indentation: begin each entry at the left margin; if the entry requires more than one line, indent each additional line of the entry five spaces from the left margin. The MLA recommends using short forms for the names of publishers, for example "Harcourt" for "Harcourt Brace Jovanovich, Inc." and "Yale UP" for "Yale University Press." If more than one city of publication is listed, give only the first. If readers might not recognize the place of publication or might confuse it with another of the same name, add an abbreviation of the name of the state or country, for example, "FL" (postal or ZIP code abbreviation) for "Florida" or "Eng." for "England."

The following examples, presented in the MLA style, include many types of sources to suggest how wide the field of research can be and to encourage you to explore new areas. Although the examples are numbered here for convenience in class discussion, in your own source list, alphabetize the entries; do *not* number them.

In each example, notice what pieces of information are given, the sequence in which the pieces appear, the punctuation that sets them off from each other, and any use of abbreviations.

1. **The first edition of a book by one author** (this requires only the most basic information—the author's name, the title of the book, and the publication data):

Carson, Rachel. <u>The Sea Around Us</u>. New

    York: Oxford UP, 1950.

2. **Another book by the same author** (instead of repeating the author's name, type three hyphens or draw an equivalent line to begin the entry. List each author's works either chronologically by publication date or alphabetically by title; whichever you choose, use the same method throughout your bibliography):

---. <u>Under the Sea Wind</u>. New York: Oxford

    UP, 1941.

3. **A book by two or more authors** (only the first author's name is in reverse order because the book will be alphabetized by that, no matter how many other authors' names are listed):

Farb, Peter, and George Armelagos. <u>Consuming</u>

<u>Passions: The Anthropology of Eating</u>.

Boston: Houghton, 1980.

4. **A book printed in two or more volumes** (give the number of volumes between the title and the publication data):

Powys, John Cowper. <u>Owen Glendower</u>. 2 vols.

New York: Simon, 1940.

5. **A book that has been reprinted** (give the year of the first edition immediately after the title):

Herriot, James. <u>All Creatures Great and</u>

<u>Small</u>. 1972. New York: Bantam, 1973.

6. **A later edition revised by the author** (use the latest edition unless another edition is significant in your research):

Robertson, J. M. <u>A History of Freethought</u>.

4th ed., revised and expanded. London:

Watts, 1936.

7. **A specially edited edition of an author's work:**

Whitman, Walt. <u>Leaves of Grass</u>. Ed. Sculley

Bradley and Harold W. Blodgett. New

York: Norton, 1978.

8. A letter published in a collection:

Hazlitt, William.   "To William Godwin."   5

    Jan. 1806.   Letter 23 in The Letters of

    William Hazlitt.   Ed. Herschel Moreland

    Sikes, assisted by Willard Hallam Bonner

    and Gerald Lahey.   New York: New York UP,

    1978. 88-89.

9. A work translated from another language:

Hesse, Hermann.   Demian.   Trans. Michael

    Roloff and Michael Lebeck.   New York:

    Harper, 1965.

10. An essay, poem, or other short work in an edited book:

Schorer, Mark.   "The Humiliation of Emma

    Woodhouse."   Jane Austen: A Collection of

    Critical Essays, Ed. Ian Watt.   Englewood

    Cliffs: Prentice, 1963.   98-111.

NOTE: Do not underline or enclose in quotation marks the titles of short poems known only by their form and a number:

Millay, Edna St. Vincent.   Sonnet 47.   Fatal

    Interview.   New York: Harper, 1931.   47.

11. **An introduction or a preface by another writer or by an editor** (use the page numbering method of the original; in this example, the inclusive page numbers of the introduction are in lowercase Roman numerals because those were used in the original):

Henley, W. E. "Robert Burns: Life, Genius,

Achievement." The Complete Poetical

Works of Robert Burns. By Robert Burns.

Boston: Houghton, 1897. xiii-lxvi.

12. **An article in an encyclopedia** (some encyclopedias give only the author's initials at the end of each article, but an index elsewhere in the set lists the author's full name. With well-known encyclopedias, and also with dictionaries, you may omit the place of publication and the name of the publisher; you may also omit the page numbers since the articles are arranged alphabetically by title. You must, however, give either the number of the edition or the date of publication because other editions may not contain the same article; always use the latest edition of an encyclopedia):

McLeod, W. H. "Nanak." Encyclopedia

Britannica: Macropaedia, 1984 ed.

13. **An article in a monthly or weekly periodical in which the pages are numbered separately for each issue** (give the full date, abbreviating the names of all months except May, June, and July):

Eltis, Walter. "The Borrowing Fallacy."

> Encounter Nov. 1986: 12-21.

14. An article in a periodical that numbers pages consecutively through all the issues of each year (give the volume number after the title of the periodical):

Wayne, Valerie. "Refashioning the Shrew."

> Shakespeare Survey 17 (1985): 159-187.

15. An article in a newspaper (give the edition, section number, date, and page number; if the article continues on another page, add a plus mark to the number of the page on which it begins):

Boyd, Gerald M. "Reagan Facing a Pivotal

> Week on Iran Scandal." The New York
>
> Times 23 Feb. 1987, late ed.: A1+.

16. An unsigned article in a periodical of any kind:

"A Guide to Color TVs." Consumer Reports

> Mar. 1987: 142-153.

17. A pamphlet (follow the forms used in examples 1 through 6 for books. In this example, the corporation issuing the pamphlet is both author and publisher, a common practice. No publication date is given, as indicated by *n.d.*, the abbreviation for *no date*):

Fidata Trust Company.   <u>Unitholder Reference</u>

   <u>Handbook</u>.   New York: Fidata Trust

   Company, n.d.

18. **A government document** (government publications
use many abbreviations; in this example, *Cong.*
stands for "Congressional" and "Congress," *GPO* for
"Government Printing Office," and *sess.* for "ses-
sions"):

United States. Cong. Joint Committee on the

   Investigation of the Pearl Harbor Attack.

   Hearings. 79th Cong., 1st and 2nd sess.

   32 vols.   Washington: GPO, 1946.

19. **A published abstract of a dissertation** (an abstract is
a summary, usually by the author, used by readers as
a quick means of locating relevant material; abstracts
of doctoral dissertations are published in *Dissertation
Abstracts International* [abbreviated as *DAI;* before
1969, titled *Dissertation Abstracts,* or *DA*], which
appears in three parts with page numbers marked *A*
for humanities, *B* for sciences, and *C* for foreign dissertations):

Franzak, Frank Joseph.   "The Impact of

   Regulation on the Distilled Spirits

   Industry: A Structural Equation

   Analysis."   <u>DAI</u> 46 (1985): 205-A.   U of

   Maryland.

20. An unpublished Ph.D. dissertation:

Worthington, Mabel Parker. "Don Juan: Theme
and Development in the Nineteenth
Century." Diss. Columbia U, 1953.

21. An unpublished letter in a collection:

Benton, Thomas Hart. Letter to Charles
Fremont. 22 June 1847. John Charles
Fremont Papers. Southwest Museum
Library, Los Angeles.

22. An unpublished letter that you yourself received:

Porter, Harriet. Letter to the author. 15
Oct. 1988.

23. An interview on a public broadcast:

Atwood, Margaret. Interview by Sherrye
Henry. WOR Radio, New York. 10 Feb.
1986.

24. A personal interview you yourself conducted:

Porter, Harriet. Personal interview. 24
Oct. 1988.

25. A lecture, speech, or address that you heard:

Heilbrun, Carolyn.   Presidential address.

    General session.   MLA Convention,

    Chicago.   28 Dec. 1985.

26. Unpublished raw data from research:

"Parking problems: Should the college enlarge

    student parking space?"   Opinion survey

    conducted by David Benson at the West

    Campus lot and Jane Phillips at the South

    Campus lot, Mayfield College, Smithtown

    OH, 8:00 to 10:00 a.m., 30 Jan. 1988.

27. A commercially available recording (begin with the name you wish to emphasize—the composer, the conductor, the soloist, or the band or orchestra; include the title, performers, conductor, catalog number, and year of issue; underline record titles, but do not underline or place quotation marks around titles of musical works known only by form, number, and key):

a.   an LP recording:

Beethoven, Ludwig van.   Symphony no. 7 in A,

    op. 92.   Cond. Herbert von Karajan.

    Vienna Philharmonic Orch.   London, STS

    15107, 1966.

Streisand, Barbra. People. Cond. Peter Matz
and Ray Ellis. Columbia, CS 9015, 1964.

b. a compact disk recording:

Mozart, Wolfgang Amadeus. The Horn
Concertos. With Hermann Baumann, horn
soloist. Cond. Pinchas Zukerman. St.
Paul Chamber Orchestra. Philips, 412
737-2, 1985. Digital compact disk.

c. an audiocassette:

Vaughan, Sarah. Songs of the Beatles.
Audiotape. Atlantic, CS 16037, 1981.

d. radio and television broadcasts:

"Goddess of the Earth, The." Narr. and writ.
James Lovelock. Nova. PBS. WNET,
Newark. 4 Feb. 1986.

Turandot. By Giacomo Puccini. With Ghena
Dimitrova, Leona Mitchell, Nicola
Martinucci, and Franco de Grandis. Cond.
Nello Santi. Metropolitan Opera.
Texaco-Metropolitan Radio Network. WGAU,
Athens, GA. 13 Feb. 1988.

28. Printed material accompanying a recording (give the author's name, the title if there is one, and a brief description, such as "jacket notes" or "libretto"):

Baumann, Hermann. Untitled pamphlet. Trans.
    Miriam Verhey-Lewis. Cond. Pinchas
    Zukerman. St. Paul Chamber orchestra.
    Horn Concertos by Wolfgang Amadeus
    Mozart. Philips, 412 737-2, 1985.
    Digital compact disk.

29. Films and videotapes (begin with the name you wish to emphasize—the whole work, a performer, the director or scriptwriter):

Color Purple, The. Dir. Steven Spielberg.
    With Whoopi Goldberg. Warner Bros.,
    1985.

Wilson, Ryall, dir. Creation vs. Evolution:
    "Battle of the Classroom".
    Videocassette. PBS Video, 1982. 58 min.

30. Live performances of drama, music, or dance (begin with the name you wish to emphasize, as with recordings and films):

Jumpers. By Tom Stoppard. Dir. Peter Wood.
    With Paul Eddington, Felicity Kendal, and
    Simon Cadell. Aldwych Theatre, London.
    3 Oct. 1985.

Ewing, Maria, soprano. Carmen by Georges
    Bizet. With Catherine Malfitano, Plácido
    Domingo, and Michael Devlin.
    Metropolitan Opera, New York. 10 Mar.
    1986.

Atlanta Ballet. Return Trip to Tango. Chor.
    Joan Finkelstein. With Maiqui Manosa,
    Matthew Wright, and Jill Murphy. Score
    by Michael Sahl based on Argentine
    tangos. Whitman Hall, Brooklyn College,
    New York. 1 Feb. 1986.

31. **Works of art** (begin with the artist's name, and give
the name of the institution where the work may be
found):

Botticelli, Sandro. The Birth of Venus.
    Uffizi Gallery, Florence.

32. **Computer software** (for a computer program, give the author's name, if known; the title, underlined; the descriptive label "computer software"; the distributor; and the date. Place a period after each of these items except the name of the distributor, which should be followed by a comma. End the entry by noting any user requirements—the type of computer, the amount of memory, and the operating system):

<u>Word Perfect</u>. Version 5. Computer software.

Satellite Software International, 1988.

256K. DOS 2.0 or higher.

33. **Legal references** (the standard forms for referring to legal documents and court cases are complex and include special terms and abbreviations. For more detailed information on legal references, consult *A Uniform System of Citation* [Cambridge: Harvard Law Review Association]. These examples illustrate several common types. Notice that the names of the cases and statutes are not underlined or enclosed in quotation marks. Follow that practice in your list of works cited; in the text of your paper, underline the name of a case but not of a law):

a. **a court case at trial level in a state court:**

Abrams v. Love Canal Area Revitalization

Agency, 132 Misc. #2d 232, 503 N.Y.S. 2d

507 (1986).

This refers to the case of Abrams, the plaintiff, against the Love Canal Area Revitalization Agency, which is number 132 in the *Miscellaneous Reporter,* second set, beginning on page 232; it is also in volume 503 of the *New York Supplement,* second series, page 507; the case was decided in 1986.

b.   a federal district court opinion:

Washington Federal Sav. & Loan Assoc. v.

Federal Home Loan Bank Bd., 526 F. Supp.

343 (N.D. Ohio 1981).

This court opinion on the case of the Washington Federal Savings and Loan Association, plaintiff, against the Federal Home Loan Bank Board is in volume 526 of the *Federal Supplement,* beginning on page 343, and was tried in the federal district court for the Northern District of Ohio in 1981.

c.   a case appealed to the U.S. Supreme Court:

United States v. Nixon, 418 U.S. 683 (1974).

This case appears in volume 148 of *United States Reports,* page 683, in 1974.

d.   a statute in a state code:

Subway Loitering Act, N.Y. PENAL LAW

§240.35(7) (McKinney 1980).

This statute appears in *New York Penal Law,* subsection 240 of section 35, part 7, published by McKinney in 1980.

e.   a statute in a federal code:

```
Racketeer Influenced and Corrupt Organization
    Act §901(a), 18 U.S.C. 1962 (1970).
```

This statute appears in section 901, subsection *a* in title 18 of the *United States Code,* section 1962, and was codified in 1970.

52a (2) Quotations and source notes: MLA style

Follow MLA conventions for quotations of prose and poetry, and for notes in your text that identify your sources. Since you will identify all your sources fully in your list of works cited, the information you give in the text of your paper can be brief.

(a) Long prose quotations   Set a long quotation, one of more than four typed lines, in a block indented ten spaces from your left margin. If you are quoting a single paragraph or less, do not indent the first line. If you are quoting two or more paragraphs, indent the first line of each an additional three spaces. If, however, the first sentence you quote does not begin a paragraph in your source, do not indent it, but do indent the first sentence of any subsequent paragraph in the quotation. At the end, two spaces after the final punctuation mark, enclose in parentheses the author's last name, if it does not introduce the quotation, and the page numbers of the source.

Example

A source note in your text would look like this:

In 1936, the editors for the yearbook of the Harvard Medical School sent personal questionnaires to graduates from 1927, 1917, and 1907, asking their opinions on their postgraduate training and, briefly, about their current income. The results were surprising:

> Most of the papers neglected the business about postgraduate training and concentrated on the money questions. The average income of the ten-year graduates was around $3500; $7500 for the twenty-year people. One man, a urologist, reported an income of $50,000, but he was an anomaly; all the rest made, by the standards of 1937, respectable but very modest sums of money.

The space at the bottom of the page had comments on this matter, mostly giving the same sort of advice: medicine

```
is the best of professions was the
general drift, but not a good way to make
money.  If you could manage to do so, you
should marry a rich wife. (Thomas 5-6)
```

If you identify the author in your introduction to the quotation, give only the page numbers in parentheses.

NOTE: This work would appear in your <u>Works Cited</u> as:

```
Thomas, Lewis.  The Youngest Science: Notes
    of a Medicine-Watcher.  New York: Viking,
    1983.
```

If you include two or more works by the same author in your list of works cited, give the appropriate title or a shortened form of it each time you make a specific reference to one of the works or quote from it. If, for example, you quoted from both books by Rachel Carson mentioned in **52a.1** and did not give her name or the titles of the books in introducing the quotations, your notes would look like these:

```
(Carson, The Sea 22)
(Carson, Under the Sea 84)
```

Other types of works documented in **52a.1** would require notes like these in the text of your paper:

A book with more than one volume:

```
(Powys, Glendower 2:185)
```

An essay or other short work:

```
(Eltis, "Fallacy" 18)
```

An unsigned short work of any kind:

```
("Guide to Color TVs" 144)
```

If a work has three or more authors, you may shorten the note by giving the surname of only the first, following it with *et al.,* an abbreviation of the Latin phrase *et alii,* meaning "and others." If two authors have the same surname, distinguish between them in your notes by giving their first initials as well.

(b) Short prose quotations   Enclose a short quotation, one of four typed lines or less, in quotation marks, incorporate it in a sentence or paragraph of your own, and give the identifying information in parentheses after the closing quotation mark. The following examples use a sentence from *The Youngest Science: Notes of a Medicine-Watcher,* by Lewis Thomas, documented earlier.

Examples

1.   A short quotation with a formal introduction:

```
We often marvel at scientific discoveries,

forgetting that hard work lies behind most of

them: "In real life, research is dependent on

the human capacity for making predictions

that are wrong, and on the even more human
```

gift for bouncing back to try again" (Thomas 82).

2.   A short quotation with an informal introduction:

Although we often forget the fact, "in real life, research is dependent on the human capacity for making predictions that are wrong, and on the even more human gift for bouncing back to try again" (Thomas 82).

3.   A short quotation with a comment inserted in it:

"In real life," although we often forget the fact, "research is dependent on the human capacity for making predictions that are wrong, and on the even more human gift for bouncing back to try again" (Thomas 82).

4.   A short quotation with the author's name inserted in it:

"In real life," Lewis Thomas points out, "research is dependent on the human capacity for making predictions that are wrong, and on the even more human gift for bouncing back to try again" (82).

(c) Long quotations of poetry   Present a long quotation from a poem—four complete lines or more—in a block indented ten spaces from your left margin. At the end of the last quoted line, two spaces after the final punctuation mark, enclose in parentheses the author's last name if it does not introduce the quotation and the page numbers of the source.

Example   A source note in your text would look like this:

In the twentieth century many American poets developed new verse forms, but some continued to use traditional meter and rhyme, as in this sonnet by a writer who became popular in the 1920s.   It begins with this quatrain:

> Loving you less than life, a little
>   less
> Than bitter-sweet upon a broken
>   wall
> Or brush-wood smoke in autumn, I
>   confess
> I cannot swear I love you not at
>   all.   (Millay 65)

381

If the source information is too long to fit easily on the final line, place it on the line below, close to the right hand margin.

NOTE: This work would appear in your **Works Cited** as:

```
Millay, Edna St. Vincent.  Sonnet XVII.  The
     Harp-Weaver and Other Poems.  New York:
     Harper, 1923.  65.
```

If you begin a long quotation after the first word in a line of poetry or end it before the last word in a line, indicate the fact by leaving an appropriate space blank:

```
The writer admits that her emotions are
confused:

                              I confess
     I cannot swear I love you not at
          all.
     For there is that about you in this
          light--
     A yellow darkness, sinister of
          rain--
     Which sturdily recalls my stubborn
          sight
     To dwell on you.  (Millay 65)
```

(d) Short quotations of poetry   If you quote only one line or less, incorporate it in a sentence of your own and give the identifying information in parentheses after the closing quotation mark, as you would with a short quotation of prose:

```
A poem written in the 1920s and beginning
"Loving you less than life" (Millay 65) is in
the form of a traditional sonnet.
```

If you quote more than one line but less than four, you may present them as a block or you may incorporate them in your own sentence or paragraph, indicating the end of each line within the quotation by a slash with a space on each side (/):

```
A poem written in the 1920s and beginning
"Loving you less than life, a little less /
Than bitter-sweet upon a broken wall / Or
brush-wood smoke in autumn" (Millay 65) is in
the form of a traditional English sonnet.
```

(e) Quotations of well-known poetry or prose   If you are quoting from a work that has been reprinted in many different editions—such as the Bible, a play by Shakespeare, a novel by Dickens, or Lincoln's Gettysburg Address—your list of works cited should include full information on the edition that you used. In the text of your paper, however, such information as chapter and verse number, or act, scene, and line number will be more helpful to your readers than page numbers because they can then find the material easily in any edition they have at hand.

If you make a specific reference to a passage in the Bible or quote from it, give the name of the book, its number, if any, and the appropriate chapter and verse numbers. You may make the identification part of your sentence or present it in abbreviated form in a note enclosed in parentheses:

```
In chapter 41, verse 15, of Genesis, Pharaoh
asks Joseph to interpret a dream.
```

or

```
Pharaoh asks Joseph to interpret a dream
(Gen. 41.15).
```

```
In verses 19 through 27 of the first chapter
of the second book of Samuel, David expresses
his grief over the deaths of Saul and
Jonathan.
```

or

```
David expresses his grief over the deaths of
Saul and Jonathan (2 Sam. 1.19-27).
```

NOTE: Do not underline (italicize) the title of the Bible or the titles of any of the books of the Bible.

You have a similar choice of methods for identifying references to a well-known play or long poem:

```
In lines 43 through 44 of the second scene
in Act 2 of Romeo and Juliet, Juliet
asks, "What's in a name? That which we call a
rose / By any other name would smell as
sweet."
```

or

```
Juliet asks, "What's in a name? That which we
call a rose / By any other name would smell
as sweet" (Rom. 2.2.43-44).
```

```
In lines 288 through 324 of the fourth book
of Paradise Lost, Milton describes Satan's
astonishment when he first sees Adam and Eve.
```

or

```
Milton describes Satan's astonishment when he
first sees Adam and Eve (PL 4.288-324).
```

With well-known novels and other prose works, identify your reference or quotation with the appropriate page number in the edition you used, but also give the chapter or section number that will help your readers find the material in other editions:

```
In chapter 21 of Bleak House, Dickens calls
Mr. Smallweed's great-grandfather "a
horny-skinned, two-legged, money-getting
species of spider who spun webs to catch
unwary flies" (268).
```
or
```
In Bleak House, Dickens calls Mr. Smallweed's
great-grandfather "a horny-skinned,
two-legged, money-getting species of spider
who spun webs to catch unwary flies" (268;
ch. 21).
```

NOTE: For the use of quotation marks, capitalization, and punctuation with quotations, see **23**.

52a (3) Quoting accurately: omissions and additions

Take special care to quote the original material accurately. If you modernize spelling, mention the fact in your paper. In quoting poetry, copy the original exactly, including capitalization and line division. Many modern poets do not capitalize the first letter of each line, and some arrange their words on the page to create visual patterns. For example, notice the arrangement of the following poem by Don R. Lee from his book *We Walk the Way of the New World* (Detroit: Broadside, 1970):

> Change is Not Always Progress
> (for Africa & Africans)
>
> Africa.
>
> don't let them
> steal
> your face   or
> take your circles
> and make them squares.
>
> don't let them
> steel
> your body   as to put
> 100 stories of concrete on you
> so that you
>   arrogantly
>
> scrape
> the
>
> sky.

Omissions from quotations   If parts of what you wish to quote are not relevant to your point, you may omit them, provided that the omission will not change the meaning of the original in any way. Indicate such omissions with three spaced periods (. . .) called ellipsis points (from Greek *elleipsis* = an omission). For example, in a paper on American history, you might wish to quote part of these sentences from Lincoln's Gettysburg Address:

```
We are now engaged in a great civil war,

testing whether that nation, or any nation so
```

```
conceived and so dedicated, can long endure.
We are met on a great battlefield of that
war.
```

The quotation, with several words omitted, might look like this when fitted into your own sentence:

```
Lincoln pointed out that the war would show
if the "nation, or any nation . . . so
dedicated, can long endure."
```

If you omit the final words of a sentence within a quoted passage, place the period immediately after the last quoted word and follow it with the ellipsis points, leaving two spaces before the next sentence:

```
Lincoln said that "We are now engaged in a
great civil war. . . .  We are met on a
battlefield of that war."
```

Place any other punctuation mark ending a quotation before or after the ellipsis points according to the relation of the omitted words to the rest of the sentence:

```
"We are now engaged in a great civil war,"
Lincoln said, "testing whether that nation,
or any nation . . . , can long endure."
```

```
Lincoln said, "We are now engaged in a great

civil war, testing whether that nation, . . .

so conceived and so dedicated, can long

endure."
```

Sometimes, because of the grammatical construction, none of the original punctuation may be needed where the words are omitted:

```
Lincoln said, "We are now engaged in a great

civil war, testing whether that nation . . .

can long endure."
```

Additions to quotations   If you add an explanation, identification, or correction to a quotation, insert it in brackets immediately after the word or word group that requires it:

```
Lincoln said, "The world will little note,

nor long remember, what we say here, but it

can never forget what they [the soldiers who

fought in the Civil War] did here."
```

If the quotation contains an obvious error, one not needing explanation, show that you recognize it by following it immediately with *sic* (from Latin = just so, thus) enclosed in brackets:

```
Martha Washington, whose spelling was often

careless, wrote her brother-in-law that

campaign problems "made the pore [sic]

General so unhappy that it distressed me

exceedingly."
```

NOTE: In formal usage *sic* used to be underlined (italicized) as a foreign word, but most scholarly journals no longer follow this practice. Ask your instructors what they prefer.

52a (4) Paraphrases and summaries

Quote a passage to support, illustrate, or explain a point if the exact wording is important or particularly clear and forceful. **Paraphrase** a passage if readers may have trouble interpreting it but you want them to know the details. **Summarize** a passage if the precise wording and details are not essential but you want readers to have the central thought.

Do not enclose a paraphrase or summary in quotation marks or present it in a block. Although the material comes from another writer, the words are yours. At the end, acknowledge your source in a note enclosed in parentheses giving the same information that you would give if you had quoted the original.

Quotation:

```
A famous definition of true love begins by

telling us what it is not:
```

> Love is not love
> Which alters when it alteration
> finds,
> Or bends with the remover to
> remove:
> O, no! it is an ever-fixed mark,
> That looks on tempests and is never
> shaken.
>
> (Shakespeare, Sonnet 116)

Paraphrase:

A famous definition of true love claims that it is not a love that changes when something changes in the loved one or that gives in to someone who tries to end the love. No, true love is a guide that is always firm and that can observe troubles without being weakened (Shakespeare, Sonnet 116).

Summary:

A famous definition of true love claims that it does not change, no matter how many changes and difficulties it must face (Shakespeare, Sonnet 116).

52b Documenting in the APA style

If your instructor asks you to use the APA style, follow the forms given in this section. Pay close attention to the kinds of information given in each example and the arrangement, punctuation, and use of abbreviations. The APA style is described in complete detail in the *Publication Manual of the American Psychological Association* (1983).

52b(1) Source list: APA style

In the APA style, the alphabetized list of sources is called the **Reference List** and includes only sources directly referred to by the writer. The information and arrangement of each entry are similar to the MLA style, with these important differences:

1. Leave only one blank space after all marks of punctuation.
2. Give only the initials of the authors' first names.
3. Give the date of publication in parentheses immediately after the authors' names.
4. Capitalize only the first letter of the first word in the titles and subtitles of articles, books, and chapters of books. With all proper names, however, including those of periodicals, capitalize the first letters of words in conventional fashion.
5. Underline (italicize) book and periodical titles and volume numbers of periodicals.

6. Do not enclose article titles in quotation marks.
7. Omit such terms as "Publishers" and "Co." in publishers' names, but give significant words in full—"Yale University Press," not "Yale UP," and "Harcourt Brace Jovanovich," not "Harcourt."
8. Give the names of the months in full—"August," not "Aug."
9. Give inclusive page numbers for essays and articles. Use "p." (page) or "pp." (pages) with page numbers of newspapers and magazines but not with page numbers of scholarly journals.
10. Begin each entry at the left margin as in the MLA style, but indent subsequent lines only three spaces.

The following examples of APA style present many of the sources given earlier in the MLA style, numbered in the same sequence for easy comparison. Do **not** number your reference list.

1. The first edition of a book by a single author:

Carson, R. (1950). <u>The sea around us</u>. New
    York: Oxford University Press.

2. Two or more works by the same author (list them in chronological order according to their publication dates and repeat the author's name):

Carson, R. (1941). <u>Under the sea wind</u>. New
    York: Oxford University Press.

Carson, R. (1950). The sea around us. New

York: Oxford University Press.

3. **A book by two or more authors** (list the authors in the order of the title page, giving last names first; use an ampersand [&] to connect the last author's name to the rest):

Farb, P. & Armelagos, G. (1950). Consuming

passions: The anthropology of eating.

Boston: Houghton Mifflin.

4. **A book printed in two or more volumes:**

Powys, J. C. (1940). Owen Glendower (Vols.

1-2). New York: Simon & Schuster.

5. **A book that has been reprinted:**

Herriot, J. (1973). All creatures great and

small. New York: Bantam. (Original work

published 1972)

6. **A later edition of a book revised by the author:**

Robertson, J. K. (1936). A history of

freethought (4th ed. rev.). London:

Watts. (Original work published 1899)

7. A specially edited edition of another author's work:

Dickens, C. (1972). <u>American notes</u> (J.
Whitley and A. Goldman, Eds.).
Harmondsworth, England: Penguin.
(Original work published 1842)

8. A letter published in a collection. (The APA *Publication Manual* does not give examples of this kind of source.)

9. A work translated into English from another language:

Hesse, H. (1965). <u>Demian</u> (M. Roloff & M.
Lebeck, Trans.). New York: Harper & Row.
(Original work published 1925)

10. An essay, poem, or short story published in an edited book:

Schorer, M. (1963). The humiliation of Emma
Woodhouse. In I. Watt (Ed.), <u>Jane
Austen: A collection of critical essays</u>
(pp. 98-111). Englewood Cliffs, NJ:
Prentice-Hall.

11. An introduction or preface by an editor or another writer:

Henley, W. E.   (1897).   Robert Burns: Life,

   genius, achievement.   In R. Burns, <u>The</u>

   <u>complete poetical works of Robert Burns</u>

   (pp. xiii-lxvi).   Boston: Houghton

   Mifflin.

12.   **An article in an encyclopedia.** (The APA *Publication Manual* does not give examples of this kind of source.)

13.   **An article in a monthly or weekly periodical in which the pages are numbered separately for each issue:**

Eltis, W.   (1986, November).   The borrowing

   fallacy.   <u>Encounter</u>, pp. 12-21.

14.   **An article in a periodical that numbers pages consecutively through all the issues of each year** (underline the volume number and omit "p." or "pp."):

Owen, C. A., Jr.   (1982).   The alternative

   reading of <u>The Canterbury Tales</u>.   <u>PMLA</u>,

   <u>97</u>, 237-250.

15.   **An article in a newspaper** (this example includes the section designation and two page numbers because the article was continued on a second page):

Boyd, G. M.   (1987, February 23).   Reagan

   facing a pivotal week on Iran scandal.

The New York Times, late edition, pp. Al,

14.

16. An unsigned article in a newspaper or magazine:

A Guide to Color TVs. (1987, March).

Consumer Reports, pp. 142-153.

17. A pamphlet (with one organization as both author and publisher):

T. Rowe Price New Era Fund. (1986). Annual

Report. Baltimore: Author.

18. A government document:

National Institute of Mental Health. (1982).

Television and behavior: Ten years of

scientific progress and implications for

the eighties (DHHS Publications No. ADM

82-1195). Washington, DC: U.S.

Government Printing Office.

19. A published abstract of a doctoral dissertation (if a microfilm copy is used, give the University Microfilms number):

Franzak, F. J. (1985). The impact of

regulation on the distilled spirits

industry: A structural equation analysis.

Dissertation Abstracts International, 46,

205-A. (University Microfilms No.

85-06,523)

20. An unpublished doctoral dissertation:

Worthington, M. P. (1953). Don Juan: Theme

and Development in the Nineteenth

Century. (Doctoral dissertation,

Columbia University, 1953). Dissertation

Abstracts, 13, 399.

21. An unpublished letter in a collection (the APA *Publication Manual* does not specifically cover such a source; if you use such material, give the name of the author, the date, the person to whom it was addressed, and its location):

Benton, T. H. (1847, June 22). Letter to

Charles Fremont. John Charles Fremont

Papers. Southwest Museum Library, Los

Angeles.

22, 23, 24, 25. An unpublished letter that you received; an interview on a public broadcast; a personal interview that you conducted; a lecture, speech, or address that you heard. Because such sources are not publicly available in recorded form, do not include them in a reference list that follows APA style. Cite them in parentheses only in the text of your paper; for example:

H. Porter (personal communication, October

    15, 1985).

26. Unpublished raw data from research (do not underline the topic; give a brief description of the material enclosed in brackets to indicate that it is not a title):

Benson, D. & Phillips, J. (1988). [Opinion

    survey on parking problems at Mayfield

    College, Smithtown, OH]. Unpublished raw

    data.

27. A commercially available recording (the APA *Publication Manual* only covers references to cassettes):

Vaughan, S. (Singer). (1981). <u>Songs of the</u>

    <u>Beatles</u> (Cassette Recording No. CS

    16037). New York: Atlantic Recording.

28. Printed material accompanying a recording. (The APA *Publication Manual* does not give examples of this kind of source.)

29. Films and videotapes (begin with the names of the originators or primary contributors in the order of their importance to your research, and specify the medium in brackets after title):

Spielberg, S. (Director) & Goldberg, W.

   (Performer). (1985). The color purple

   [Film]. Los Angeles: Warner Brothers.

30, 31. Live performances; works of art. Because such sources are not publicly available in recorded form, do not include them in a reference list that follows APA style. Identify them as fully as you can in the text of your paper.

32. Computer software (end with the information necessary for identification and retrieval, enclosed in parentheses):

Fernandes, F. D. (1972). Theoretical

   prediction of interference loading on

   aircraft stores: Part 1. Subsonic speeds

   [Computer program]. Pomona, CA: General

   Dynamics, Electro Dynamics Division.

   (National Aeronautics and Space

   Administration Report No. NASA

   CR-112065-1; Acquisition No. LAR-11249)

33. Legal references (follow the style presented in example 33 of **48a.1**, and consult *A Uniform System of Citation* [Cambridge: Harvard Law Review Association]).

52b (2) Quotations and source notes: APA style

The APA system for presenting and documenting quotations is similar to the MLA system, but some details are different. Set **long quotations** (40 or more words) in a block indented five spaces from the left margin, beginning with the first quoted line, whether or not it is the first line of a paragraph. Indent the first line of any subsequent paragraphs in the quotation an additional three spaces.

Introduce each long quotation with the author's last name, followed by the date of publication in parentheses. After whatever punctuation mark ends the quotation, give the page numbers of the original, enclosed in parentheses and followed by a period.

Example

A source note in your text would look like this:

In 1936, doctors who had graduated from the Harvard Medical School in 1927, 1917, and 1907 gave some surprising answers to a questionnaire. Thomas (1983) reports:

> The average income of the ten-year graduates was around $3500; $7500 for the twenty-year people. One man, a urologist, reported an income of $50,000, but he was an anomaly; all the rest made,

by the standards of 1937, respectable but
very modest sums of money (5-6).

NOTE: This work would appear in your **Reference List** as:

Thomas, L. (1983). <u>The youngest science:</u>
<u>Notes of a medicine-watcher</u>. New York:
Viking.

Incorporate **short quotations** (less than 40 words) in your own paragraph. Identify the source by either of these methods:

Examples

1. A short quotation without mention of the author's name:

In his reminiscences, a doctor mentioned
that, according to a questionnaire sent out
by the Harvard Medical School in 1936, "the
average income of the ten-year graduates was
around $3500" (Thomas, 1983, p. 5).

2. A short quotation with mention of the author's name:

In his reminiscences, Thomas (1983) mentions
that, according to a questionnaire sent out

by the Harvard Medical School in 1936, "the
average income of the ten-year graduates was
around $3500" (p. 5).

52b(3) Punctuation and mechanics in quotations: APA style

Certain features of the APA style are identical with
the MLA style. When quoting in APA style, follow MLA
style (52a.2–3) for ellipsis dots to mark omissions and
brackets to enclose additions. For the use of quotation
marks, capital and lowercase letters to begin quotations,
and punctuation following the last quoted word, see 23.

52c Content notes

Content notes serve a different purpose and are not
like notes documenting sources. Use a content note to
provide material that does not fit smoothly into the general style of your paper, such as a critical comment, an
explanation, a definition, or an illustrative anecdote. You
may place each note at the bottom of the page as a foot-
note, numbering it, and adding a matching number in
your text immediately after the material to which it refers.
Or you may, instead, place all such notes together at the
end of your paper as endnotes, just before your list of
sources (for examples, see the second sample research
paper, 53b). In either case, number the notes consecutively. If such a note requires documentation of its own,
give it in parentheses at the end of the note, applying

whichever system you use for your list of sources. Remember to include full documentation in your list of sources for any work referred to in a content note.

If you have only a few content notes, not more than one on any page, and if you present them as footnotes, you need not number them. Instead, place an asterisk at the beginning of the note and another in your text immediately after the material to which it refers.

52d Latin words and phrases in documenting

If you use scholarly sources published before the 1970s, you may find Latin words and phrases in footnotes and endnotes. Do not follow this practice in your own writing. The most common are:

loc. cit. Abbreviation for *loco citato,* meaning "in the place cited," referring to the same page in the same work documented in the preceding note.

op. cit. Abbreviation of *opere citato,* meaning "in the work cited," referring to a work cited earlier but not in the immediately preceding note. Usually followed by *p.* or *pp.* and the page number or numbers.

ibid. Abbreviation of *ibidem,* meaning "in the same place," referring, like a ditto mark, to the work documented in the immediately preceding note. Followed by *p.* or *pp.* and the page number or numbers if different from those in the preceding note.

supra Meaning "above," indicating that the topic, work, or writer concerned was mentioned a little earlier; often abbreviated as *sup.*

passim Meaning "scattered about" or "in different places," indicating that references to the topic, work, or writer can be found repeatedly in the chapters or between the pages whose numbers are cited.

cf. Abbreviation of *confer,* meaning "compare," referring readers to another part of the book for comparison.

53 ◆ SAMPLE RESEARCH PAPERS

Two examples of student research papers follow. After each paper is the student's personal description of doing the research and of the process of composing the paper. The difficulties they encountered and the solutions they found are typical of the problems of writing based on research and critical analysis.

As you read each paper, notice the following features:

1. The methods by which the student presents a thesis and develops support for it

2. The way the student uses notes in the text of the paper to document sources:
   a. The form of each note
   b. The placement of each note in the structure of a sentence
   c. The punctuation used before and after each note

3. The way the student quotes other writers:
   a. The placement of short quotations within the structure of the student's own sentences

    b. The punctuation before and after each short quotation

    c. The placement of long quotations in relation to the text of the paper

    d. The relationship between long quotations and the words or sentences introducing them

    e. The documentation in the text for each quotation

4. The style for presenting information in the Works Cited list at the end of the paper

    a. The method for alphabetizing the entries in the list

    b. The kinds of information given in each entry

    c. The punctuation to divide the parts of each entry

5. The use of capital letters in the title of each paper

6. The position of the title in relation to the first line of the text and to the page as a whole, and the position of the student writer's name and other identifying information

NOTE: If your instructor asks for a title page, use the title page of the second research paper as a model (see **53b**).

53a Research paper #1

    The writer of the following paper composed it early in 1986 to fulfill this assignment:

Examine one issue in each of five periodicals (newspapers and magazines) covering approximately the same period of time. Focus on a particular part of the content, the opinions expressed, or an aspect of style, and develop a thesis based on this. Compose a paper of 2,000 to 3,000 words in which you present and defend your thesis. Keep a log recording all important steps in the project and hand it in with the paper.

The log kept by the student throughout the project follows the paper and traces the many revisions in the plans and the writing that resulted in this final draft.

The student uses **APA style** documentation.

5

R. D. Miller

English 101

As 1986 Begins

How will 1985 go down in history? What
lies ahead in 1986? A look at three major
news magazines and three major newspapers as
1986 begins suggests that 1985 was a year
that will be remembered for disasters and for
financial and political difficulties, many of
which will continue to threaten us in 1986.

Probably most of us would agree that any
list of important events in 1985 should
include such natural disasters as the
earthquakes in Mexico and Colombia, which
caused over 44,000 deaths, and the famine in
Ethiopia, where thousands have died, and also
such man-made disasters as the many air
crashes around the world which killed almost
2,000 people, making 1985 the worst year in
the whole history of civil aviation. The

year was also notable for terrorist attacks:
782 people were murdered. One of the ugliest
killings was that of Leon Klinghoffer, an
elderly cripple, who was shot by terrorists
on a cruise ship in the Mediterranean and
then pushed overboard. Another was that of
an 11-year-old American girl in the terrorist
shooting spree at the Rome airport just after
Christmas. Other bad news was the further
evidence of racial oppression in South
Africa, where the government continued to
enforce apartheid and punish protesters,
notably Winnie Mandela, whose husband, Nelson
Mandela, a black leader, has been in prison
there for over twenty-one years. AIDS made
more headlines as the number of cases
increased across the country. Since 1975
more than 8,000 have died of AIDS, and Rock
Hudson's death called new attention to the
disease.

    Many Americans will also remember 1985 as

the year that added a record-breaking $200
billion to the federal deficit, bringing the
total to almost $2 trillion, the biggest
deficit in U.S. history. The financial news
was mixed. Many savings and loan
associations needed government help to stay
afloat, and 115 banks failed, the highest
number since the Depression, and many farmers
throughout the country went bankrupt and lost
their farms.

On the positive side, we may remember
1985 as the year when the stock market went
higher than ever before, despite some
predictions at the end of 1985 that it would
crash. The Dow-Jones average rose above
1,500 for the first time in history and
stayed there. We may also remember 1985 as
the year when a large number of people were
generous: Live Aid concerts, given on the
same day in Philadelphia and London, raised
$72 million for African famine relief. The

personal triumphs of two popular figures also cheered their many fans: Bruce Springsteen's album <u>Born in the U.S.A.</u> sold 15 million copies, and Pete Rose made his 4,204th hit, breaking the record set by Ty Cobb in 1928.

The January 6 issue of <u>Time</u>, which appeared on December 30, concentrated on international matters in reviewing 1985. The editors chose Deng Xiaoping, the leader of China, as the magazine's "Man of the Year." In a letter to readers, Richard B. Thomas, the publisher of <u>Time</u>, explains the choice:

> In choosing the 59th Man of the Year, the editors considered such headline makers as Mikhail Gorbachev, the vigorous new Soviet leader; Nelson Mandela, the jailed black South African who symbolizes the struggle against apartheid; Bob Geldof, musical fund raiser for African famine relief; and once again, the terrorist.

The editors eventually decided to look
beyond the day-to-day news and examine a
phenomenon with enormous potential impact
on history: China's sweeping economic
reforms, which have challenged Marxist
orthodoxies and liberated the productive
energies of a billion people. For
introducing these far-reaching changes,
China's leader, Deng Xiaoping, was made
<u>Time</u>'s Man of the Year for 1985. (4)

The magazine sent a team of thirty-three
people--editors, writers, reporters, and
researchers--to China for five days to gather
information and then devoted over thirty
pages of the January 6 issue to a description
of Deng, his policies, and the economy and
everyday life in China. Although the general
tone of the <u>Time</u> study is positive, George
Church, in the lead article, reminds us that
Deng's "success cannot be taken for granted"

(41). Church points out that there has been
a sharp increase in corruption in China and
that industrial management lacks modern
business skills. Moreover, under Mao's brand
of communism people became accustomed to the
security of lifetime employment even for the
incompetent and redundant, so that many now
on the payrolls are unwilling or unable to be
productive workers. The future of China,
Church thinks, depends on Deng's being able
to create a new blend of communism and
capitalism, and his success in doing so is by
no means guaranteed. Incidentally, a change
is surely long overdue in the label "Man of
the Year." A title such as "Newsmaker of the
Year" would recognize that there is at least
the possibility, however remote it may seem
to Time's editors, that a woman may someday
deserve the honor.

In the first 1986 issue of Newsweek,
which, like Time, is dated January 6 but

appeared on December 30, the cover story is on the "Abandoned," the mentally ill discharged from institutions with nowhere to live but the streets. For them, 1986 would seem to promise only continued misery and degradation. One note of social progress, however, is a chart titled "The Capitol's Slowly Changing Face" (5), which shows that the number of blacks and women elected to the House of Representatives has gone from 9 blacks and 10 women in 1969-71 to 19 blacks and 23 women in 1983-85. While they still form only a tiny fraction of the 435 members of the House, the increase is a sign of social progress. In a feature called "Portrait 85," Newsweek describes several "men and women who mattered in 1985." It includes six who have achieved conventional types of success: Ronald Reagan, Mikhail Gorbachev, the billionaire businessman Ted Turner, and the stars Don Johnson, Lily

Tomlin, and Bruce Springsteen. Perhaps as a reminder that 1985 saw much news that was tragic, the feature includes five people who are noteworthy because of the suffering they endured or inflicted on others: Omaira Sanchez, a little girl who died after being trapped for sixty hours in a mudslide caused by the earthquake in Colombia; Rock Hudson, who died of AIDS; Winnie Mandela, the civil rights leader in South Africa; Bernard Goetz, who claimed self-defense in shooting four teenagers in the New York subway; and a nameless, hooded terrorist, symbolizing any of those who attacked civilians in the past year.

The year-end issue of U.S. News & World Report, which also appeared on December 30, takes an extremely optimistic view of 1985 and 1986. On the cover is a photograph of the torch of the Statue of Liberty with two cheerful predictions on each side:

BUSINESS	WORLD
More Growth	US Takes
Ahead	The Lead
NATION	MONEY
The Can-Do	Where to
Mood in	Invest
The States	Now

In the first feature article, "America's Rekindled Spirit," David Gergen begins by stating that "the good times are still rolling at least for now" (20). He mentions in passing that the farm belt is enduring its worst crisis since the Depression and predicts that "the woes of the underclass will continue unabated" (20). Nevertheless, he concludes with a repetition of his optimistic forecast: "Across the broad expanse of the nation, 1986 promises to be upbeat. Approaching the new year, polls show the sense of national well-being as high as

any time in fifteen years" (20). He does
not, however, name the polls or describe
where and how they were conducted, so that
his forecast does not inspire the reader's
confidence.

   To reinforce Gergen's optimistic
description, a large photograph of twelve
smiling people spreads across most of the two
facing pages. Recent immigrants who will
become citizens in 1986, they are quoted as
expecting life in the United States to be
very happy, the fulfillment of their dreams.

   In the business section, Monroe W. Karmin
and Richard G. Elbo continue the optimistic
tone in "The Growth Will Steam Right on
through '86." In a special box, they list
twenty varied experts whose predictions for
the rate of economic growth in 1986 range
from 1.5% to 4.8%, but on the same page in
their article they admit that the 1985 growth
rate of 2.6% was not impressive, especially

when compared to 1984's rate of 6.8% (79).
The reader is left wondering what Karmin and
Elbo mean by concluding that the economy is
"now in the upswing again" and "will still be
going strong at the end of 1986" (82).

The final feature in U.S. News & World
Report, "Portraits of the American Family" by
Martin Baker (118-122), presents four married
couples with their children, presumably
selected as typical Americans. They are all
quoted as being satisfied with their lives,
but one man, a commercial architect, mentions
that he does not watch the news on TV because
it depresses him, and one woman, a
pediatrician, notes that racial
discrimination is still a major problem in
America and that the government is spending
too much on defense and not enough on social
programs. The final impression created by
the account is not at all as optimistic as
the editors probably intended it to be.

418

On the first day of 1986, the news in three of the nation's major newspapers was also not likely to encourage much optimism for the year, although all three papers tried to soften the bad news by including cheerful items. The front page of the <u>San Francisco Chronicle</u>, for example, has three large photographs of people celebrating the new year in the financial district by tossing piles of ticker tape around, but the banner headline and the feature story tell of the New Year's Eve plane crash that killed Ricky Nelson, his fiancée, and five members of his band, adding more deaths to the tragic air-crash total for 1985. Elsewhere on the front page is " 'Dr. Ruth' Goofs in Sex Guide for Teenagers," reporting on a proofreading error that may cause a host of unwanted pregnancies, and "Lebanon Killer Squads Shake New Peace Pact," reporting on more violence in that war-torn country.

In the <u>Chicago Tribune</u> for January 1,
"HAPPY NEW YEAR" is the banner headline on
the front page, and the first column, which
is much wider than the others, lists major
upcoming events, particularly sports. The
rest of the page, however, emphasizes
problems--political, financial, local,
national, and international. The top story,
occupying five columns, is on a local problem
that is bound to cause difficulties in 1986:
the new trade center in McCormick Place will
not be ready in time for the 1986 trade show.
A photograph of a Lake Michigan tugboat
completely covered with ice occupies much of
the middle of the page, a reminder of the
bitter cold weather to be expected in the
coming weeks. Next to it is an account of a
bombing in Beirut, and below is a story on
Italy's reduced tolerance of the PLO after
the December massacre in the Rome airport.

At the bottom of the page is a report that
the Regional Transportation Authority failed
to meet the budget deadline for the new year
and another that South Africa has imposed new
racial bans. All in all, the local and
international pictures are distinctly gloomy.

The front page of the New York Times
features a large photograph of bombed cars in
Beirut and a slightly smaller one of police
in South Africa scattering supporters of
Winnie Mandela. Front-page stories report
that the U.S. trade deficit has set a new
record, that a State Department study claims
to have found a link between Libya and the
most recent terrorist attacks, that the
Agriculture Department is ordering farmers to
repay their loans or face foreclosure, and,
the one hopeful note, that Afghan leaders
have informally presented a plan for the
withdrawal of Soviet troops from their

country. Elsewhere in the paper are more
pieces of bad news: farmers in southern
California are suffering from the competition
of cheap fruits and vegetables imported from
Latin America; two 12-year-old girls in a
small town in Georgia were kidnapped,
imprisoned, and raped by a man who then
joined the search party and pretended to look
for them while keeping them locked in a
closet; the PLO had made new threats against
the safety of hostages held in Beirut; and
reports from China indicate that Deng's
agricultural policy is failing to produce
enough grain, especially rice, to feed the
people because, now that they have a choice,
the farmers prefer to raise easier crops.
George Church's fears for the future of
China, printed only a few days earlier in
Time, would seem to be coming true already.

On the last page of Newsweek, the

columnist George F. Will labeled 1985 a
"tolerably adequate year," despite an
assortment of bad news he listed. Let us
hope that 1986 will at least not be worse,
even if the news at the start is not
encouraging.

Reference List

Anderson, Harry. "Holiday of Terror."
Newsweek 6 Jan. 1986: 26-30.

Baker, Mark. "Portraits of the American
Family." U.S. News & World Report 30
Dec. 1985/6 Jan. 1986 [combined year-end
issue]: 118-122.

"Beirut Militia Chief Survives Grenade
Attack." Chicago Tribune 1 Jan. 1986,
natl. ed.: 1.

Burns, John F. "Facing a Decline in Its
Grain Fields, China Retreats on Policy."
New York Times 1 Jan. 1986, late ed.: 2.

"Capitol's Slowly Changing Face, The."
Newsweek 6 Jan. 1986: 2.

Church, George. "China." Time 6 Jan. 1986:
24-41.

"'Dr. Ruth' Goofs in Sex Guide for
Teenagers." San Francisco Chronicle
1 Jan. 1986, two-star ed.: 1.

Gergen, David. "America's Rekindled Spirit."
U.S. News & World Report 30 Dec. 1985/6
Jan. 1986 [combined year-end issue]:
20-21.

Gwertzman, Bernard. "Afghan Informally
Presents Peace Plan." New York Times 1
Jan. 1986, late ed.: 1.

Hershey, Robert D., Jr. "U.S. Trade
Deficit." New York Times 1 Jan. 1986,
late ed.: 1.

Karmin, Monroe W., and Ricardo G. Elbo. "The
Growth Will Steam Right on through '86."
U.S. News & World Report 30 Dec. 1985/6
Jan. 1986 [combined year-end issue]:
78-82.

Keller, Bill. "State Dept. Study on Terror
Group Cites Libyan Link." New York Times
1 Jan. 1986, late ed.: 1.

"Lebanon Killer Squads." San Francisco
Chronicle 1 Jan. 1986, two-star ed.: 1.

Lindsey, Robert. "New Food Patterns Affect
    Strike in West." New York Times 1 Jan.
    1986, late ed.: 6.

Morgenthau, Tom. "Abandoned: The Chronic
    Mentally Ill." Newsweek 6 Jan. 1986:
    14-17.

"Ricky Nelson Killed." San Francisco
    Chronicle 1 Jan. 1986, two-star ed.: 1+.

"Portrait 85." Newsweek 6 Jan. 1986: 35-49.

Schmetzer, Uli. "Italy Rethinks Its Support
    of PLO Actions." Chicago Tribune 1 Jan.
    1986, natl. ed.: 1.

Schneider, Keith. "Agriculture Dept. to
    Order Farmers to Pay Late Debt." New
    York Times 1 Jan. 1986, late ed.: 1+.

"Searcher Charged with Kidnapping." New York
    Times 1 Jan. 1986, late ed.: 7.

"South Africa Imposes New Bans." Chicago
    Tribune 1 Jan. 1986, natl. ed.: 1.

20

Thomas, Richard B. "Letter to the Reader."
Time 6 Jan. 1986: 4.

Unger, Rudolph. "RTA Fails to Meet '86
Budget Deadline." Chicago Tribune 1 Jan.
1986, natl. ed.: 1.

Will, George F. "A Tolerably Adequate Year."
Newsweek 6 Jan. 1986: 68.

Log for Research Paper Assignment

<u>Day 1</u>: Went to the library and glanced over current magazines displayed in periodical room <u>Forbes</u>, <u>Business Week</u>, <u>US News</u>, <u>Time</u>, <u>Newsweek</u>, <u>Sports Illustrated</u>, <u>People</u>, <u>US</u>. Want to use weeklies and biweeklies for project because they cover a lot of the same subjects--the monthly magazines all go off in different directions. Started with magazines because they will be harder to match up than newspapers, which overlap more because they're limited to most recent news. <u>Newsweek</u>, <u>Time</u>, and <u>US News</u> would make a good trio, alike but different. I'm not really familiar with any of them. Sticking to recent ones though, so I'll know something about the news. Someone in class is doing it on a Civil War battle, but it would take too long to do all that research. Got recent back issues of <u>Newsweek</u> to help me choose a week to concentrate on.

Best issue of <u>Newsweek</u> was first one for '86--with a review of '85 and forecasts for '86. Found out that <u>Time</u> and <u>US News</u> did the same thing. I can use them and a couple of newspapers.

Talked the project over with some classmates in the dorm. M.J.'s a business major and wants to do something on the stock market. C.S. wants it to be something on sports, probably on the Bears; A.K. is going to check out reviews on jazz and rhythm and blues; and R.G. wants to compare the car ads from the 1920s with the current ones.

<u>Day 2</u>: Back at the library for a closer look. <u>US News</u> has a year-end double issue instead of one on Jan. 6 (like <u>Time</u> and <u>Newsweek</u>), but it's the same general idea. Listed article titles for each one and skimmed the main ones. For newspapers, <u>New York Times</u> is the obvious choice--the Big One. Periodicals librarian suggested <u>San Francisco Chronicle</u> and <u>Chicago Tribune</u> to

give me different parts of the country. I
only need two of them, but three newspapers
will balance three magazines. Decided to use
Jan. 1st papers because they've got some of
the same kind of year-end-review articles.
And the librarian says the magazines really
came out on December 30 or 31, in spite of
the date on the cover, so the papers were
following up on the same events. Listed the
main topics of the front page stories and
took notes on their general layout.

Back in my room, looked over notes and
lists. Made a list of possibilities for a
thesis. Can think of only two general
approaches: concentrate on the news stories,
or compare and contrast the periodicals
themselves. For the first one, I could
concentrate on overview or on a particular
story. For the second, I could concentrate
on layouts, on news selections, or on
opinions. Have to decide soon.

<u>Day 3</u>: Looked over notes for possibilities
for thesis. Chose comparison/contrast of
layouts because I'd thought about it before.
Went back to the library to measure the size
of the feature stories, headlines, and photos
and to check out the arrangement of the
stories. Realized I don't know enough about
journalism to do this. Looked back at list
of possibilities. Don't want to do just one
or two big news stories--the choices are too
limited. Before class, everyone was talking
about it. And having problems, too.

<u>Day 4</u>: Back to library. Spread out all the
periodicals on one big table for an overview.
What interested me was looking back at '85
and guessing about '86. <u>That</u> can be my
topic. Reviewed notes with this in mind.
Listed the big events of '85. And I bet
it'll be more of the same in '86--terrorism,
deficits, hunger, and maybe a little
progress. Can my views and the periodicals'

views on that idea work as a thesis on the topic? Hardly an earthshaking idea.

Day 5: Checked my notes and lists. Made a rough outline of materials, grouping it under "important people," "disasters," "successes," "forecasts," etc. Returned to the library to read closely and try to determine writers' attitudes toward subjects. Photocopied some feature stories. Tried to draft an opening paragraph, but need clearer idea of the main body first. Choices for organizing: start with magazines, then do newspapers, or vice versa; either do local, national, international news, or vice versa. Whatever way I choose, there will be lots of repetition because my sources overlap and have similarities. Better go by publications, then by featured news, to avoid jumping around, since I have six publications but dozens of stories. Start with Time among the magazines because it's the oldest and best known; same goes for New York Times

among newspapers. Newsweek second because
it's so close in style to Time; that puts US
News third. With newspapers, go
geographically east to west, since geography
was the basis for choosing them. Will that
seem logical to readers? Hope so.

Day 6: Started writing. Thesis statement
will serve as opening for now--come back to
it later. Wrote up my list of events in '85,
then on to Time and its big stories, then
Newsweek. Getting bogged down in all the
details--pages and pages just explaining my
own list of events and then what the
magazines featured. Made a more detailed
outline for the main body. Started cutting
down on what I'd written. Back to the
library to check on some details. Wrote
rough draft of section on US News.

Day 7: Wrote rough draft of section on
newspapers. Back to the library to check
which articles are from news services and
which have bylines. Remeasured the length of

some stories. Made notes all over my rough draft; it's getting illegible with all the changes.

Day 8: Read the whole rough draft in order. Too long. Can't cut the facts, but have to cut the words down. Need more support for my criticism of US News--some hard facts. Reversed the order for covering the newspapers. San Francisco Chronicle had better come first because it's almost all local news; at the end of my paper it would be a letdown. Reread my whole paper quickly, then wrote a rough ending. Read it all again slowly, chopping down the wordy parts, but adding a few specifics for support. Found a good quote in Will's Newsweek article to strengthen my conclusion.

Day 9: Reread the whole paper just for word choice and sentence structure. Made more cuts and condensed more. Alphabetized the list of sources. Started typing. Back to

the library for inclusive page numbers on two
articles and spelling of some names.

Day 10: Finished typing, including the
"Works Cited." Proofread. Retyped three
pages and "Works Cited" because of errors.

Day 11: Proofread again. Found some minor
typos, but corrected them in ink. Added the
title, my name, etc., to first page.

Day 12: Submitted paper.

General conclusions: Two most difficult
things were deciding on the organization and
making good notes--full enough to be
accurate, but short enough to be handled
easily. Most interesting thing was the
differences among all the publications and
how much more detail they give than the TV
news. I had never read the New York Times
before or ever even seen the other papers.

53b Research paper #2

The writer of the following paper composed it to fulfill this assignment:

> Select a short poem (under 150 lines) from the course anthology. Examine the criticism (books *and* periodicals) available in the library. Compose a four- to six-page paper in which you discuss the form, diction, and themes of the poem. Use at least *five* secondary sources in your paper—as background, as support for your own views, or as critical positions you wish to disagree with.

A note by the student follows the paper, describing the planning and research that resulted in this final draft.

The student uses **MLA style** documentation.

The text of the poem that the student selected, Percy Bysshe Shelley's "Ozymandias," follows here for convenient reference:

Ozymandias

I met a traveller from an antique land
Who said: Two vast and trunkless legs of stone
Stand in the desert. . . Near them, on the sand,
Half sunk, a shattered visage lies, whose frown,
And wrinkled lip, and sneer of cold command,
Tell that its sculptor well those passions read
Which yet survive, stamped on these lifeless things,
The hand that mocked them, and the heart that fed:

And on the pedestal these words appear:
'My name is Ozymandias, king of kings:
Look on my works, ye Mighty, and despair!'
Nothing beside remains. Round the decay
Of that colossal wreck, boundless and bare
The lone and level sands stretch far away.

Shelley's "Ozymandias"

By

Charles Davis

English 125

Section 8

"Ozymandias" is Shelley's best-known and most often anthologized sonnet. The poem's popularity is probably due, as one critic suggests, to Shelley's strong use of irony in writing about delusions of grandeur (King-Hele 93). Despite the popularity of the poem, very little critical or scholarly treatment has been given to it, except for articles dealing with Shelley's possible sources for the poem.[1] Three of the features of the poem, however, deserve special attention: the unusual rhyme scheme, the closely related themes of the power of the artist and the power of time, and the use of irony.

Although Shelley is basically writing a poem in the Italian sonnet form, the rhyme scheme that he uses in "Ozymandias" is very unorthodox. Traditionally, an Italian sonnet contains fourteen lines of ten syllables

each, and it has a rhyme scheme that goes
abba, abba, cde, cde. Variations in the
rhyme scheme of the last six lines are
common. Some widely used alternatives are
cdc, cdc; or cdc, dcd; or cd, cd, cd
(Crutwell 5). As a result, the Italian
sonnet form has either five different rhyme
sounds in its basic pattern or only four
rhymes in some common variations.

Unlike these traditional patterns,
however, "Ozymandias" rhymes abab, acdc, ede,
fef. Only the a and e rhymes occur three
times; all of the others occur only twice.
No rhyme repeats four times, as the a and b
rhymes do in the traditional Italian sonnet
pattern. In addition, no two lines in a row
rhyme with each other, so Shelley does not
create the sound effect of the two pairs of b
rhymes that the usual Italian sonnet has.

The unusual rhyme scheme gives Shelley
two advantages. The more different rhymes he

uses, the easier it is for him to find appropriate words that rhyme. By increasing the number of different rhymes from five to six, Shelley simplifies one of the problems that poets writing in English have always had in using the Italian sonnet form. As one authority indicates, "[The Italian] scheme is much more difficult in English, a language with comparatively few rhymes, than in Italian, a language with many . . ." (Crutwell 5). The second advantage is that each rhyming sound is less conspicuous because it occurs less often. Reducing the prominence of the rhyme is desirable in this poem because it makes the traveller's story sound more conversational and more like ordinary human speech. As a result, our attention goes to the details of the narrative and to the main irony.

Shelley uses another device called near-rhyme that also helps to de-emphasize

4

the rhyme scheme in the eye and ear of the reader. Near-rhymes are words that sound similar but do not rhyme exactly. The b rhyme of stone and frown provides one example, and the e rhyme of appear, despair, and bare provides the other.

Shelley's interesting use of internal rhyme is also an important feature of the poem's sound pattern. The third and fifth lines of the poem not only rhyme with each other as two a rhymes, but they also both begin with words that are a rhymes, stand and and. That same a rhyme sound occurs prominently in two other places in the poem, in the word hand in the eighth line and in the middle syllable of the name of Ozymandias himself in the tenth line. If we add seven more occurrences of the word and and the word sands in the last line, then there are fourteen a rhyme words in all. They unite the poem with their repeated sound, and they relate the poem's most important ideas to the name of Ozymandias. The linking of stand-sand-command-hand-Ozymandias emphasizes words that are keys to the theme of the poem.

The poem's two major themes have to do with power. On the one hand, there is the power of the artist in contrast with the power of the king; on the other, there is the power of time in contrast with the power of human beings. The power struggle between the sculptor and king is the major subject of the first eight lines of the poem. Here, the artist has the power to cut the truth into stone, and the truth that he has carved is the image of a cold, sneering tyrant. The king's power is quite different. He has the power to command people and to command the artist to make a statue, but he does not have the power to see the truth that the artist has captured in stone. The artist is more powerful because in the end he defeats the king by showing him not as powerful but as tyrannic. As one critic puts it, "Although the words and work of Ozymandias are ruined by age, the truth perceived by the unknown artist is carried intact through time, by the power of his imagery" (Hall 20).

The second power struggle in the poem is on a larger scale. Shelley shows us that time has the power to control both men and truth. Like the first theme, this one is not plainly stated; in fact, the word time does not even appear in the poem. Only the word antique in the opening line and the use of the ancient Greek name Ozymandias for the Egyptian pharaoh Rameses II are clues to how much time is involved. The broken condition of the statue, however, and words like survive and decay make very clear to us the power that time has. In a crude way, time has been more powerful than either the sculptor or the king because both of them are

dead. Time has taken away the sculptor's
name and has made the king's great statement
an empty boast. But in a subtler way, time
has given a second victory to the artist.
Even though the statue's face is all
shattered, time has preserved all the broken
pieces that we need to see the artist's truth
and to see his power. By contrast, the
king's power is now as completely destroyed
as his statue. Time has preserved the truth
and strengthened it because we can still see
the king for the tyrant that he was, and we
see the weakness of his kind of power.

Shelley's use of irony in "Ozymandias"
makes these two themes strong and clear. The
major irony of the poem results from the
clash between the words of the king, which he
must have meant to be awe-inspiring, and the
wrecked statue, which inspires awe for the
artist's skill and for the power of time.
Desmond King-Hele suggests that as readers we

take pleasure in feeling superior to the king. "The poem subtly flatters our vanity. We feel after reading it that we are wiser than Ozymandias, who never knew the irony of his inscription, and wiser too than the traveller, who seems unaware of any moral to be drawn from his plain tale" (94).

There is a second irony which results from Shelley's use of the word mocked. For modern readers, the word mocked means "made fun of" or "derided," but in Shelley's time the word also meant "copied," "mimicked," or "imitated" (Reiman and Powers 103). The artist has done both things. He has made fun of the king and the king's ambitions, and he has done it by copying his features truthfully. The power of time has reinforced the irony of the word mocked because time has preserved the copy and has made additional fun of the king by destroying all of his works.

    With these three important features of
Shelley's poem in mind, we have a clearer
idea of how the poem works. The rhyme scheme
and internal rhyme focus our attention on the
words that are most important to the poem's
themes. Because those themes are never
spelled out plainly, the added emphasis on
these words is important in conveying the
themes and pointing our attention to them.
Shelley's use of irony is flattering to the
reader, and the irony sharpens our response
to the poem. We can appreciate more fully
the power of the artist and the power of time
to assist the artist in communicating the
truth.

Note

¹William V. Spanos discusses the problem
of articles dealing with Shelley's sources:

> Much scholarly ink has been spilled
> over the question of the literal
> identity of the "traveller" who
> provided Shelley with the
> description of the shattered
> monument and the inscription on the
> pedestal. . . . For a summary of
> this scholarship and an exhaustive
> list of possible candidates see
> Johnstone Parr, "Shelley's
> 'Ozymandias,'" Keats-Shelley
> Journal, VI (1957), 31-35. (14)

In addition to Parr 31-35, three other
articles deal with Shelley's possible
sources: Bequette, Richmond, and Thompson.
The longest critical discussions are: Hall
(19-24), King-Hele (92-95), and Spanos.

Works Cited

Bequette, K. K.   "Shelley and Smith: Two
    Sonnets on Ozymandias." Keats-Shelley
    Journal 26 (1977): 29-31.

Crutwell, Patrick. The English Sonnet.
    London: Longman, 1966.

Hall, Jean. The Transforming Image: A Study
    of Shelley's Major Poetry. Urbana: U of
    Illinois P, 1980.

King-Hele, Desmond. Shelley: His Thought and
    Work. 3rd ed. Rutherford, NJ:
    Humanities, 1977.

Parr, Johnstone. "Shelley's 'Ozymandias.' "
    Keats-Shelley Journal 6 (1957): 31-35.

Reiman, Donald H., and Sharon B. Powers, eds.
    Shelley's Poetry and Prose: Authoritative
    Texts and Criticism. New York: Norton,
    1977.

12

Richmond, H. M.   "Ozymandias and the
    Travelers."   Keats-Shelley Journal 11
    (1962): 65-72.

Spanos, William V.   "Shelley's 'Ozymandias'
    and the Problem of the Persona."   CEA
    Critic 30.1 (1968): 14-15.

Thompson, D. W.   "Ozymandias."   Philological
    Quarterly 16 (1937): 59-64.

Comments on Researching My Paper

    I chose Shelley's poem for my paper for
two reasons: I liked the other poem we read
by him this semester, and I liked the other
sonnets that we read by Shakespeare and
Milton.

    I began work on my paper by going to the
library and locating the books on Shelley. I
was disappointed to discover that only two of
the many books had more than one sentence
about the poem. I photocopied the pages from
those two books, and I photocopied the title
pages too so that I wouldn't have to write
out the information. My assignment was to
use at least five sources, and I knew that
none of the one-line comments about the poem
would be of any real use, so I started to
look for articles in scholarly journals.

    I went to the reference librarian for
help in finding articles. He told me that I
should look in the bibliography of PMLA,

which is published every year and lists all
the articles for a given year. The librarian
also told me that there was a similar
bibliography published every year in the
Keats-Shelley Journal. In addition to those
bibliographies, there are several
bibliographies that deal only with the
writers of the Romantic movement. It took me
five hours just to go through all those
bibliographies. I photocopied all the
entries that I found that dealt with the
poem.

When I was through, I had ten articles
that I had to find. Each time I found one of
them, I photocopied it and the cover of the
journal it was in so I'd have all the
information for my notes and bibliography. I
took all this material home, and I began to
study it along with the poem to see what I
could write about.

As I looked over my materials, I realized
that very little of what I had was really

criticism or interpretation of the poem.
Most of it was stuff about the sources of the
poem, and there was nothing I could say that
wasn't already in the articles by Parr,
Richmond, and Thompson. Summarizing those
articles didn't seem like a very worthwhile
paper topic, and besides, I really wanted to
write about the poem itself, not about its
sources.

In order to write about the poem itself,
I needed to know more about the form of the
sonnet. I went back to the library and
looked up books on the sonnet as a form in
poetry. I found several promising things in
the card catalog, and the books did give me a
good idea for Shelley's poem. His poem is
very different from the normal Italian type
of sonnet. One book in particular was very
clear about the sonnet form and the different
rhyme schemes that are usually used in it. I
photocopied the information from it and its
title page too.

I now had enough information for my
paper. I could write about Shelley's rhyme
scheme and use the sonnet book; I could write
about Shelley's theme by using one of the two
critics I had found; and I could write about
Shelley's use of irony by using the other
critic. Finally, I could also use the names
of all of the critics who had written about
Shelley's sources to indicate that that's
what had been written about most.

I did find one critical article, the one
by Spanos, but I'm not 100% sure I understood
his point, and I don't think I agree with him
if I do understand him. His discussion of
"persona" didn't fit well with the things I
wanted to say, but one of his notes looked
like a useful summary of the problem with
Shelley's sources, so I decided to use it in
my own notes but not really in my paper.

I made one dumb mistake that cost me an
extra trip to the library. When I
photocopied the material from one book, I

didn't notice that the date and place of
publication were on the back, not the front,
of the title page. I recommend always
photocopying both sides of the title page to
avoid this error.

Another thing that took a lot more time
than I had expected was the forms for the
entries in the bibliography and the notes.
These forms are different from what I learned
in high school, so I had to retype those
pages with our college handbook open right
next to my typewriter to be sure that I was
getting all the punctuation right.

Part Eight
BUSINESS
WRITING

54. Business Letters

54 ◆ BUSINESS LETTERS

The business letter usually has five parts, in addition to the message itself. Before the message come the heading, the inside address, and the salutation; following the message come the complimentary close and the signature. The model letters at the end of the section illustrate these parts.

1. The **heading** includes the date and the sender's address, occupying three lines in the upper right corner. Place them far enough to the left to allow the longest line to end at the right-hand margin. Businesses use stationery with their name and address; on such stationery, add only the date, either near the right margin or centered under the printed heading. Include the ZIP code and the two-letter state abbreviation.

2. The **inside address** gives the name and address of the person or firm to whom you are writing, as on the envelope. Start at the left margin at least two lines below the date. Skip more lines if you are arranging a short letter on a large page.

   If you are directing a letter to the notice of a particular person in the firm, include the word *Attention,* a colon, and the person's name or title on the second line below the inside address.

3. The **salutation** appears at the left margin, two lines below the inside address or attention note, and contains the formal greeting. Whatever the occasion, follow these rules:

a. Choose a salutation that matches the inside address in number and gender, disregarding any intervening attention note.
b. Choose a salutation of suitable formality for the occasion.
c. Capitalize the first word and all nouns.
d. Punctuate with a colon—nothing more.

For a formal salutation when you do not know whether you are addressing men or women, or when you know that you are addressing both, use one that includes both sexes.

To one recipient	To more than one recipient
Dear Sir:	Dear Sirs and Mesdames:
or	*or*
Dear Madam:	Ladies and Gentlemen:
Dear Committee Member:	Dear Committee Members:
Dear Classmate:	Dear Classmates:

If you know the sex, use *Gentlemen* or *Sirs* for men and *Mesdames* for women. When you know the name and sex, choose among these conventional phrases:

To a male	To a female
Dear Sir:	Dear Madam:
My dear Mr. Blank:	My dear Miss (Ms., Mrs.) Blank:
Dear Mr. Blank:	Dear Miss (Ms., Mrs.) Blank:

NOTE: In the plural, for *Mr.* use *Messrs.;* for *Mrs.* and *Madam* use *Mmes.; Ms.* is both singular and plural.

"My dear _____" is slightly more formal than "Dear _____" (British usage is the reverse). "Dear Sir" and "Dear Madam" are the most formal salutations. Do *not* write "Dear Gentlemen" or "Dear Ladies." For a less formal salutation, simply use the full name: "Dear John Blank" or "Dear Jane Blank."

4. The **complimentary close** should begin far enough from the right margin for your name and title, if any, to end before the right margin. Place them at least two lines below the last line of your letter. Again, you may add more lines for arrangement's sake. The complimentary close employs a conventional phrase:

```
Yours truly, Very truly yours,
  Yours very truly,
Sincerely yours, Yours sincerely,
  Sincerely,
Cordially yours, Yours cordially,
  Cordially,
```

The choices in the first group are impersonal, those in the second are friendlier, and those in the third are the warmest. Choose a close that matches the formality of your salutation. Capitalize only the first word, and end with a comma.

5. **Sign your name** directly under the complimentary close, and type your name under your signature. If you are writing in any official capacity, give your title below your name:

```
            Jane Blank
            President
            Journalism Club
```

As for social titles, a man never signs himself *Mr.;* it is taken for granted. But a woman may wish to indicate whether she prefers to be addressed as *Miss, Ms.,* or *Mrs.* for the convenience of the person replying. Because those titles are not part of a legal signature, they are enclosed in parentheses:

for an unmarried woman	(Miss) Jane Blank
for a married woman (traditional style requires both names)	Jane Blank (Mrs. John R. Blank)
for a married woman in business or a woman formerly married	(Mrs.) Jane Blank
for any of the above	Ms. Jane Blank

The two pairs of initials that appear at the left margin of a business letter opposite or below the signature are those of the sender and the secretary who typed it. You do not need these initials when you are writing your own business letters.

Abbreviations Use the abbreviations *Mr., Mrs.,* and *Ms.*—these forms are never written out. Other common abbreviations are *Dr.* and (after names) *Jr., D.D.S.,* and *M.D.* You may use initials for first names (especially if the people themselves do), in the names of businesses if they themselves do (Sears, Roebuck and Co., H. & R. Block), and in directions (238 E. Grand St., 32 Vermont Street NW) designating a section of a city. Names of countries, except *U.S.A.* and *USSR,* are not abbreviated, but those of states usually are when they are part of a written address. Use the two-letter abbreviations authorized by the U.S. Postal Service, followed by the ZIP code. Other abbreviations (months, street names, etc.) are not customary in business letters.

Format Observe conventional format for your letter:

1. **Type your letter** on a good grade of white paper of standard size (8½ by 11 inches).
2. **Make a carbon,** printout, or photocopy to keep as a record; it may prevent many problems later.
3. **Arrange your whole letter** carefully on the page so that it will look like a picture in a frame:
   a. Space the parts—the heading, inside address, and so on—to fit with the length of the message.
   b. Leave at least one inch for each of the four margins, with the bottom one slightly larger than the others; the shorter the message, the wider your margins should be.
   c. Use single-spacing, with double-spacing between paragraphs. The extra space between paragraphs makes indenting the paragraphs

unnecessary. If, however, you prefer the more traditional look of indented paragraphs, indent the first line of each paragraph five spaces. For very brief letters, use double-spacing throughout to avoid the lonely look of two or three lines of message, and indent the paragraphs.

d. Be concise; keep to a single page. If your letter must be longer, be sure that at least three lines of the message are on the last page. Number each page after the first.

e. *Never* write on the back of a sheet of paper.

4. **Use full-block or semiblock style** for the parts of your letter.

a. In **full-block style,** all the lines of the heading, salutation, complimentary close, and signature begin at the left margin.

b. In **semiblock style** (see example), all the lines of the inside address begin at the left margin, as does the salutation. All lines of the heading, the complimentary close, and signature begin about twenty spaces inside the right margin, so that each part does not need more than one line.

c. The only punctuation *ending* these parts is a colon after the salutation (but a comma is conventional in a social letter) and a comma after the complimentary close.

d. The only punctuation *within* these parts is a comma in the traditional style of date, separating the day and year, and in the address, separating the town or city name from that of the state.

5. Use a **white envelope** of the same quality and finish as your paper. The standard small size (3¾ by 6½ inches) will take a one-page letter comfortably. For a longer letter, use the standard business size (4¼ by 9½ inches).

   a. Make the outside address identical with the inside. Place it in the lower half of the envelope, beginning approximately one-third of the distance from the left-hand edge.

   b. Place your name and address in the upper left corner.

   c. Place any special directions such as "Attention: Personnel Director" or "Please Forward" in the lower left corner.

```
Lee Cooper
210 W. Oak Street
Greenvale, PA 18360



           Arnold Clothing Store
           634 Main Street
           Smithtown, OH 33501


Attention: Accounts Dept.
```

6. **Fold the letter** so that the recipient can withdraw it easily.

   a. Fold a one-sheet letter in half, then turn it sideways and fold it in thirds.

   b. Fold a longer letter in thirds by bringing the bottom edge of the pages about two-thirds of the way to the top and the top edge down close to the resulting crease.

54a Letter of inquiry, order, or complaint

For a letter making an inquiry, placing an order, or voicing a complaint, use the basic form already described and also follow these directions:

1. **Be precise and explicit.** Include enough details to make a definite reply easy. A letter asking for the rates for hotel rooms is pointless if you omit the date you want to reserve and the type of rooms. Make your inquiry so clear that the reply can be an answer instead of a request for more specific information. In making a complaint, clarity and precision are essential; your case will depend on the accuracy of your explanation.
2. **Be courteous.** Even when you know that the person or company to whom you are writing wants your business, remember that *please* and *thank you* are still standard good manners.
3. **Be brief.** Include all the necessary details but nothing that is beside the point. Requesting information about a company product, you may appropriately mention how you plan to use it, but a long description of your hobbies would probably be irrelevant.

54b Letter of application and résumé

Letters of application may be the most important letters that you ever write. If you are applying for an award, admission to a special program, or a job, your letter may change your life.

1. **Make the letter appealing.** Courtesy and clearness are all you need for inquiries, orders, and complaints, but the application letter is essentially a sales letter.

   a. *Think first of the viewpoint of your prospective readers.* They are interested in what you may be able to contribute to the field, not in your purely personal considerations. You are "selling" your skills, not yourself. "Because of my long interest in popular music and because I have been taking piano lessons for the past three years, I believe I can be useful in your record store" is more likely to appeal to the store owner than "I want to work for you because I like your employee discount on records" or "because my friend works in a store across the street and can give me a ride."

   b. *Do not be too modest.* Remember that readers know only what transcripts and letters of recommendation show and what you tell them about your skills and accomplishments.

   c. *Do not be boastful.* A statement such as "I have always outranked every other student in my class" may be perfectly true, but it is likely to antagonize readers. Let others supply such information in letters of recommendation.

   d. *Do not sound superior* to whatever you are applying for. No reader will be won by such remarks as "I am willing to work for you until I can find a more suitable position" or

"My education has been in places with more prestige than yours."

e. *State honestly the achievements that are relevant* to whatever you are applying for. What may be an important asset in some applications may be irrelevant in others. "In high school I spent my spare time helping in a sports program for neighborhood children" would be valuable in applying for work as a camp counselor or for admission to a child psychology program but not for work in accounting.

f. *Try to make your letter stand out favorably* from the others. Your prospective readers may receive many letters from qualified applicants, so you must try to make them notice yours. Avoid, however, anything "cute" or "gimmicky"; your letter should sound serious and dignified.

2. **The content of your letter of application** will fall into five main sections: introduction, personal data, qualifications, list of references, and conclusion.

a. Your **introduction** will depend on your particular situation. If you are answering an advertisement or announcement, begin with a reference to it. If you learned indirectly of the job opening, award, or program, mention how you learned of it. If you have no definite knowledge of an opening but are hopeful that one may develop, begin with some mention of your reasons for applying to the particular firm, college, or committee to which you are writing.

b.   Give the **personal data** relevant to the situation—a list of facts, such as your age, sex, marital status, or other items, such as health or citizenship, that are pertinent.

c.   Give the **qualifications** that fit you for whatever you are applying for—education, experience, interest, aptitudes.

d.   List your **references**—the names, official positions, and addresses of those qualified to recommend you as to both character and ability. (Obtain permission before using them as references; afterward, thank them for recommending you.)

e.   **Conclude** your letter with something to ensure a reply: a request for an interview; a reminder that you have enclosed a stamped, self-addressed envelope for your reader's convenience; an indication that you hope for an early reply.

3. **Compose a résumé** (data sheet). This is a separate listing of factual information (personal data, qualifications, references) arranged under suitable headings so that readers can consult it easily. You may present information in chronological order, beginning under each heading with the earliest date, or in reverse chronological order, beginning with the most recent date. Reverse order is widely used because readers are likely to want to know the most recent information first (see example).

NOTE: The writer of the sample résumé includes statistics on her height and weight because these are relevant to the job involved; for most jobs this information would be unnecessary.

Sample letter and résumé

Box 254, Watson Hall
Mayfield College
Smithtown, OH 33501

March 12, 1989

Mrs. Constance Lopez
Director, Camp Towanda
537 South River Road
Greenvale, PA 18360

Dear Mrs. Lopez:

I am writing to apply for a position as a junior counselor at Camp Towanda this coming summer.

My work last year as a student aide in the playground program in my hometown has convinced me to major in child psychology. In the program, I particularly enjoyed seeing how organized games encouraged the shyer children to join in while helping the more aggressive ones to work off their energy and learn to cooperate.

I am interested in a position at your camp because Lois Brown, a basketball coach here at Mayfield, has told me that you have a strong program for six- to nine-year-olds, which is the age group I worked with most often.

If there is any chance of an opening for which you can consider me, I would be glad to come to Greenvale for an interview at your convenience. I can make the trip on any

Saturday, and I am also free on most
Thursdays.

My résumé, which is enclosed, includes the
names and addresses of three people who know
my work and who have kindly consented to
write to you about me at your request.

I hope to hear from you soon.

                         Sincerely yours,

                         Jennifer Howard

                         (Miss) Jennifer Howard

Jennifer Howard

Position desired: camp counselor

Home address
  610 West Elm Street
  Newbury, OH 33526
Phone: (513) 232-3247

College address
  Box 524, Watson Hall
  Smithtown, OH 33501
Phone: (513) 426-7500

Personal data
  age: 19
  height: 5'5"
  weight: 124 lbs
  health: excellent

citizenship: U.S.
marital status:
  single

Education
  1987-1988 Mayfield College
    Will have completed 34 credits toward B.A.
      by June
    Probable major: child psychology
    Extracurricular activities
      Member freshman women's basketball team
      Member Freshman Debate Club
  1983-1987 Smithtown High School
    Academic diploma with honors

Work experience
  September 1985-June 1986 Hamilton Elementary
      School, Newbury
    Teacher's aide in after-school playground
      program
    Organized and supervised games for groups
      of 10 to 12 children
  December 1986 Arnold's Clothing Store, Main
      Street, Smithtown
    Part-time salesclerk (two days a week)
    Arranged displays and sold merchandise on
      main floor

References
  The following people have agreed to write
  references for me at your request:

Mrs. Eleanor Thornton
Director, Playground
  Program
Hamilton Elementary
  School
Newbury, OH 33526

Dr. M. L. Farber
Department of
  Psychology
Mayfield College
Smithtown, OH 33501

Mr. James Ryan
Personnel Department
Arnold's Clothing Store
634 Main Street
Smithtown, OH 33501

Ms. Lois Brown
Athletics Department
Mayfield College
Smithtown, OH 33501

EXERCISES

A. Write a letter of application and a résumé for a summer job at a camp or resort in whatever area of activity and for whatever age group you think you would prefer. Include an envelope addressed to the director.

B. Write a letter of application and a résumé for a summer internship as an office assistant for a firm in whatever line of business interests you most.

C. Write a 150-word essay on the two letters you wrote for exercises **A** and **B,** analyzing the differences in the information you selected and emphasized.

D. Write a letter of inquiry about the accommodations at a hotel or motel in a place you would like to visit. Include questions about features that are important to you (such as a beach or pool, evening entertainment, or types and prices of food in the restaurant) and about facilities in the room (such as "wet bars," refrigerators, bathtubs or stall showers, cable TV, and 24-hour room service).

GLOSSARY
OF USAGE

A glossary is a list of special words for which explanation is necessary. The word *glossary* comes from the Latin *glossa*, meaning "a foreign or strange word," which in turn comes from the Greek *glossa*, meaning "tongue or language," and *usage* means "customary practice." This glossary lists the words and phrases that most often cause difficulties for writers using the English language. The words and phrases in the glossary and the decision to call them formal, informal, colloquial, or dialect, and standard or nonstandard are based on the most recent editions of the three major college dictionaries, the earliest and latest unabridged editions of the major American dictionary, and the *Oxford English Dictionary*.

For your convenience, the items in the glossary are arranged alphabetically. Additional points of usage are discussed in other parts of the book. Check the index for page numbers. Notice particularly the list of the principal parts of common irregular verbs (**6j**); the discussion of nouns with plurals not formed by adding *s* (**4a**); and the list of homophones and homonyms, words that are easily confused with each other (**2b**).

all ready, already   *All ready* means "completely ready." *Already* means "before that time."

The food was all ready to be served.

When we arrived, the movie had already begun.

all right, alright   In formal, standard English, *all right* is written as two words. *Alright* is considered a misspelling.

all together, altogether   *All together* means "everyone or everything concerned, taken as a group." *Altogether* means "completely" or "thoroughly."

The players were all together at one end of the field.

The party was altogether successful.

all ways, always   *All ways* means "all methods or paths." *Always* refers to time.

They examined all ways of solving the problem.

They have always lived in Texas.

a lot, alot   Always write *a lot* as two words; *alot* is a misspelling.

alternately, alternatively   *Alternately* describes switching back and forth between two actions, things, or persons. *Alternatively* describes the second of two choices.

The guests alternately swam and sunbathed.

We plan a holiday in Florida or, alternatively, in California.

among, between   Use *among* as a preposition when referring to three or more things or persons. Use *between* as a preposition when referring to two things or persons.

For the main course, we could choose among five dishes.

For dessert, the choice was between pie and cake.

amount, number   Use *amount* when you are discussing anything that cannot be counted in separate units; use *number* for anything that can be counted in units.

> The lake contained a large amount of water, but only a small number of fish.

and etc.   Omit the redundant *and*. The abbreviation *etc.* of the Latin words *et cetera* means "and other things." See also **etc.**

any one, anyone   *Any one* refers to one member of an identified group. *Anyone* means "any person at all."

> Of the six students, any one could answer the question.

> Anyone can learn to play checkers.

NOTE: The same distinction applies to *any thing* and *anything, every one* and *everyone, every body* and *everybody,* and *some one* and *someone.*

anything, any thing   See **any one, anyone.**

any way, anyway   *Any way* is a noun modified by an adjective and means "any path or method." *Anyway* is an adverb and means "in any case," or "anyhow."

> They could not find any way out of the jungle.

> They did not like the cake, but they ate some anyway.

anyways   Dialectal or colloquial for *anyway.*

anywhere   In formal, standard English, *anywhere* is always written as one word. *Anywheres* is dialectal or colloquial.

as, because   Do not use *as* to mean "because"; readers may think you are using it to mean "at the same time as," which is one of its accepted meanings.

> Our picnic was spoiled because (*not* as) the weather changed.

as, if, whether   Do not use *as* or *as how* to mean "if," "whether," or "that" after such verbs as *feel, know, see, seem,* or *think.*

> We do not know whether (*not* as) we should tell you the news.

> We think that (*not* as how) you must be right.

a while, awhile   *A while* is a noun modified by an article and means "a length of time." *Awhile* is an adverb meaning *"for* a length of time."

> After arguing for a while, they compromised.

> After they compromised, they stayed awhile longer in the room.

bad, badly   *Bad* is an adjective, and *badly* is an adverb. *Bad* may follow a verb when acting as a subject complement. *Badly* should modify verbs, verbals, adjectives, or adverbs.

> They felt bad about their poor grades.

> They performed badly on the test.

because   Do not combine *because* with *reason.* A reason is a cause, and therefore *reason* is redundant with *because.* Instead of "The reason we have won is because of our hard work," write "We have won because of our hard work" or "The reason we have won is our hard work."

being as, being that   These are nonstandard for *because* and are dangling modifiers (see **11b.2**).

beside, besides   *Beside* is a preposition meaning "next to"; *besides* is an adverb meaning "also," or "moreover," but it may be used as a preposition meaning "in addition to."

The cat slept beside the dog. *(preposition)*

They own a cat and a dog, and two canaries besides. *(adverb)*

They own two canaries besides a cat and a dog. *(preposition)*

between, among   See **among.**

both   *Both* means "the two" (from Old English *ba* = both + *tha* = the). Writing "The both of them were late" is redundant; instead, write "Both of them were late."

but   *But* is redundant and awkward in sentences such as "They can't help but do it" or "I don't know but what he's right." Instead, write "They can't help doing it" and "He may be right," "I don't know that he's right," or "I'm not sure that he's wrong."

can, may   In formal English, use *can* to indicate ability and *may* to indicate permission. (See **6g.**)

We can start the test when the instructor says that we may.

can't help but   See **but.**

center around   The center of anything is a specific point; it cannot be a circle.

The movie centered on (*not* around) the life of Napoleon.

compare to, compare with In formal English, use *compare to* when you claim that two things are similar; use *compare with* when you examine two things to find similarities and differences.

The critics are comparing him to Picasso.

We compared his paintings with Picasso's.

different from In formal English, use *from* after different.

The test was different from (*not* than) what we had expected.

disinterested, uninterested These words are not synonyms, and the distinction between them can be useful. *Disinterested* means "impartial"; *uninterested* means "not caring" or "lacking in interest."

The judge gave a disinterested verdict, even though he was uninterested in the case.

done *Done* is the past participle, not the past tense, of *do.* Do not write "We done the work" or "We done finished the work"; instead, write "We did the work" or "We have finished the work."

due to Use *due to* to mean "attributable to," not as a substitute for the prepositional phrase *because of.* In formal English, *due to* usually acts as a subject complement after the verb *be.*

The famine was due to the long drought.

People suffered because of (*not* due to) the famine.

either . . . or Remember that when *either* acts as a correlative conjunction to introduce a clause or a verbal phrase, it must be followed by *or* introducing a matching clause or verbal phrase.

equally as In this expression, *as* is redundant. Do not write "Their team is good, but ours is equally as good"; instead, write "Their team is good, but ours is equally good" or "Our team is as good as theirs."

etc. An abbreviation of the Latin *et cetera, etc.* means "and other things." It is not incorrect to write "The courses include geology, botany, chemistry, etc.," but "and so on" or "and so forth" is preferable, except in technical writing.

every body, everybody; every one, everyone; every thing, everything See **any one, anyone.** (For help in deciding whether to use these as singular or plural words, see **section 5g.**)

farther, further Most writers prefer to use *farther* for physical distances, as in "They drove farther down the road," and *further* for abstract references, as in "Further evidence changed the case" or "They examined the problem further."

few, fewer; less, little; many, much Use *few, fewer,* and *many* to describe something that can be counted; use *little, less,* and *much* to describe something that cannot be counted.

Few cars were on the road, so there was little danger.

Fewer cars were on the road, so there was less danger.

Many cars were on the road, so there was much danger.

first . . . second Remember that if you use *first* to introduce a statement, you must follow it with *second,* introducing another.

formally, formerly *Formally* means "in a formal manner"; *formerly* means "in the past" or "at an earlier time."

former, latter *Former* refers to the first of two persons or things; *latter* refers to the second of two. When you discuss more than two, use *first, second, third,* and so on.

further, farther See **farther.**

good, well In formal English *good* always acts as an adjective; *well* may act as either an adjective or as an adverb.

Chris is good at tennis, and Pat plays golf well.

"Chris plays good" is nonstandard English.

had better This is a synonym for "ought to." Remember to include *had* or "We had better go" or *'d,* as in "We'd better go."

had ought This is nonstandard English. Write "They ought to leave early" or "They ought not to be late," and so on.

hardly, scarcely These words imply a negative meaning. Do not use *not* or other negatives with them. Do not write "They could not hardly lift the box" or "They couldn't scarcely see us"; instead, write "They could hardly lift the box" or "They could scarcely see us."

hopefully *Hopefully* means "filled with hope." It should therefore modify an action performed by a person capable of hoping, as in "The beggar asked for money hopefully." To indicate a general wish, use "It is hoped that . . . ," "Let us hope that . . . ," or "I (you, they, *etc.*) hope that. . . ."

We hope that our foreign policy will succeed.

Let us hope that our policy will succeed.

imply, infer   In formal English, use *imply* to mean "suggest" or "hint" and *infer* to mean "draw a conclusion."

The defendants tried to imply that they were innocent, but the jury inferred from the evidence that they were guilty.

inferior than   This is nonstandard for *inferior to*.

irregardless   This is nonstandard for *regardless*.

is when, is where   Do not use *when* or *where* after *is* when defining something. Do not write "A simile is where (*or* is when) you describe something by making a comparison"; instead, write "A simile describes something by making a comparison" or "A simile is a description that uses a comparison."

kind, sort   *Kind* and *sort* are nouns in the singular; their plurals are *kinds* and *sorts*. Use *this* or *that* with the singular; use *these* or *those* with the plural.

This kind of oak is never tall.

Those kinds of trees grow quickly.

kind of, sort of   These are informal English. Use *somewhat* or *rather* in formal English. Do not write "The movie was kind of dull"; instead, write "The movie was rather dull" or "The movie was somewhat dull."

later, latter   *Later* describes time; *latter* refers to the second of two persons or things previously mentioned (see *former*).

The show began later than usual.

We used a saw and an axe, but the latter was not ours.

lay, lie   *Lay (laid, laid, laying)* is a verb meaning "put" or "place" something; it is transitive and must have an object. *Lie (lay, lain, lying)* is a verb meaning "rest" or "recline"; it is intransitive and should *not* take an object. (See **6i**.)

They lay (*or* laid, have laid, are laying) the logs on the fire.

They lie (*or* lay, have lain, are lying) awake in bed.

learn, teach   *Learn* means "acquire knowledge"; *teach* means "impart knowledge."

The experience may teach us a lesson.

We may learn from our experience.

leave, let   *Leave (left, left, leaving)* is a verb meaning "depart," "abandon," or "go away from." We often follow it with an infinitive, as in "We shall leave to go to Chicago" and "They left Chris to run their house." *Let (let, let, letting)* is a verb meaning "permit" or "allow." We usually follow it with a bare infinitive (see **11b.4**), as in "They let Chris run their house." Do not write "They can leave Pat finish the job" or "Leave us talk in peace"; instead, write "They can let Pat finish the job" or "They can leave Pat to finish the job," and "Let us talk in peace" or "Leave us to talk in peace."

less   See **few**.

let, leave   See **leave**.

let's us *Let's us,* as in "Let's us go," is nonstandard and redundant. Write "Let us go," or, less formally, "Let's go."

liable, likely *Liable* indicates "having an obligation or duty"; *likely* indicates probability.

> The owner of the dog was liable for the damage it caused.

> A poorly trained dog is likely to cause trouble.

lie, lay See **lay.**

like, as In formal, standard English, *as* is a conjunction, and *like* is a preposition. Do not use *like* to introduce a clause.

> We slept late as (*not* like) we always do on weekends.

likely, liable See **liable.**

little See **few.**

loose, lose These are often a spelling problem. *Loose* is usually an adjective or an adverb, but *lose (lost, lost, losing)* is always a verb. In spelling the two words, you may find it helpful to remember that *loose* rhymes with *goose* and both have *oo.*

many, much See **few.**

may be, maybe *May be* is a verb composed of the auxiliary *may* with *be; maybe* is an adverb, meaning "perhaps."

> They may be here for dinner. *(verb)*

> Maybe the weather will improve. *(adverb)*

may, can See **can.**

much See **few.**

myself This is a reflexive pronoun. Use it to emphasize another pronoun or to make a reference clear. Do not use it as a substitute for *I* or *me.*

not . . . no, not . . . none Two negatives cancel each other. These are nonstandard if the meaning is negative. Do not write "They have not eaten no lunch" or "They haven't got none"; instead, write "They have eaten no lunch" or "They have not eaten any lunch" and "They have none" or "They haven't any."

not only . . . but also Remember that if you have *not only* in a sentence, you must follow it with *but* or *but also* to complete your meaning, as in "They not only surfed in Hawaii but also skied in Vermont." *Not only* and *but also* should introduce the same kinds of constructions. If you write "They surfed not only in Hawaii," the rest of the sentence should name another place that they surfed, as in "They surfed not only in Hawaii but also in California," not another action such as skiing.

number, amount See **amount.**

of Do not write *of* when you mean *have.* A mistaken *of* instead of *have* is particularly likely to occur with the auxiliaries *could, would, may,* and *might.* Do not write "They should of left earlier"; instead, write "They should have left earlier" (formal) or "They should've left earlier" (informal).

on the one hand If you use this phrase, be sure to complete the thought with *on the other hand. . . .*

per *Per* is a Latin word meaning "for," and we use it to mean "for each" or "for one," as in "cost per annum," meaning "cost for each year." Use *per* in technical writing; avoid using it to introduce English words, as in "the fees per student." *Per* is not a substitute for *according to,* so do not write "The store will close early, per the manager"; instead, write "The store will close early, according to the manager."

plus *Plus* has become popular in informal usage as a substitute for *also, and,* and *moreover.* In formal writing, use *plus* only in mathematics, as in "Two plus two equals four." Do not use *plus which* to connect two clauses, as in "They spent all their money, plus which they lost their car keys"; instead, write "They spent all their money and also lost their car keys."

prefer, preferable Each of these words should be followed by *to,* not *than,* when making a comparison. Do not write "We preferred fish than meat for dinner"; instead, write "We preferred fish to meat for dinner."

prejudiced Remember to write the final *d* when using the past tense and past participle of *prejudice,* even though it may not be heard in speaking, as in "They made a prejudiced decision."

raise, rise *Raise (raised, raised, raising)* is a verb meaning "lift up" something; it is transitive and must have an object. *Rise (rose, risen, rising)* is a verb meaning "move upward"; it is intransitive and should *not* take an object. (See **6i.**)

They raise (raised, have raised, are raising) the flag.

They rise (rose, have risen, are rising) to their feet.

reason is because See **because.**

rise, raise See **raise.**

scarcely See **hardly.**

set, sit *Set (set, set, setting)* is a verb meaning "put or place" something: it is transitive in almost all uses and takes an object. *Sit (sat, sat, sitting)* is a verb meaning "seat oneself"; it is intransitive and does *not* take an object. (See **6i.**)

>The waiters set (have set, are setting) the food on the table.

>The guests sit (sat, have sat, are sitting) down to eat.

some one, someone See **any one.**

such . . . that When you use *such* in formal English, remember to complete your meaning with words introduced by *that* to show the result, as in "We had such a good time at the party that we did not want to leave."

supposed to Do not forget the *d* ending for *supposed,* as in "The show is supposed to start in five minutes."

teach, learn See **learn.**

than, then *Than* is a subordinating conjunction and is used in introducing a comparison, as in "Lead is heavier than gold." *Then* is usually an adverb referring to time, as in "They played golf and then swam." In spelling, notice that *than,* like *compare,* has an *a,* whereas *then,* referring to time, rhymes with *when.*

that, which Traditional, formal usage distinguishes between these pronouns. In formal English, use *that* to

begin a restrictive modifier, one that identifies which of
two or more things or persons is meant, as in "The oranges
that we bought today are ripe, but the oranges that we
bought yesterday are not." Use *which* to begin a non-
restrictive modifier, one that refers to something that
needs no identification, as in "Oranges, which supply vita-
min C, grow in Florida, Texas, and California." Many writers substitute *which* for *that* in sentences that also contain
that as a subordinating conjunction or demonstrative adjective. (For more discussion of restrictive and non-restrictive modifiers and how to punctuate them, see **18, rule 4.**)

their, there, they're   Remember to spell each of these
correctly. *Their* is the possessive form of *they,* as in "The
students opened their books." *There* is an adverb or expletive, as in "He left his book on the table, and I found it
there" and "There are six books on the table." *They're* is
the contracted form of *they are,* as in "When they're
ready, we can start working."

then, than   See **than.**

there   See **their.**

these, this   In formal English, use *these* and *this* to modify or refer to persons or things that have already been
identified. Instead of "I saw this great movie last week,"
write "I saw a great movie last week."

these kind, these sort   See **kind.**

they're   See **their.**

this, these   See **these.**

to, too, two   *To* is a preposition, *too* is an adverb, and *two*
is a numeral that can act as a noun or adjective.

They went to the store. *(preposition)*

They bought two or three shirts. *(adjective)*

We also bought two. *(noun)*

We bought socks, too, but they were too small. *(adverbs)*

(In choosing between *to* and *too,* it may help to remember that *too,* which can mean "also," "very," or "extremely" and therefore suggests something additional, has an additional *o.*)

toward, towards Both forms are considered standard English.

try and, try to It is usually illogical to write *try and,* as in "I will try and pass the test," because that is really saying that "I will try and I will pass the test." Instead, write "I will try to pass the test."

unique *Unique* means "the only one of its kind." It is illogical to write that one thing is *more unique* than another or *most unique.* Instead, use *rarer* or *rarest,* or *more unusual* or *most unusual.*

used to Remember to add the *d* when meaning "accustomed to."

want for The *for* is redundant in this expression. Instead of "They want for us to come," write "They want us to come."

where Do not use *where* as a substitute for *that.* "We saw on the news where Congress passed the bill" means that we saw the place where Congress passed the bill. Instead, write "We saw on the news that Congress passed the bill." (See also **is where.**)

whereas *Whereas* is a subordinating conjunction. In legal writing, in which there are often many long subordinate clauses, those beginning with *whereas* are often punctuated as if they formed complete sentences, even though they do not. In any other kind of writing, do *not* punctuate clauses beginning with *whereas* as if they were complete sentences.

which, that See **that.**

which, who Use *who* to refer to persons, *which* to refer to everything else; *that* may refer to persons, animals, or things.

while Use *while* to mean "at the same time as" or "during the time that," as in "We stayed home while it rained." The informal use of *while* to mean "in contrast" can cause confusion. For example, "Chris works at the supermarket, while Pat goes to college" seems to suggest that Chris is working during the time that Pat goes to college. Use *but* or *whereas* to suggest a contrast.

would like for The *for* in this expression is redundant. Instead of "They would like for our team to win," write "They would like our team to win."

would of See **of.**

ACKNOWLEDGMENTS

INDEX

Abbreviations and Symbols

Your instructor may use abbreviations and symbols in correcting your paper. Refer to the sections listed.

abbr	use the standard abbreviation, or spell out completely	27
act	use the active voice	6d
adj	use adjectives to modify nouns or noun substitutes	7a
adv	use adverbs to modify verbs, adjectives, or other adverbs	7b
agr	make this verb agree with its subject, or make this pronoun agree with its antecedent	4k 3e, g
awk	rephrase this awkward expression	8
cap	use standard capitalization	28
case	use the correct case of this pronoun	4b
cs	comma splice; use appropriate punctuation	15
d	diction; use a more appropriate word	1c, 32
dev	develop this idea or paragraph more fully	35
dm	dangling modifier; relate this modifier to an expressed word in the sentence	11b.2
doc	documentation; use correct footnote, endnote, or bibliographical forms	52
emph	revise this sentence or passage to emphasize the main idea	30
fig	revise this figure of speech to make it suitable	32
frag	fragment; make this into a complete sentence	14
fs	fused sentence; use appropriate punctuation	15
gl	consult the glossary of usage at the end of the book to correct this word or expression	
ital	use italics or underlining	24
lc	lowercase; do not use a capital letter	28
logic	logic; correct this passage to make it logically consistent	33
ms	use conventional manuscript form	41
no ¶	do not begin a new paragraph	34
num	use words to express this number	29
org	revise the organization of this paragraph	34
p	correct the punctuation	17–26
ʼap	apostrophe	25
[ ]	brackets	22
	colon	20